## Management for Professionals

The Springer series *Management for Professionals* comprises high-level business and management books for executives. The authors are experienced business professionals and renowned professors who combine scientific background, best practice, and entrepreneurial vision to provide powerful insights into how to achieve business excellence.

More information about this series at http://www.springer.com/series/10101

Jan De Visch • Otto Laske

# Practices of Dynamic Collaboration

## A Dialogical Approach to Strengthening Collaborative Intelligence in Teams

Springer

Jan De Visch
Connect & Transform, Mechelen,
Catholic University of Leuven - Flanders
Business School (FBS)
Leuven, Belgium

Otto Laske
Interdevelopmental Institute (IDM)
Gloucester, MA, USA

ISSN 2192-8096 ISSN 2192-810X (electronic)
Management for Professionals
ISBN 978-3-030-42548-7 ISBN 978-3-030-42549-4 (eBook)
https://doi.org/10.1007/978-3-030-42549-4



This Springer imprint is published by the registered company Springer Nature Switzerland AG
The registered company address is: Gewerbestrasse 11, 6330 Cham, Switzerland

*We dedicate this book to Adelheid Maekelberg and Nadine Boughton, our wives, with gratitude for their clarity, wisdom, and patience.*
*Above all, with gratitude for their love. Without them, the book would not have come into being.*

# Foreword

As a reader of *Practices of Dynamic Collaboration*, I have had the good fortune of reflecting anew on my work with Otto Laske, one of the co-authors, as a client and collaborator. While I have been a student of adult development and organization design influenced by Otto's and Jan De Visch's work for over a decade, only now do I get to turn the pages of one of their books I helped research.

Otto and I had the opportunity to intervene in an organization comprised of about 100 people who have spent years attempting to apply models such as Holacracy, Lean, Agile, GTD, and a myriad of other frameworks to "working on the business." What we began observing was that these ideologies and their associated instruments, although meant to transform a business, led to thought fixations that further separated cultural ideals from extant ways of working and organizing.

Rather than to import "models" to help get people closer to real-world dynamics as they show up in organization's conflicts (or "tensions," as we called them), through semistructured *real-time* interviews Otto and I began to uncover the adult-developmental realities of individuals and teams that no pre-fabricated, out-of-time model is able to capture. In short, we started to work as what this book describes as *critical facilitators*.

In doing so, we came to understand that and how people's *inner workplaces*—including our own—were the original source of the imbalances between working on visionary strategy and the daily delivery of work (which kept us employed). To my surprise, I discovered that the dilemmas of people's and teams' inner workplace could not be resolved by processing those tensions within an imported holonic organization design.

In fact, it was the formality of the holonic model the organization was following that led to the tensions the model was meant to solve (and I had been hired to fix). Rather than focusing on how to metabolize the natural conflicts that arise within developmentally diverse teams *internally*, the holonic model zapped the rich complexity that makes up "the organization" of its energy and flow, in particular on account of the fragmented de-collage of meeting practices, software applications, and, to boot, an almost religious adherence to idiosyncratic working agreements.

Specifically, we noticed early on that the executive team, of which I was a part, was divided, not only behaviorally but adult-developmentally. On the surface, this division looked like a split between the CEO and I, on one side, and the CFO and CMO on the other. While we were focused on an agenda of transformation, with the aim of differentiating profit centers through including new startups into the business portfolio, the CFO and CMO were focused on growing the still strong core of the business through its legacy functional areas. Under circumstances in which three of us stood in opposition to the CEO as we attempted to reform the team toward a more common purpose, I found the executive team's division exacerbated by my now heightened awareness of its developmentally sourced, counterproductive dynamics.

After reading *Practices of Dynamics Collaboration*, I now have the language to understand what we were dealing with was a "downwardly divided" team, if not organization. While it looked like the team was divided down to a level of operational efficiency because of the 2:2 stalemate, in reality we were downwardly divided because our team could not even produce a developmentally more mature member that could coach teammates to find a consistent "we-space,"—not even the CEO.

While terms such as "downwardly divided," "developmentally mature," and "we-space" may be new to you, through reading this book you and your teams can begin to become aware of the developmental realities that lie behind what was, at least for us, an emotionally wrought and conceptually confusing situation these new terms precisely represent. These terms do not only represent a sob story in all cases. What stood as entirely "emotionally negative" conflicts in my memory before reading this book became a collection of insights into the developmental limitations of the executive team I and Otto had worked with.

While new terms can become their own obstacles, my bet is by reading *Practices of Dynamic Collaboration*, lingering conflicts in team dynamics you have experienced, once you relive them in terms of the book, may offer you a deeper experience of the developmental realities of human systems. In this book, Jan and Otto demonstrate how real-time communication between different types of teams brings to light that what is viewed by each of them as "real," unbeknownst to them dramatically differs from one to the other team, even though their members use similar words, phrases, and modes of interaction.

Because the differences within and between teams determine the quality of an organizational transformation, as I have briefly highlighted above, in my view working on team members' and teams' dialogue *in real time* is today of greater importance than ever for any organizational culture's future. After all, it is by speaking with one another in teams that we gain access to our colleagues' otherwise hidden thought process. While thinking is only one of two forms of adult development Jan and Otto teach us about, how sense is made of the real world is crucially relevant for how members link to their team, and for linking teams' performances to the totality of their organization.

As we learn from this book, upwardly and downwardly divided teams communicate with one another in distinctly different ways because they operate in adult-developmentally different *dialogue-spaces* (we-spaces). How we speak with one another in real time reflects how we think, and since thinking precedes action, assuring high-quality dialogue becomes paramount when composing sets of actions for achieving larger organizational outcomes.

Importantly, Jan and Otto take us beyond behavioral notions of communication. As a result, the book makes its readers realize that they communicate with each other based on their internal mental process (what the authors call their *internal dialogue*) in which thinking and use of verbal language become entirely meshed. On account of this merger, people bump into developmental limits of what they can communicate precisely, relative to their present understanding of how the "real world" works.

Having also worked as an organization designer and strategist in some of the largest companies in the United States, such as American Express, PepsiCo, and General Electric, I can tell you that to succeed in realizing complex initiatives through matrixed organizations with entrenched political climates, answering questions, such as "how are the teams I am initiating developmentally composed?" and "do I have a grasp of the capacity of my team adult-developmentally speaking," would have served my clients and their missions well.

Consultants and executives alike benefit from reading this book as a guide to designing and developing teams and scrutinizing the conceptual quality of their communications, that is, of the ways in which team members' internal dialogue is translated into their external dialogue with each other.

You will be relieved to know that the book's authors have given you a shovel to dig yourself out of the complicated meeting practices and frameworks you may presently be using, which bury simple and clear communication with your colleagues. While you might be initially surprised by how Jan and Otto lift you from the malaise of conventional management thinking, do not be dissuaded by their unorthodox style. The book's style exactly fits the subject matter they are trying to convey, in order to provide you with a more realistic and practical way of working.

Please enjoy reflecting on *Practices of Dynamic Collaboration* as I have.

Brooklyn, NY, USA
Winter Break 2019

Nathan Snyder

# Preface

Dear reader,

Just before the publication of this book, the World Economic Forum published its Davos Manifesto (Schwab 2019). The manifesto documents the growing awareness that we not only need to reconceive of organizations but that to do so, a different dialogue culture is required. Without a greater awareness of the quality of our dialogues, we may be unable to tackle issues such as climate change, inequality, and trade conflicts in an integrative way. A different conversation is needed at all levels of society. Such a dialogue is characterized by greater critical realism due to a greater awareness of our thinking.

In your company, you are surely confronted with the consequences of the fourth industrial revolution. The simultaneous emergence of new technologies—artificial intelligence, robotics, blockchain, chatbots—is exerting a profound influence on how jobs and collaborations are evolving. Project and teamwork play an increasingly decisive role, and the quality of the dialogue, both between individuals and in teams, influences whether a company can maintain its competitive position. Perhaps you share our frustration about the low quality of the dialogue culture now in place in your company.

You may even have noticed a direct link between the way innovations and improvements are *spoken about* and the fact that the results they yielded do not match your expectations. You may also have noticed that initiatives meant to shift the balance between hierarchy and self-organization have failed to lead to a higher quality of decision-making.

Let us give you a better idea of what this book is about: the book is designed to make you aware of the dimension of *thinking* that empirically underlies the functioning of collaborative intelligence. Specifically, the book describes how teams at different levels of work complexity ("We-Spaces") think and fail to think together. The book's uniqueness lies in its focus on what is grounding role identity, decision-making, foresight, and action in the context of team collaboration. To accomplish our intention we move beyond behavioristic views of what it means to plan and deliver work, compose teams and networks of teams, and boost human resources. We do so grounded in our own experience of working with teams, especially in organizations transitioning from hierarchical arrangements to self-organization. Every day, just like you, we see how people struggle over collaborating in concert. This led us to ask: what is missing from teams' thinking?

We are well prepared for writing this book: over the past 20 years, we have been exploring a new paradigm of thinking for the sake of collaboration in teams and have extensively tested it with our clients. The new paradigm focuses on what we call executives' and employees' *sense-making*. From this vantage point, we pay focal attention to how the faculty of making sense of the world conceptually—in contrast to making meaning emotionally—evolves across adulthood, and how this evolution can dramatically change people's life and work. Throughout the book we show in detail, practice by practice, how contributors transfer their understanding of the world at large to how they deliver work at different levels of work complexity. We show in particular how contributors' sense-making determines the way in which they naturally interpret the organizational practices they carry out as a function of their level of cognitive development, and thus also what they pay attention to, or bypass, in their daily work.

After a decade of team facilitation with a focus on their movements-in-thoughts in real time, we come to the conclusion that contributors' interpretive processes are the arbiters of the quality of their dialogues when collaborating. The new paradigm we have adopted gives rise to entirely new dialogue practices that we have tested and successfully implemented in a wide range of companies. The new paradigm has enabled us to create employee ownership, achieve coherence in action, build cultural common ground, take an innovative approach to employee and manager development, and, above all, get more out of meetings.

Specifically, we have written this book for posing for you the challenge of viewing your organization as a huge *dialogue-space*. Taking a dialogical approach, we are focusing your attention to how contributors "think" when speaking to themselves and others in real time. As we see it, such an approach to organizational work uniquely promotes self-organization and leads to success in the global market. In our experience, the quality of the dialogue nurtured in an organization's teams transfers to the dialogue with its clients and other stakeholders. By "dialogue" we mean a way of being together in real time as interlocutors willing to stop themselves when speaking, to "think twice" about the concepts just brought into play in real-time exchanges of information and ideas.

How does our thought-centric paradigm work? The stop sign we teach interlocutors to put up for each other has to do with more deeply inquiring into "what was just said" that was meant to lead to mutual understanding. We have had very good success with redirecting speakers' momentary awareness to how they "create," rather than merely describe, realities, in the process of speaking. We have seen this "stopping to think twice" creates a new organizational work culture. Our notion of speech behavior is that language by nature does not describe, but rather "creates" World and that this World is indeed all we can know about what we call the "real" world.

As a result, the "facilitation" we are providing to clients is a way of making possible high-quality team dialogues. In these conversations, each team member functions as a critical thinker who takes responsibility, not only for his or her own speaking and thinking, but also that of others, and does so as an integral part of his or her role mandate, thereby acting as a *sense-making officer*. For us, doing so forms the basis of creating collaborative intelligence.

Because human thinking does not come out of nowhere but develops to higher levels of complexity over an adult's entire life span, we find it necessary to issue to executives and employees an unusual invitation. The invitation is: to begin to absorb key insights from research in adult development into the way adults make meaning and sense of each other, and how, consequently, they interact with each other according to their present level of emotional and cognitive maturity. The challenge the book poses is thus to take seriously that we adults are all on a developmental journey, both regarding the way we function emotionally and intellectually. In this book, we show extensively that where we are in this development over the life span at a particular moment in time has direct consequences for how we deliver work, interpret the environment in which we work, and link our work to our life. In order to make this challenge easier to take on and absorb, we make distinctions between a number of organizational practices in three different dialogue- or "We"-Spaces: *(1) continuous improvement, (2) rethinking value streams, and (3) business model transformation*. These distinctions allow us to show the dramatic difference in how a practice such as "holding a meeting" pans out differently in different domains of organizational functioning. In each of the dialogue- or We-spaces we discuss, the same organizational practice (such as a meeting) is shown to take different forms. In short, we differentiate the notion of "teamwork" by giving an outline of "how teams think based on how its members speak" at the three different levels of work complexity just introduced.

To sum up, we show in this book that an organization's teams are delivering work in three distinct dialogue- or We-Spaces, and that how they differ from each other is grounded, above all, in how they communicate with each other on account of the way they make sense of themselves and the world at large *at a specific level of development*. We show that how a team makes conceptual sense of its internal and external workplace determines its mandates and sets of goals, and that the difference between one team and another in large part reflects the quality of dialogue possible as well as required in each of them.

The framework we use is not simply a descriptive, but also a prescriptive and pedagogical, one. Throughout the book, we make a considerable number of recommendations, and give examples, for achieving higher-quality dialogues in each of the three We-Spaces and detail what is the thought structure of such dialogues. We conceptually detail the dialogue-spaces we distinguish by pointing to the specific *thought forms* that carry a team's dialogue. Finally, we show that, differently in each adult-developmentally defined We-Space, the collaborative intelligence follows its own dynamics, either "downward" to failure or "upward" to success. Throughout the book we demonstrate the importance of having teams work with a "critical facilitator," but also that critical facilitation is learnable and teachable by contributors.

As a CEO, CFO, manager, and team member, you will learn from this book how to reshape organizational practices in the direction of becoming self-organizing. We are about to demonstrate to you that the ideal of working in an "agile" and "lean" way hinges on the fluidity of thinking more than the speed of action. Our concern in this book centrally regards the challenges of developing collaborative intelligence, and of doing so against the background of an adult-developmentally sourced understanding of human thinking. We demonstrate through the book that human thinking is much broader, as well as deeper, than logical thinking, and that cognitive maturity has to do with overcoming thinking's own instrumentalism, thereby waking it up to the deep gap between "how the real world works" and "how humans think."

As the reader journeys with us through different organizational practices, it becomes clear to him or her that taking executives' and employees' phase of adult development into account not only leads to more effective collaborations, but potentially also a more humane organization. In our view, humane organizations are those in which all stakeholders continually interlace the richness of their personal developmental transformation over the life span with the transformation of their work practice. The book concretizes how jointly people can meet the practical challenges of the World Economic Forum and respond better to the complexity of the evolutions we are facing as a civilization.

Essentially, then, the book invites you personally to consider the impact of your adult development on your life and work. The challenge we pose for you is to ask: "what are the limits of my present functioning at work, and how can I transcend them by forming a crisp notion of my emotional and cognitive resources?" In this sense, this book is about YOU, and about what you yourself can do to make your organization a more collaboratively intelligent one, starting with yourself.

We hope, dear reader, you will find this challenge mind-changing, not just inviting, and wish you a mind-opening reading journey.

Leuven, Belgium
Gloucester, MA
January 2020

Jan De Visch
Otto Laske

# Acknowledgments

"Who is wise? He who learns from everyone." (The Talmud)

We want to thank the many people, too numerous to name, who have shaped our thinking and been supportive of our efforts. This includes, first of all, our clients in many companies and various industry sectors who dared to step into dialogue experiments and new ways of organizing work; the many students in the portfolio of programs we teach who learned complex thinking "the hard way"; as well as our colleagues in critical facilitation and organizational development who provided encouragement for implementing our approach and gave us feedback.

We also want to thank the thought partners we have felt most attuned to throughout our learning journey, Roy Bhaskar and Elliott Jaques.

# Contents

# About the Authors

**Jan De Visch** is Managing Director of Connect & Transform (www.connecttransform.be) and Executive Professor at Flanders Business School (by Catholic University of Leuven). He co-creates systems of work and systems of change. He concentrates on making complexity manageable. His current focus is on critical facilitation and creating collaborative intelligence. He can be contacted at jan@connecttransform.be.

**Otto Laske** is the Founder and Director of IDM, the Interdevelopmental Institute (www.intedevelopmentals.org), and the originator of the *Constructive Developmental Framework* (CDF). As a teacher and consultant, he assists individual clients and teams in re-assessing their way of thinking and emotional stance in the workplace through real-time dialogue with them. He can be contacted at otto@interdevelopmentals.org.

# Understanding Developmentally Sourced Diversity as a Key to High-Quality Dialogue and Collaborative Intelligence

1

*The fundamental flaw in management thinking is that the concepts used are often seen as ingredients of what is thought to be "reality."*

**Abstract**

This chapter introduces the structure and content of the book, as well as the central experiences, ideas, and assumptions from which the book evolved. In critically reviewing contemporary management thinking, we show the stark limitations of Tayloristic ideologies, including those in now fashionable, digitally streamlined, forms. To substantiate the calamity of these limitations, we introduce findings from empirical research in adult development which substantiate that the developmental homogeneity of teams is a fiction and that this fiction hides limits of using digital tools. We demonstrate, in contrast, that and how team members' adult-developmentally differentiated profiles determine the quality of team collaboration. In order to provide alternatives to Tayloristic shortcuts for organizational work arrangements, we introduce a framework for actively boosting dynamic collaboration in teams. At the end of the chapter, we help readers prepare themselves for taking note of, and reviewing, behavioristic misconceptions in five practices: holding quality meetings, developing commitment and ownership, creating coherent collaborative action and common ground, and promoting an organization-wide dialogue about individual development of contributors that amplifies administering "human resources."

In this chapter, we introduce the structure and content of the book, as well as the central ideas and assumptions from which the book evolved. We do so against the background of a review of management thinking, deriving from Taylorism. To show



J. De Visch, O. Laske, *Practices of Dynamic Collaboration*, Management for Professionals, https://doi.org/10.1007/978-3-030-42549-4_1

the stark limitations of Tayloristic ideologies in their now fashionable upgraded forms (expressed particularly by digital apps), we introduce the topic of adult-developmental diversity that determines team collaboration. Based on this content, we then introduce a framework for enabling dynamic collaboration, detailed in five practices. In discussing each of these practices, we point to what is absent from contemporary management theory and from ideas about integrating algorithmic intelligence into human work delivery. In this way, we set the tone for a detailed investigation of practices that together compose organizational functioning, shedding light on them from an adult-developmental "constructivist" and critical perspective.

When we published our book *Dynamic Collaboration* in 2018, we were unable to assess the outcomes of the fundamental paradigm shift we proposed for looking at the nature of work, especially in teams. In that book, we only began to look at collaboration in a fundamentally different, namely *developmental*, way.

Concretely, we started from the perception that cooperation in most organizations is problematic, especially in light of the reductionist ideology of human resources that is a legacy in most organizations. This ideology is rooted in an enormous simplification of what is the nature of work and, as a result, that of the worker. In contrast to the conventional pared-down picture of work delivery in organizations—especially from the perspective of the adult-developmental sciences—the notion we have today of those who deliver work is immensely more complex than Taylorism had allowed for.

The main point of difference between the "Taylor = made" human resources ideology and the psychological and social reality of work is that contributors must be characterized as individuals who work on realizing their own agenda, based on highly idiosyncratic ways of thinking, intending, and acting that change dramatically over their adult life span. Due to their own emotional and cognitive complexity, they both reinforce and limit each other through their actions and are, on average, developmentally profoundly different one from the other and incompatible in their capabilities.

The tensions that arise in the workplace are equally complex, especially in teams. Contributors lock each other in and out, and negotiate values and ideas in fundamentally different ways, namely, based on their developmental history. They develop ways of working together based on a multitude of psychological and developmental factors that the conventional notion of the "worker" in human resources never acknowledged.

Contributors even function as politicians, where depending on their power, they set up intersecting spheres of autonomy. Not only are they free to keep subjects on or under the table, they can also unconsciously or consciously ignore them, avoiding those they prefer not to look at, or consider them as irrelevant. In short, in the human resources field, we benefit from addressing a highly complex interweaving of work-determining factors that not even contributors themselves have—and constitutionally are able to have—an inkling of.

In contrast to the complex picture of work delivery drawn up in our previous as well as the present book, organizational experts, managers, and even researchers of organizations have acted mainly, and continue to act, as "terrible simplifiers" when thinking about *human capital.* They usually look at human resources phenomena from the perspective of persons as objects of observation. They focus on behavioral strengths and personal preferences, thereby reducing the human condition in complexity far beyond what makes business sense. For them, solutions to managing human capital are often restricted to strengthening kinds of behavior believed to reinforce intended outcomes and thus focused on reducing the impact of personal idiosyncrasies to hypothetical norms that are too simplistic to do justice to how the social world works. Compared to what we know about people's behavior and adult development today, we are dealing with "terrible simplifications" throughout the field of human resources. This very fact makes bringing the existing complexities to consciousness in organizations very difficult indeed, as we daily experience ourselves.

What today's aficionados of agile and flat organizations are settled with is the fact that looking at human capabilities from a vantage point of behavioral practices alone is alarmingly insufficient as well as inefficient. The range of methods for strengthening employees' self-observation, complexity handling, fluidity of thinking, and perspective-taking is woefully inadequate. This is precisely because they set themselves the primary goal of influencing organizational behavior predominantly in favor of shared intentions and cultural consensus, forgetting to acknowledge findings of empirical research in adult development since 1975.

For instance, from the tradition of Taylorism—however updated by now—derives the overall conviction that there exist relatively simple solutions for issues presented by collaboration. These simplistic solutions are currently finding their way into a large number of digital frameworks (templates) for upgrading the quality of collaboration. These initiatives aim to alter meeting practices, make role agreements explicit, steer the evaluation of colleagues, reroute information flows, and much else. The basic idea behind these "best practices" is the conviction that there exists one best way of working together and that the practices proposed can be used anywhere anytime.

Below, we distinguish in these *best practices* three unexamined beliefs: *the belief in efficiency, in motivating employees*, and *in strategy.* As we attempted to show in our previous book, the notion of a single "best way" lacks cogency since it disregards stark differences between organizational cultures, as well as developmental differences between contributors. More importantly, there is a disregard for the fact that employees are *adult thinkers* and thus, consciously or unconsciously, unceasingly interpret concepts such as the above in a highly complex way that moreover changes dramatically over their lifespan. As meaning-makers who are under lifelong development, they do so based on their present peculiar *frame of reference* that determines their world view, both in life and at work.

**The human condition we are dealing with is best addressed as *epistemological.* It has to do with how knowledge is generated in human minds (episteme = knowledge) due to how movements-in-thought are structured when articulated in real-time**. Being subject to, rather than in control of, their personal development, adult thinkers have no choice but to enter into dialogue with themselves and others in a way predetermined by their level of maturity. Whether contributors, manager, or CEOs, they "sit in the same boat" because they are, as adults, without exception on a developmental journey and therefore share world views they can decipher as "too narrow" only when they get to the next following stage of their adult development.

To see more clearly, the fallacies implicit in the conventional, behavioral line of thinking about organizational work let us briefly review modern management thinking.

## 1.1 Management Thinking and Its Focus on the "Best Way"

Although managers have not been reduced in their human capabilities to the extent that workers have, throughout the twentieth century, even managerial resources have been seen in a behaviorally reduced light. Managers were left unsupported in developing a vocabulary for articulating their cognitive and emotional resources to the fullest. In their majority, they remained "other-dependent" and internalized what they were thought to be about and capable of by others than themselves. As a result, managers developed a "professional" persona that significantly differed from their personal one, indirectly shaping (and often reducing) the latter as well. The self-estrangement that occurred gradually led to depleted thinking capabilities that were "brought into shape" by business schools teaching rigid curricula, as well as organizational cultures in which hierarchy, and thus control, were considered more important than collaboration.

The three salient characteristics of managerial thinking that emerged (discussed below) bear this out. They account for what today hampers managers in their ability to engage with employees as full-blooded adults and find innovative ways of working with them.

### 1.1.1 The Belief in Efficiency

The belief in efficiency as the standard of work delivery originated in the early twentieth century when Frederick Taylor looked for ways to do away with existing inefficiencies in the workflow. His rational thinking told him that you had to reduce work to its smallest components first, and then find a single, "best," way for each component to be delivered. The novelty of Taylor's method was on a par with its brutality: that by standardizing goals, they would become calculable. In his *Principles of Scientific Management* (1911), he developed the concept of division of labor and explained the tasks of managers in terms of it. The manager was able to plan the job, and if the planning was right, the result was achieved automatically since workers had no say in it, nor could they have a say in it.

Taylor's analyses made efficiency a standard of production, as well as human performance. They became the basis of performance rewards. In a factory, workers were forced to work at the speed of the assembly line, which defined the standard of efficiency. Taylor's idea was based on the financial self-interest of both the worker and the owner of the factory. The first wanted to maximize his wages; the other wanted to maximize his profits. Efficiency was, therefore, in the interests of both parties (or so he thought). The model of employees Taylor used is that of "homo economicus" who focuses on his own interests and acts rationally toward that end.

In recent years, many variants of this approach have been formulated based on ideas about the division of labor. Business Process Engineering and Lean Six Sigma have become very popular. All of these approaches look at nothing than some abstractly envisioned output, thus never at how it is produced in real time. They all define "work" negatively as something in the course of which to avoid "unnecessary" steps of no benefit for the final product or service to the customer. It is a starkly reductionist kind of thinking that does not take how employees' mind works into account.

### 1.1.2 The Need to Motivate Employees

To make up for the reduction of employees to appendices of machines, it seemed necessary to "motivate" them to abide by what they were forced into. This could be approached by making a "clear" distinction between thinking and doing: managers are good at thinking, workers at doing. This dichotomy between two aspects of work, which cast workers as automata, became widely accepted. To balance this crude distinction, finding ways of motivating employees (compensating for the reduction imposed on them) became part of a manager's job. It took a lot of "research" to remind oneself of the single-minded brutality of the distinction between thinking and work.

Elton Mayo's (1933) research indicated that employees (surprisingly) have wishes and desires that one cannot express in terms of wages. He started with the physical characteristics of the workplace itself, investigating how to improve production by changing the lighting in the workplace. He concluded that employees' productivity increased, not so much because of changing circumstances or pay but because employees felt part of a team and did not feel they were being coerced. His finding was that it motivates people to feel they are essential to an organization.

Strange as it may seem today, Mayo is considered as the founder of the *human resources* movement. Following up on his work, researchers like Douglas McGregor (1960) and Peter Drucker (1967) elaborated on the concept of self-motivation of employees and managers. According to them, the manager's most important task was to ensure that the personal goals of employees and the goals of a company were aligned. In their view, measuring performance was a means of self-control and improvement. A lot of the management literature today is about how employees and managers can improve themselves. Steven Covey's (1989) books on the seven characteristics of effective leadership are an excellent example of this way of thinking.

The human resources tradition has inspired many researchers. McKinsey's well-known 7-S model (Samygin-Cherkaoui 2005) is based on the need to align shared values, strategy, structure, system, style, staff, and skills. It is the task of the manager to build one coherent story around these components of organizational work. Irregularly, a new story is needed to deal with changing circumstances, and subsequent stories have increasingly weakened the notion of employees as automata.

Approaches to new organizational forms or self-directed teams fit in well with the human resources approach. As a legacy of unabated Taylorism, the central question is always how to motivate people to deliver the best possible performance. The permanent assumption made in these approaches is strictly behavioral: people are seen as responding to "stimuli," consciously or unconsciously. In different theories, stimuli take on various forms, moving increasingly closer to how the human mind works: reward, self-direction of a team, a story, and shared values. The fact that the mind is not just a processor of stimuli or "information" did not get a hearing before theories of adult development came upon the scene in the 1970s. Up to today, these new theories are received in organizations only quite whimperingly.

### 1.1.3 The Importance of Strategy

Since Taylor, the importance of strategy in management has increased and simultaneously changed in significance. Where previously strategy was designed by business owners, this is now often a task of managers. Strategy precedes budget, which in turn precedes the execution of activities. It is a concept that must be put into practice in the real world. Strategy primarily concerns the following questions: which customers does the company want to serve, with which products or services, and in which markets? There are numerous models and schemes to help managers answer these questions. A commonly used analysis is the SWOT analysis: list the strengths and weaknesses of a company in a specific environment relative to opportunities and threats. The models range from very simple (such as the STEP analysis or the Boston Consulting Group matrix) to more complex canvases (such as the Business Model Canvas).

In our experience, managers see working with strategic models as a mere filling-in exercise. Such models are not used for reflecting in-depth or for testing assumptions made in calculations or practice. For instance, it is easy to forget that it is only possible to perform a SWOT analysis after it has been determined which products or services will be delivered to which customers in which markets. Such investigations usually try to capture reality in simple, linear stories, projecting the past into the future and populating it with simple characters or personas. It is a kind of storytelling without checking how the real world works.

## 1.2 The Fundamental Flaw in Management Thinking

It is a shock to see that the three strands of modern management thinking (efficiency, employee motivation, and strategy) by themselves do not reveal the ultimate goal of management as a discipline. What is the purpose of management? It is also striking that the question of effectiveness is not addressed much. In the management literature, the goal of delivering work usually remains implicit. When it is detailed, it is abstractly and ideologically referred to as *value creation*. In short, its realization, at least until recently, has remained restricted in its meaning to what is assumed to be of relevance to shareholders. It is the task of the manager to ensure that sufficient value creation occurs to satisfy shareholders. Management thus becomes a particular way of thinking and doing for the sake of creating value for an abstraction called "shareholders." The essential questions, however, are as follows: what value means, for whom value is (to be) created, and how it is to be created optimally in real time.

If we look at current management practices, answers to these questions are increasingly recentered on *investors*. It is the task of a manager to ensure that investors obtain the maximum possible profit. The customer serves as a means for achieving this. By extension, every activity in the company must *add value*. This train of thought is concretized in the value chain model by Michael Porter (1980). This model presumed to cover all possible process steps in a company. It ranges from incoming logistics, production, outgoing logistics, marketing, and sales to service provision. In this reasoning, it is also necessary to manage suppliers, for example, by partial strangulation of contracts, because even purchasing has to add value.

To accomplish value creation, the manager uses three concepts, namely that of the business model, the market, and the organizational model. The business model is the manager's hypothesis. It explains which markets are to be developed in which way and how a company brings together talent, capital, and suppliers, so that it can make money. The assumption is that the business model works because each party gets something of value if it pursues its interests in a particular market. The customer receives his product or service; the employee gets work and salary, the supplier receives his income, and the investor gets his return.

In fact, it is possible to come up with a business model for every step in the Porter value chain. In each step of the business process, one can envision new variations and market combinations. It is also possible to rearrange the sequence of the different steps or to skip steps. For example, webshops are based on direct delivery to customers without the intervention of other parties or stores. In all choices concerning value creation, there are also choices concerning markets, whether these are sales markets, markets for labor, capital, or raw materials. The strategy aims to outsmart the competition in these markets. Here, too, managers have a large number of support frameworks at their disposal. Porter's five-force model is such an example. It serves as a tool for looking at all parties and markets in the vicinity and formulating how one can be different from them.

Finally, to realize value creation, the manager designs a model of organizational functioning. Thereby, he determines the boundaries of the organization. He decides what happens inside or outside of its boundaries and determines which activities of the value chain take place where—inside or outside the organization. Is it better for the organization to make its parts or to purchase them? Can another company perform certain activities better or cheaper? Managers decide which activities are to take place in which sections of the organization, or at which locations.

The common feature of the three concepts used by the manager is that the boundary between the "concept" and the "reality" of value creation is never (made) clear. **The fundamental flaw in management thinking is that the concepts used are often seen as ingredients of what is thought to be "reality."** Unquestionably, this reality needs to be continuously *improved*. Managers usually assume that the causal reasoning they engage in is in total harmony with fact, without second thoughts about holistic real-world causality. A manager looks at abstract causes as drivers or triggers of "change" and focuses on continuous improvement, whether it is profit, cost, or errors in the production process. He or she assumes that "reality" corresponds with what was calculated and conceived in advance, remaining unaware of the assumptions s(he) made and the cultural environment they are deriving from. What is more, he or she assumes that there are no realities beyond those presently visible. There are no absences and emergences; because for positivistic thinking, it is too arduous to anticipate how to cope with them.

By doing so, managers forget a fundamental lesson from developmental psychology and developmentally sourced epistemology: people experience what is "reality" for them, based on their individual developmental history, that is, their frames of reference, specific beliefs, assumptions, and models. These artifacts and abstractions are rooted in their emotional as well as cognitive processing or "thinking," something that dramatically differs between people at different adult-developmental levels and in different universes of discourse (domains of competence).

The notion of "strategy," for example, has an entirely different meaning for people in different organizational environments. Some see it as comprising steps of a plan with which to achieve goals. For others, "strategy" is synonymous with policy, while still others associate it with an ongoing conversation of adjusting to evolving circumstances. The failure to recognize these differences in interpretation makes staying realistic very difficult. The stubborn desire to reduce reality to a set of agreed-upon logical definitions necessarily leads to significant errors, unexpected situations, disappointments, and the feeling of not being able to control things. In the end, the so-called "VUCA" world is rooted in one's own strictly logical thinking that is unable to deal with transformations, and barely with "change."

## 1.3 Dynamic Collaboration Under Conditions of Interpretive Diversity

One of the insights we arrived at in our book *Dynamic Collaboration* is that organizational theory has a very undeveloped theory of how people think. It conceives of human thinking, and thus behavior, in a way that simply does not correspond to how people naturally navigate the real world. The reasoning the theory gives rise to certainly is out of line with what adult-developmental theory would suggest. Not every employee in an organization is primarily oriented toward efficiency and profit maximization. Not everyone looks at the immediate usefulness of something or someone for achieving results. Not everyone logically reduces the complexity he or she encounters to independently solvable problems or chooses the most obvious way to tackle a challenge. In fact, these epistemological hypotheses reflect the very lowest level of adult maturity, as we show throughout the book.

### 1.3.1 The Neglect of Adult-Developmental Research in Contemporary Management Doctrine and the Approach to Self-Organization

Management doctrine denies that, in reality, people identify with different ways of living, working, and thinking and do so not just for personal reasons but on account of their present developmental level. It is a reductive theory that brutally simplifies how the social world works. The doctrine denies key findings from adult-developmental research. The critical insight in that research is that individuals evolve throughout their lives in the way they interpret the real world around them as something meaningful to them, individually as well as a group. Management theory thus shows itself ignorant of, or denies, differences in people's levels of development (or reduces them to differences in behavioral strengths) and makes it appear as if certain organizational practices were universally valid.

For example, the meaning people give to the term "plan" plays a vital role in its execution. Some will give strong weight to their personal objectives. Others will exclude certain customer expectations in their planning in search of consensus. Still others use overarching considerations and value systems (they largely remain unaware of) to make choices between conflicting options when realizing a plan. The boundaries between optimism, wishful thinking, and self-deception are quite narrow. And when an initiative fails, it is often thought that this is due to changing circumstances or because some manager did not do "a good job."

However, the real world, both inside and outside of managers, is dramatically more complex—not just complicated—than management theory's predictions allow for. In today's organizational reality, conventional concepts of division of labor have become dubious, teams are playing an increasingly important role, and digitization is creating a range of new issues and functions. The distinction between thinking and doing—never very sound—is increasingly obsolete, and differences in how employees and managers construct "reality" depending on their level of maturity are becoming increasingly evident.

Recently, a lot of attention has been paid to the notion of "self-organization." Principles of self-organization emphasize the interdependence of thinking and acting. Self-organizing teams work autonomously. According to Hoda and Murugesan (2016), they work within minimal critical specifications, can handle variations in their environment (requisite variety), are characterized by the interchangeability of team members (cross-functionality), and follow a variety of practices of continuously improving their way of working (learning to learn).

In practice, it is never easy for self-directed teams to respond to the evolving wishes of customers, realize interchangeability, make valid estimates of their workload, and achieve team member autonomy. Despite of using a "state of the art" approach to self-direction, more than 60% of self-directed efforts fail. Within a short time, an orthodox hierarchy has been re-established within "cutting-edge" collaborative contexts.

In our work with teams, we found that self-organizing approaches are often nothing but a re-packaging of anachronistic management logic. Their focus on practices of interacting and cooperating camouflages old ways of thinking. Essentially, the focus is on behavior, not on the structure of team members' thinking. As is the tradition in management theory, the emphasis is put on behavioral practices such as sharing information, giving and receiving feedback, planning jointly, resolving conflicts, making decisions, and so on. What is not attended to are those factors that determine the quality of individual and team *dialogue* in an organization. There is also no acknowledgment that the real world (not just the social world) is highly complex and therefore highly unpredictable. As a result, the shared thinking required to configure a focal problem and enhance its transparency for participants frequently remains unrealized.

The assumption shared by many current approaches to self-organization is that behavioral processes exist that make collaboration predictable and manageable, an assumption that starts from the flawed management thinking described above. Practices are characterized in strictly logical ways, as a series of steps with no attention paid to other than linearly causal relationships between them. Holistic causality that is nonlinear is simply denied. Accordingly, methods developed for enhancing self-organization have remained based on breaking down problems into their most straightforward facets and then solving subfacets. Schemes and procedures are formed around these subfacets, for example, around "nonviolent communication," "decision-making in the absence of objections," "role interviews," etc., which quickly take on the character of ideological orthodoxy.

### 1.3.2 The Importance of Adult-Developmental Differences in the Workforce

In our book *Dynamic Collaboration*, we proposed a more holistic and systemic management theory than positivistic thinking has so far permitted to develop. This model builds on an evolutionary perspective, both regarding organizations and their managers and other contributors, including clients. We did so informed of robust findings in research on adult development available since 1975. According to these findings, adults, whether CEOs, employees, or managers, evolve in maturity in "stages" whose unfolding extends over their entire lifespan and to their death. It follows from this: how complexity is handled; the way a person takes a perspective on what is real and makes decisions, etc.; and whatever activity might come into focus is under the influence of emotional and cognitive development. While emotional differences between contributors have to some extent been a topic of organizational assessment, phases of cognitive development, except for E. Jaques and Cason (1994), have never even been sighted. Consequently, how contributors speak to and dialogue with each other based on their momentary thought process in real-time has remained com-pletely in the dark in management theory.

A genuinely human-centered (humane) organization does not spring from tools and processes obtained from "out there" but is determined by the quality of the dialogue employees engage in among themselves "in here." When tools, who have their specific conceptual structure, are blindly followed (i.e., without a recognition of their conceptual structure), they often suppress the quality of the reflections they enable. Incorporated into toolboxes said to promote self-organization, they result in rigid (logical) thinking that forces teams to narrow their objectives and reduce the agility of their functioning.

The most crucial insight emerging for us from *Dynamic Collaboration* is that the quality of team dialogue, both of people with themselves ("internal") and each other ("external"), determines the pace and outcome of collaboration. The quality of the conversation, in turn, is strongly influenced by the level of maturity and fluidity of the thinking of those involved. Maturity is both an emotional and a cognitive issue. It has to do with the level of self-awareness from which team members communicate with themselves and each other.

A typical behaviorist assumption about adult development equates adulthood with getting better at one's work by way of accumulating skills and knowledge. Empirical findings in developmental science lead to a very different picture. According to Laske (2008), for instance, becoming an adult is not about learning new things (adding things to the mind seen as a mere container); it is instead about the transformation of the adult mind, thus the shift to consecutively more complex frames of reference. Mental growth is about changing the way one experiences oneself and the real world, essentially a movement away from ego-centrism. While social-emotional development points toward the development of an autonomous value system, cognitive development unfolds in the direction of the fluidity of thinking and the breadth and depth with which a person explores reality.

More specifically, the cognitive development of adults has to do with building increasingly complex thought structures by which one develops an understanding of oneself and things. The more complex the structure of a person's thinking, the more complex is the world in which the person finds himself or herself. An increase in the ability to handle conceptual complexity develops alongside fluidity of thinking, and thus of taking multiple perspectives on oneself and the world. In addition, the more complex thinking becomes, the more the person leaves behind the fixation on the real world as static and begins to see it as being in motion, composed of elements intrinsically related to each other. In this book, we refer to the development of thinking "transformational" of the person as a whole, including emotionally.

Given this theoretical background, it becomes understandable that empirical findings of adult development are centrally important in understanding the functioning and failure of teams. Since teams comprising members acting from the same developmental level are nearly nonexistent, developmental diversity in teams is a significant determinant of team functioning. This is so because the way team members see the world and workplace, and thus collaborate, is to a large extent determined by their level of emotional and cognitive development.

As the majority of adults, employees, as well as managers are generally unaware of their developmental stage, the interpretative framework associated with it, and how both affect the quality of their dialogue, the cognitive and emotional quality of dialogue team members are able to conduct with themselves and, based on that, others directly feed into team members' interpretation of the real world. Also, since people are not in control of, but subject to, their adult development, team members are necessarily unaware of the specific developmental position they assume relative to each other. Add this to their being unaware of the structural quality (maturity) of their thinking, and you understand why one and the same concept has dramatically different meanings for different team members.

In our experience, team members can be taught to pay more attention to the thought structures they use in real time to interpret what is happening around them. Acquiring self-awareness of one's emotions and thinking is typically possible only for very mature individuals, of which there are few, even on the upper echelons of an organization (empirically, less than 7% of mortals). This fact goes a long way toward explaining why prefabricated "toolboxes" tend to stifle rather than promote flexibility of thinking. Very often, they remain "dumb tools" seen as something outside of the thinker instead of something invigorating team members' movements-in-thought.

In addition to individual differences in adult development, different levels of organizational responsibility also present challenges. Assignments at higher management levels differ from those at lower levels of an organization because as an individual climbs the corporate ladder, the nature of work changes, often dramatically. At higher levels of work complexity, the social environment one encounters becomes more complex, thus requiring different competencies and capabilities. In contexts where self-organization prevails, the values a team strives to adopt and follow are fundamentally different from those in which team functioning is other-dependent (rooted in immature, less than self-authoring, value systems). For example, some teams focus on the qualitative delivery of a set of services or products, while others focus on continuous improvement and still others on the rethinking of transversal (operational) processes. For this reason, we speak of teams as functioning in different "We-Spaces" that are characterized by conceptually different ways of dialoguing.

The stratification of organizational systems as reflecting levels of adult cognitive development has been a topic ever since Elliott Jaques. Jaques hoped to turn management theory into a scientific discipline that would override the unceasing fashions that still dominate the management field today. His central insight was that in a "requisite" (naturally organized) organization, work levels differ by level of cognitive development of role holders. To achieve the effectiveness of work, each level of work needs to be staffed with individuals characterized by a distinct level of thought fluidity and complexity handling ability that is commensurate with the mandate and goals of the work in question.

Accordingly, Jaques' organizational systems theory identifies differences between levels of work based on time span of decision-making, thus thought complexity is required. Also, each level of work focuses on a specific value-adding theme providing a unique contribution to the organizational workstream, and no level is more important than another. Higher levels that do not add value beyond the lower ones are to be eliminated. Consequently, finding the right fit between individuals and levels of work complexity is the crucial determinant of organizational success.

How a team deals with real-world and social-world complexity is a crucial determinant of organizational effectiveness. As a consequence, aligning a team's mandate and goals with its members' developmentally sourced capabilities is a precondition of effectiveness if the team is to add value.

As a consequence, wherever team members' level of maturity of sense and meaning-making is incommensurate to the complexity of their task, a *downwardly* directed team dynamics emerge. Such dynamics foster team dialogues whose participants reduce assignments to their narrowest common denominator and make decisions accordingly. Inadequate perspective-taking commensurate with the full complexity of a task then assures that decision-making and team effectiveness decline. Conversely, it is the broadening and deepening of a team's perspective-taking on real-world functioning that defines upward team dynamics.

To sum up, working with findings of developmental research makes it evident that individual developmental differences in teams exert a strong influence on team dynamics. Such differences engender different ways of making sense and meaning of the real world and consequently differentiate work agendas in terms of what gets a hearing and what does not.

In our previous book, *Dynamic Collaboration*, our attention focused on understanding how teams deal with the task and personal complexity in more general terms. In this sequel, we detail our findings by addressing a selected number of essential practices that together make up "organizational work." As in the former book, we focus on the cognitive processes team members engage in and on how these processes influence the quality of the dialogue that ensues in the team (both those that team members have with themselves and with each other). The key question in fostering a genuinely dynamic collaboration in teams is this: how to create teams in which team members' dialogical self is strengthened rather than reduced to a common denominator. A related question is how to enhance the quality of conversations rooted in team members' self-understanding in each of the different practices we address.

## 1.4 A Framework for Enabling Dynamic Collaboration: Five Practices

In most day-to-day interactions, there is a tendency to assume that "people say what they mean and mean what they say" and that what is said is consciously intended. Developmental sciences challenge this assumption. Since each team member thinks and speaks based on underlying frames of reference different from that of another, what he or she "means to say" is different from other individuals might understand or say. Also, an individual's level of maturity determines the dimensions of the role with which he or she identifies, thus governing not only his or her professional identity but also the thoughts and actions flowing from that identity.

When the same message is naturally interpreted in often dramatically different ways by members of a team, it is essential to strengthening everybody's ability to be explicit about what and how he or she is thinking. For this purpose, this book provides teachable conversational tools that help people become explicit about what they "mean" when they speak up in dialogue with each other. Using such tools, referred to as "dialectical sense-making tools," reduces the occurrence of oversimplifications. The tools, all derived from Laske's DTF (Dialectical Thought Form Framework, 2008), make it easier to get every team member to articulate "what they really mean to say." When mastering such tools, team members become able to deal with divergent, often conflicting, viewpoints brought to the table—viewpoints that often remain unclear when team members have no understanding of the "thought forms" they employ when speaking.

In addition to learning to use new "thinking tools," it is also essential in teams, to pay attention to the structure of the conversational space individuals create for themselves. In addition to using complex thinking tools, the conversational space has to be such as to encourage flexible, critical thinking and allow for mutual openness of team members toward each other. Only when these conditions are fulfilled, can questions be asked, deep listening occurs, and heretofore not envisioned designs emerge.

As is well known, each organizational practice is associated with a peculiar dialogue that is grounded in specific competencies, challenges, and expectations of success. In each of the chapters below, we look at how team dialogue is conducted within a particular practice.

To promote high-quality dialogue, organizations frequently use templates, diagrams, and tools derived from organizational theory. Most of such templates never disclose the thought processes they result from, keeping them buried, so that they become taken for granted by their users. The risk in using templates of that nature is that they may be mistaken for windows on how the real world works while in reality, they reduce the real world to a manageable size far beyond what is productive. As such tools get widely distributed and accepted, the thought processes they derive from move underground or are reinterpreted if not completely forgotten. As a consequence, taken as an inert thought object, the template chosen hinders fresh thinking and reduces the depth of thinking dramatically.

As an example of the risks indicated above, take the notion of *lean management*, initially developed by Japanese system thinkers. In western practice, this notion has been reduced to suggesting a linear, step-by-step strategy as a result of which it has lost most of its power. Such a simplification is due to detaching the outcome of thinking from the process that engendered it. The approach, labeled after its source, then degenerates into a checklist. Questioning stops, and a "best practice" is born.

Aware of the fallacies introduced by templates sees as road maps for finding solutions, in this book we discuss ways of enriching team dialogue through *thought form templates* of a more universal character that, while not bound to a specific practice, can be adapted to it by team members making an effort to think matters through in an untrammeled way. These thought forms stem from research in adult cognitive development. Different levels of cognitive complexity are distinguished depending on the depth to which thought forms are consciously used in teamwork. On account of knowledge-generating thought forms, the number of options and choices that can be created from a single concept (as a focal point) multiply, whatever a team's chosen topic or goal may be. Throughout the book, we discuss how this knowledge-creation approach contributes to initiating and deepening team members' dialogue, both with themselves and others.

As said, in most organizational venues, cooperation is not easy to bring about. Working together tends to lead to disagreement, discord, struggle, and controversy about how to support a vision not truly common to all participants. In pursuit of their vision, people fight for recognition, reward, inclusion, and improvement of position. Their involvement is grounded in that something is at stake for them. Often, team members feel unengaged or feel they have to compromise their role identity and authority for the sake of something they do not entirely understand or subscribe to. They may resend the dependency on others that surfaces, although it is developmentally intrinsic and thus hidden to them.

### 1.4.1 The Strategy Followed in This Book

It is not easy to choose from the broad range of practices through which an organization daily takes shape. Every choice made excludes others and is, in a way, arbitrary. The decision we made for this book is based on our many years of experience in guiding organizational development processes. We have chosen the practices of which we have found that dialogue regarding them delivers major benefits. We follow our experience that the evolution of each of the dialogue practices discussed in the book helps bring about a humane organization and a consciously development-oriented culture in which employees and organizations may flourish.

The set of practices we discuss has been shown to accelerate mental growth in the direction of self-organization. Each practice discussed invites the reader to take a critical look at the dialogue structure employed in a collaboration. For example, how do we discuss planning, how do we interpret the feedback process, and how could we design it more optimally?

Regarding each practice discussed below, we invite the reader to ask two questions:

- What is the conceptual complexity of the dialogue that takes place?
- In what way can the negative impact of team members' ego-centrism be mitigated, and the positive aspects of their self strengthened?

In selecting practices, we have taken into account practices used in a whole range of approaches to self-management, such as Semco, Cybernetics, Holacracy, Spotify, Agile, Lean, Sociocracy 3.0, LiquidO, and many more.

Noticeably, many companies striving to reduce the hierarchy of managerial layers start with a rather opportunistic approach. Inspired by ideas eclectically chosen from presently fashionable methods, they work by trial by error. Some organizations decide to follow a single promising approach (e.g., Holacracy) without thoroughly checking which building blocks do or do not fit their present business model.

### 1.4.2 Structure and Content of the Book

We start our research on dialogical practices with an exploration of the idea of autonomy. Ideas about autonomy and dependence are pervasive in organizational cultures, whether implicitly or explicitly. In most cases, these aspects of work delivery are viewed as behavioral "traits," or ways of acting, of an individual, rather than also as aspects expressing his or her level of emotional and cognitive maturity.

The set of practices we have chosen to discuss are arranged along two axes.

Along the vertical axis, we distinguish between structuring and generative practices, respectively. For example, role descriptions, meeting formats, agreements on objectives, project planning mechanisms, dashboards, and key performance indicators have a structuring effect. Others, such as clarifying value choices, mission, collaboration rules, and strategy, specify frameworks of cooperation and are thus generative. The generative practices create dimensions of intersubjectivity and commonality.

Along the horizontal axis, we distinguish between practices that primarily focus on the individual or the collective, respectively. By combining these two axes, four fields representing groups of practices in discernible relationships to each other come into being. Figure 1.1 summarizes the practices. Each chapter of this book is devoted to a separate underlying theme in each of the practices.

In the top-left quadrant, the idea is that of commitment and ownership. In this quadrant, we can situate the dialogue practices that are intended to provide mutual

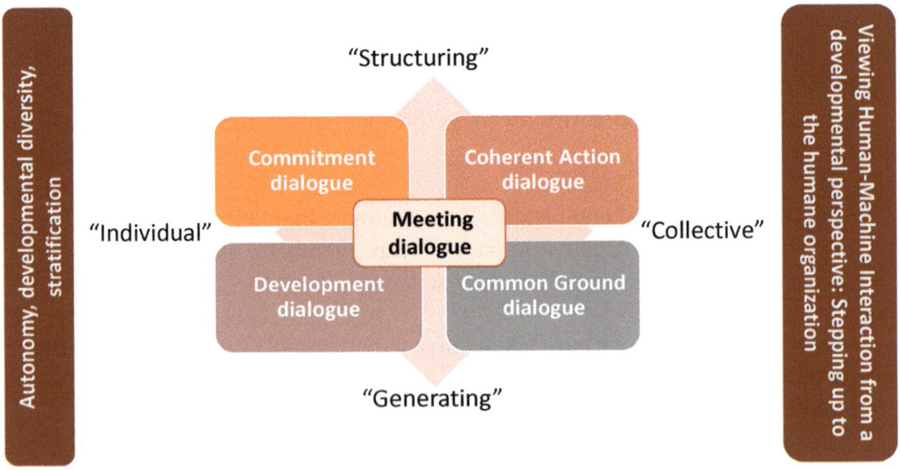


**Fig. 1.1** A framework for enabling dynamic collaboration

clarity about who does what. This includes job description conversations, agreeing on key performance indicators, modifying individual performance, and agreeing on personal priorities. The theme of commitment is central to these discussions. In Chap. 5, we explore the building blocks of commitment. We see them as shaped by how individual contributors conceive of their role both emotionally and conceptually, rather than in terms of some organizational abstractions found in typical role definitions. We make use of findings from adult-developmental science to recast roles as something co-constructed by interpretive processes. Commitment arises when an internal dialogue is combined with the transparent exchange of reciprocal expectations.

In the top-right quadrant, the theme is the dialogue that leads to coherent coordination. We look more closely at the dialogical dimension of collaborative action. This includes conversations on structure, work systems, information flow, feedback processes, decision-making, planning, and dashboards. In Chap. 6, we address the issue of how organizational coherence is created through real-time dialogue. For this purpose, we distinguish four configurations of teamwork giving rise to collaborative action in successively more complex ways: coordination, cooperation, co-constructing, and co-modeling. We hypothesize that the cognitive (sense-making) process underlying teamwork encompasses two contrasting dynamics which derive from the kind of reflections and questions participants raise in working together. We describe the interweaving and interpenetration of two different tendencies in the same dialogue. We reflect on themes that ensure coherent action, as well as on the areas of tension entailed by organized collaboration.

In the lower right corner, the theme is the creation of common ground. This includes the range of conversations around purpose. In concrete terms, we are thinking of conversations about mission, vision, strategy, rules of cooperation, values, and culture. What these discussions have in common is that they aim to achieve a common perspective on the desired collaboration. We observe that developing a culture is easier written than executed. Seventy percent of efforts to transform an organizational culture fail (Dewar and Doucette 2018). Employees do not commit to the desired culture, notwithstanding the combinations of different levers and methodologies. The dominant idea in most approaches to collaboration is that with the right steps, you can realize values agreed upon by all employees. We know from developmental science that ideas, as well as the "real world," are constructed by individuals according to their developmental level which makes that idea noncogent. In Chap. 4, on the membership dialogue, we highlight the interplay between taking perspectives on the real world, going along with a team's decision-making, and understanding oneself in relation to others, showing the essential role it plays in what performance level an individual can achieve.

The last quadrant, bottom left, revolves around the theme of individual development. We discuss the organizational conversations necessary to enabling individual employees' mental growth (rather than the only accumulation of "skills"). Here, the question arises of how an organization's culture shapes the growth of individual employees. Traditionally, the emphasis has fallen on becoming aware of one's behavioral strengths and weaknesses. In the context of self-direction, such a focus is insufficient. One must also include how participants' level of adult maturity can be enhanced that underlies strengths and weaknesses.

Specifically, we discuss in Chap. 7 what it takes contributors to grow in their capability of taking on the complexities of the real world that get lost in purely logical-analytical thinking. We propose that enhancing the critical realism of employees' thinking entails two consecutive steps. The first is becoming aware of the thought form structure of one's own thinking; the second is beginning to experience one's thought as a ceaselessly available resource for oneself and others. We describe how these two steps are tied together by what we name "double listening," with an outcome of mental growth especially in the cognitive sphere of delivering work.

Central to the framework depicted by Fig. 1.1 are *meeting practices*. In this book, they are considered the fundamental link that connects the various subdialogues. Meeting practices are of structural importance since people spend one-third of their professional time in meetings, and half of them complain about the quality of the session they attend. In Chap. 3, we focus on the function as well as the pitfalls of meetings. We emphasize that meeting participants are not all cut from the same cloth but are, in what they do and do not, limited by how they position themselves toward others social-emotionally and psychologically, as well as by their conceptual grasp of situations that occur in, or are referred to, in meetings. To better understand what happens in meetings, we integrate findings from research in adult cognitive development with Tomasello's research (2014). He conceptualizes collaboration as based on shared intentionality. More specifically, we show that and how meeting participants import into meetings their *internal workplace*—the mental space they construct for themselves when interpreting their role in contrast to the role assigned to them externally (their external workplace). It is this mental workplace that is the crucible of every meeting, whatever its topic.

Dialogue practices have to be seen against a background of digital and technological developments. In Chap. 8, we return to the Taylorist idea that lies at the heart of many automation initiatives. We discuss in what way the instrumentalist approach they are following does not enhance either users' adult development or the complexity of their thinking. Against this background, we outline the principles of humane collaboration.

**Key Insight and Practice Reflections**

For the transition to dynamic collaboration to proceed smoothly, it is necessary to think through the relationships between possible actions flowing from these different practices. It is not taking many initiatives that is essential. Instead, one ought to think about which limited number of initiatives could be mutually reinforcing. By thinking through organizational practices of central importance in their mutual relationships, a DNA of self-direction emerges.

The transition to dynamic collaboration is usually a process of several years; it does not take place sequentially. Initiatives often start in one quadrant. Such a start initially creates a lot of enthusiasm, which is difficult to maintain if initiatives from the other quadrants do not support the efforts undertaken. In this way, companies start to work on transforming their culture. The less the interplay of roles, feedback mechanisms, and employee development are taken into account, the less culture transformation worthy of this name results.

Practice shows that the most successful change initiatives follow a process comparable to creating a choreography in which a company examines the next steps that need to occur to complete an envisioned movement. Each subsequent action needs to be based on the evaluation of what is emerging, taking steps that can further deepen the desired transformation.

**Practice Reflections**

The following four questions can serve as a guide to choreographing organizational change:

1. How does dynamic collaboration presently fit into the broader picture (business model, strategy) of our company?
2. What is spontaneously evolving within partnerships in our company, and what practice could accelerate this spontaneous evolution?
3. What initiatives taken so far reinforce or weaken each other, and how can the relationships between them be detailed and refined?
4. How could we test the boundaries of dynamic collaboration in our organization to understand more clearly where more coordination for the sake of coherence is needed?

# Critical Practices Strengthening Autonomy, Developmental Diversity, and Stratification

# 2

*The prevailing notion that teams are developmentally homogeneous—in the sense that all team members function on the same level of maturity and can act autonomously—can be called fictitious.*

**Abstract**

In this chapter, we review empirical research on adults' social-emotional and cognitive development over the life span that has a direct bearing on management theory, not just the theory of human resources. Specifically, we briefly review "stages" of social-emotional, and "phases" of cognitive, adult development that have found broad consensus in the developmental research community. Together, a contributor's stage and phase of development are thought to make up his or her *developmental profile* at a specific point on his or her life journey. In addition, such a profile is shown to anchor a contributor's *frame of reference* in the broad sense of "interpretive framework" and "world view."

On account of this review, the reader is enabled to engage with what we call the three "We-Spaces" or "dialogue-spaces" that together constitute an adult-developmental outline of organizations' mental architecture: the continuous improvement We-Space, the rethinking value stream We-Space, and the rethinking business model We-Space. We show each of these dialogue-spaces to produce dramatically different team dynamics that directly shape collaborative practice.

In this chapter, we review empirical research on adults' *social-emotional* and *cognitive* development that has a direct bearing on management theory, not just the theory of human resources. We introduce concepts pervasively used in subsequent



J. De Visch, O. Laske, *Practices of Dynamic Collaboration*, Management for Professionals, https://doi.org/10.1007/978-3-030-42549-4_2

chapters. The wake-up call issued here is overdue by more than 40 years: organizational theory, in particular management theory, has so far failed, even to take note of new empirical research on human capabilities and their development over the life span. However, to do so is of the highest importance for making sense of, and promoting, the integration of algorithmic intelligence into human work delivery.

Specifically, we briefly review the "stages" of social-emotional and the "phases" of cognitive development that have found broad consensus in the developmental research community. The notion of "stage" entails that a manager cannot be at stage 4 if he or she has not been at stage 3. Importantly, nobody neither "is" in his or her stage nor functions at a single stage but rather is grounded in a "center of gravity" surrounded by lower and higher stages that define risks of regression and unrealized potential. The notion of "phase" indicates that cognitive development is not strictly linear since different individuals make their journey into fluidity of thinking and efficient complexity handling in idiosyncratic ways, following what we refer to as the *CPRT Sequence*, where C = context, P = process, R = relationship, and T = transformation. It is the telos of cognitive development to integrate these four components, thereby enabling organizational contributors to understand not only "change" but also "transformation."

It is important to note that a contributor's stage and phase of development together are thought to constitute his or her *developmental profile* at a specific point along the life journey and that this profile amounts to more than a description of competences but is rather an outline of a contributor's "frame of reference" in the broad sense of "interpretive framework" and "world view."

As a result of this review, the reader will be able to fully understand what we call the three "We-Spaces." These mental spaces are dialogue-spaces in which teams realize high level collaboration to the degree that their members can listen to themselves as well as each other in constructive ways and can externalize their own "internal dialogue" through team discussions. As a result of our notion of "team dialogue," we are able to formulate cogent hypotheses as to how to improve the quality of collaboration both within and between teams. We thereby rethink a slew of organizational practices, including meetings, that without an understanding of what we call "dialogue" cannot be deeply understood and, based on this understanding, improved.

Central to our discussion in this chapter are the contrasting notions of "autonomy" and "dependence" which color all thinking about role identity and role assignment.

Ideas about *autonomy* and *dependence* are pervasive in organizational cultures, whether implicitly or explicitly. In most cases, these aspects of work delivery are viewed as behavioral "traits," or ways acting, of an individual, rather than also as aspects that express different levels of adult maturity, emotional as well as cognitive. In this chapter, we introduce some significant clarifications regarding the concept of maturity, both individuals and teams, that facilitate reading the subsequent sections of this book.

The extent to which individuals act autonomously varies enormously from one to the other. Some individuals take ownership of things that need to be done quickly, while others continue to fall back on traditional ways of working or want to be managed. The idea of cross-functionality does not seem to be easy for the latter to grasp. Some employees colonize tasks within their domain of expertise, thereby limiting others' communication with them about a shared project. The situations just referred to exemplify very different meanings of the notion of "autonomy" in a specific role.

Autonomy is often associated with acting based on one's wishes, beliefs, and values, in contrast to being based on the opinions of a partner, parent, colleague, or employer. The basic idea seems to be that we can only be responsible for our own actions and, therefore, for our lives, if we can be in charge of them ourselves.

For instance, role holders have many choices to adress issues of customer demand for more support and flexibility, higher speed or lower price come up. Having options entails not only having to act responsibly as a decision-maker but also becoming aware of one's professional convictions compared to that of others. It also involves having to review one's dependence on others, given the need for shared decision-making. In any organizational context, dependencies abound. Even autonomous decision-making is truly independent only when it takes the interdependency of associated work roles into account.

Developmental scientists investigating cognition have empirically shown that human adults far surpass adolescents in conceptualizing their experience of the real social and physical world. By way of different but largely coinciding theories of how adults develop both emotionally and cognitively, they have shed light on the fact that whatever reaches an individual's mind is interpreted by him or her in a highly personal way. Interpretations are internally "constructed" by individuals and therefore depend on the individual's present level of adult maturity that determines the individual's present "world view" (frame of reference).

To put it differently, each of us unceasingly constructs his or her own "world," and while this world is sharable by way of language, the meanings attached to the same word or concept by different individuals vary widely.

Given what we know from developmental science today about how "the mind" works, it is easy to fool oneself both regarding one's cognitive independence of others and the scope of the real world at large, not to speak of the quality of one's own thinking. We can say that personal identity is the product of lifelong development, and so is the level of a person's autonomy that is attached to it. Researchers in adult development have built outstanding theories about the succession of stages of development of both emotional and cognitive autonomy that adults achieve. They have also shown that about 60% of adults never make it to the level of self-authoring that is consistently assumed in the management literature.

As developmental scientists tell us, a person's sense of autonomy is closely tied to that person's *frame of reference*. A frame of reference is the lens through which the world he or she lives in is emotionally interpreted as well as conceptualized and thus *experienced*. Overall, a distinction has to be made between a person's physical and mental age, which means that a younger person can be mentally more mature than a physically older one. This notwithstanding, the general tendency adult development over the lifespan follows is that by passing through successive developmental stages (longitudinally), individuals become increasingly aware of, and better able to assess, their relationship to themselves, others, and the world and thus also who they are in contrast to others.

Each successive phase of emotional and cognitive development is characterized by a transformational mental shift away from ego-centrism. Since each developmental stage is associated with a coherent pattern of how the world is interpreted and acted upon, any shift amounts to embracing a different "world view" as well as a distinct sense of one's own personality. For instance, while at one stage of emotional development we act as internally dependent on others, defining ourselves by their expectations, at a higher developmental stage, we are able to follow our own value system regardless of what doing so might mean for others.

In short, the mental transformations that occur over the adult life span lead to changes in the way we know and understand ourselves and the real world. We can speak of a transformational shift as a personal "Copernican Revolution." Over an adult's life span, there is a constant shift away from a large ME (subject) to a small one and, concomitantly, from the world as a small object "out there" to a large object of which we feel to be a very small part (even though we coconstruct the world with others).

Developmental changes are unnoticeable, even to us, but unceasing and extend over our entire life span until death. We are subject to them rather than controlling them since they occur unconsciously. Think, for a moment, of rereading a management book that inspired you 10 years ago about dealing with customers in a new way. Although the information you now absorb from reading a book is the same (the same words, the same edition), the way you experience and understand the book (and the world) in a second reading is fundamentally different.

In sum, we can say that mental growth has to do with gradually escaping our inbuilt ego-centrism and thereby broadening the frame of reference by which we experience life and work. Such growth is "development" in the sense of an unfolding of potential. It takes place along different tracks. The two most researched tracks are that of adult ego development and cognitive development. With the inclusion of the psychological dimensions, these two tracks determine what a person finds crucial and feels responsible for in life and work. Therefore, an experience of possible freedom, or lack of freedom, is always to be evaluated in terms of the specific developmental phase in which a person presently finds herself or himself.

## 2.1 Ego: Autonomy and Socioemotional Maturity

Otto Laske (2006), building on Kegan (1982), describes four specific developmental stages. The transformational shift a person goes through moving from one stage to the next one involves changes of what, as an individual or "subject," one takes for granted and can make an "object" of reflection of. When taking something for granted, one experiences one's assumptions as self-evident and, as a consequence, does not investigate them further.

In this movement toward a higher level of awareness, each step requires a subject–object shift. Such a shift is one from what we do not yet question to making it the object of research that we can analyze, assess, and adjust to. The general notion in developmental research is thus that the more we can take our life as an object of reflection, the clearer we see ourselves, others, and the world at large. For example, a subject–object shift may occur in the evolution of one's professional identity. In such a shift, both we, the subject, and our world, the object, change in its meaning.

For instance, when we are young, our professional identity is often an extension of our study choice, diplomas, and role models. In most cases, we are not able to analyze or question our beliefs as to who we are at work. As we grow older, our understanding of our professional identity is altered by career changes, technological evolutions, and the networks in which we operate. However, these changes by themselves may not lead to higher levels of reflection regarding our own life and work. It is only if we can step back and analyze our inner positioning to the world (our *frame of reference*) as it shows up in our behavior, feelings, desires, and needs that true personal autonomy is given a chance to develop.

Roughly speaking, it makes sense to describe social-emotional development in four stages (as explained above): *the instrumental, other-dependent, the self-authoring, and the self-aware stage*, where "stage" refers to a way of knowing the world, or *world view*. Far from being merely psychological, or linked to behavior, a stage is a peculiar frame of reference within which a person "at" a specific stage, thinks, feels, acts, and experiences life, including all of his or her behavior. Nobody is acting from a single stage but oscillates between lower and higher stages—regression and potential—around a consistent center of gravity.

Given that no person is ever at a single stage but usually in a *zone* comprising three or more intermediate stages, we can think of a stage as a center of gravity below and beyond which a person can move while staying connected to his or her emotional center (behaviorally often referred to as "comfort zone"). The "center" metaphor leads us to think of development focalized on a *center of gravity* as a kind of oscillation. Oscillation always entails the risk of falling below, and the potential of rising above, the center. This is the tension in which we emotionally lead our lives until death.

A center of gravity is a point of equilibrium to which the person tends to return when he or she is most solid and grounded. When this equilibrium gets disturbed, we say that the person is acting "below" his present center of gravity, or else, with appropriate boosting by others, is rising "beyond" it. Importantly, each center of gravity is associated with a peculiar "world view" that characterizes how the person tends to view and thus act in the social world and positions himself or herself toward others internally. At each center of gravity, the "reality" of the world seen and experienced is a different one; it also makes the person concerned be a "different person" compared to others he or she is linked to.

Work delivered at each of these stages looks very different as well, not only in terms of output but also in terms of the contributor's sense of his or her autonomy in delivering the work and the value system that underlies doing the work. Not all individuals can move to the highest possible stage, however. This is especially true for the move to the self-authoring stage. Specifically, in Western countries, between 60% and 65% of the population never outgrows the stage of other-dependency (which may be camouflaged by external props of self-authoring such as attitude and manners). Unbeknownst to themselves, individuals at an other-dependent stage lack a sense of independence of self. As a result, their thinking, belief systems, and feelings are "conventional" in that they follow others, rather than behaving in terms of their idiosyncratic value system.

A snapshot of each of the four stages of development (frame of reference; world view) follows below.

### 2.1.1 The Instrumental Stage

At the instrumental stage, the emphasis lies on one's own interests and desires. The transactional aspect is paramount when entering into relationships. Colleagues, customers, suppliers are seen as a means of meeting one's own needs. People at this stage act in a customer-oriented manner not because they care about the customer's experience but because attending to customers has positive consequences for them. Such people are customer-focused out of fear of the consequences (e.g., missing a bonus), not because they find customer-centricity important but because they are ready to act on it.

Also, at this stage, individuals follow a large number of rules, models, and "best" practices. They do so not because they believe in them or understand them deeply but because they need to gain awards and avoid disadvantages. A person operating from this stage will refrain from cheating neither because he or she fears the consequences nor because doing so conflicts with his or her values. In addition, at this stage, a person will be focused on systems of influence and control, believing that social power is to be followed. As a result, the "autonomy" we can speak of at this stage has to do with the feelings and desires by which a person defines himself or herself, and which that are never questioned: a "me-first" attitude.

### 2.1.2 The Other-Dependent Stage

At this stage, a socialization process sets in. This process provokes a shift to being able to detach (step by step) from one's own needs and desires, and gradually to integrate others' perspective into one's own frame of reference. The young adult identifies with what his or her social network finds important: he or she internalizes others' convictions, and his or her experience begins to be colored by what he or she thinks is expected of him or her and modeled by others.

For example, at this stage, a person identifies with the viewpoint of his or her boss ("He thinks I'm not customer-focused enough") or makes it part of his or her subjective experience to live up to a challenge posed. Beginning at this stage, people no longer see others purely as a means to their own ends but acquire the ability to take others' perspectives, at least where it is seen as supportive of one's own social position. In their interpretation of "customer orientation," for instance, they look for external validation and let their sense of self-esteem depend on a customer survey.

However, judgments and evaluations remain mostly conventional, in the sense that they need to be reinforced by others to become one's own. A manager, for example, "knows" whether a particular meeting was successful or not, only if said so by others. As well, compliance with others now leads to taking responsibility for others' experience of oneself, since an authentic value system of one's own is not yet in place. As a side effect, people avoid giving confrontational feedback since it could result in losing others' recognition; they are risk averse.

Importantly, at this stage, people do not yet have acquired an independent self-concept. Such a concept is based on an authentic value system, one's own. The value system enables one to follow through with thoughts and actions even if they encounter resistance from others, and even when there is a risk to be ostracized by others for one's thoughts or actions. Although such people think they know what they want, what they consider "their" identity, and needs associated with it, derives from having internalized others' expectations, including those "best practices" that define their profession.

As a result, a person at this stage finds it challenging to identify with standards, ethical or competential, of other professional groups than his or his own. Also, the fear of losing respect when going one's way is always present. It hinders such a person from being a good change agent, or even giving constructive feedback since it could be perceived as deviating from agreed-upon procedures.

In his or her thinking, an other-dependent person usually identifies with ideas stemming from his or her discipline, finding it hard to transcend it cognitively. The person adopts ways of working in harmony with the self-concept he or she has developed, or else waits for instructions. Complying with others' expectations, such a person tends to avoid risks, and any action that could lead to being excluded from the groups he or she defines his or her identity by.

### 2.1.3 The Self-Authoring Stage

The transition to self-authoring is long and often painful, having to do with being ethically "one's own man," even if one is at risk to lose social acceptance. In Western cultures, only 25% of adults reach this stage of meaning-making. Although many people referred to as, and believed to be, "managers" never reach this stage, it is self-authoring, not other-dependent, people who make the best supervisors and change agents, due to the consistency of their value system and adherence to a high level of responsibility. The autonomy they exude and practice does not entail that they decide everything on their own without taking into account others, nor does it mean that they act in a way disconnected from the real world. It is, rather, a specific kind of being in relationship to others that marks a self-authoring individual. Such people respect others as peers, especially when they are equally self-authoring, and otherwise have various degrees of compassion for those who remain other-dependent. Nor is being self-authoring psychologically easier than being other-dependent. It is precisely the tensions and conflicts a person experiences with others that leads them to decide things by themselves after having consulted others. With their hard-won ability to make and adhere to choices, such people express their superior form of identity.

Contributors who operate from a self-authoring stage are referred to as "post-conventional," not because they live by breaking conventions but because they intensely reflect on conventions and weigh their validity against what is required in a particular moment of time or real-world situation. For this reason, they can "take a stand," can set limits, and formulate their own judgments uninfluenced by fears of being disapproved of. However, such a person is rarely able to see the limitations of his or her own present value system and is thus at risk to act autocratically or even blindly.

Self-authorers develop an internal sense of direction and the ability to determine and follow their course. They can take responsibility for their inner states and emotions and explain them to others. For example, when a customer asks them to bypass a procedure, they can react with "I don't feel comfortable with what you ask of me, it violating what is important to me." Equally, such people can say: "what you propose might work but would be done at the risk of endangering other people and their self-concept, so for that reason, I would question it." This kind of approach would seem to be ego-centric, were it not balanced by a self-authorer's ability to explore others' thoughts and feelings and have compassion for them.

Reaching the self-authoring stage is also a high point in team functioning. It is likely to change a team's entire dynamics. While most ideas about self-directed teams assume that all team members operate from a self-authoring position, empirically, this is true of less than 25% of them. This explains why "self-organization" is often no more than a slogan that leaves "business as usual" untouched.

### 2.1.4 The Self-Aware Stage

At the self-aware stage, a person's self-concept is no longer bound to particular identities or roles but is continuously created by exploring one's self-concept and roles in real time in interaction with others, at a high level of reflection. The self-aware person fully lives *in the moment*, compassionate with others less developed. Nevertheless, he or she is open to working, indeed keen on, working with others in authority or less developed, and humble about his or her achievements.

People who act from this stage question their own as well as others' authority. They are no longer held captive by their own identity. They are fully aware of the complexity of life, strive not just to change but to transform themselves, and seek every possible opportunity to do so, open to their own and others' potential. In this sense, they are continually reinventing themselves, able to hold many thoughts and ideologies at the same time without remaining attached to them. For this reason, they find it easy to understand and reframe situations from different perspectives. They strive for moral clarity, able to make their entire personality an object of reflection, not only in launching their own initiatives but also participating in those of others.

The notion of “autonomy” has as many meanings for people as there are developmental stages from which they operate, including intermediate stages falling between the four “main” stages (in fact, about 16). A person’s stage of social-emotional maturity is best seen as a “lens” through which a person constructs and interprets “reality.” “Stage” is thus a frame of reference through which the real world is interpreted in light of a person’s developmental profile both in regard to emotion (which is fast) and cognition (which is slow).

In approaching a task, for instance, a person may experience that a specific approach so far pursued no longer feels right. This often directly has to do with the fact that the person has taken the next developmental step. The step taken was not merely a tactical, or even a strategical, one but reflects the fundamental reorganization of the person’s entire meaning-making system which often also initiates a cognitive broadening of how the person interprets the world. This reorganization of meaning-making can equally be triggered cognitively, by moving to another phase of complex thinking.

In teams, the fact that team members are usually positioned at different developmental levels easily creates a disturbance factor that hinders self-organization from materializing. Since teams whose members are making meaning from common level are rarely found, the multiplicity of meaning-making systems in the same team easily becomes an obstacle to self-organization. Since team frame of reference differs from one person to the other, what they experience as “true” or even “important” may vary widely.

For example, when discussing customer orientation, those acting from an instrumental perspective will likely focus on whether the approach adopted ties in with their notion of self-improvement. Those functioning from an other-dependent perspective have built their self-esteem on long-established methods and will thus feel having to change their approach to customers continually implies a critique of their current way of functioning. Self-authored members see a direct connection between customer orientation and their professional values. And so forth.

Without thinking developmentally, a manager or team leader will have a hard time improving self-organization. How decisively these differences can be dealt with by team members largely depends on the conceptual quality of their dialogue that, if high, can compensate for social-emotional differences and tensions. However, in general, the way of thinking of team members at an instrumental (stage “2”) or other-dependent level (Stage “3”) cannot match the level of self-authored thinking. The two strands of adult development are closely intertwined, with the cognitive strand often initiating social-emotional transformations in a person. Overall, how a team deals with developmental diversity—the presence in a team of different developmental levels—determines whether the approach to customer orientation, for instance, ends up being broad or narrow.

## 2.2 Autonomy and Cognitive Development

Cognitive development over the life span has to do with growing to maturity the "thought structures" or "thought forms" a person is endowed with from birth. As has been empirically shown (Basseches 1984; Laske 2008), this type of development differs from social-emotional development in that it regards not simply the social but the physical world in which the social world is embedded. Cognitive development is one beyond purely logical thinking, consisting of the acquisition of systemic, holistic, and what we refer to as "transformational," thinking in which logical thinking is fully embedded. This development is spoken of as occurring in "phases" rather than "stages" since consistent and unchangeable lines of demarcation of levels of complexity of thinking have not been found by researchers.

Often, cognitive development is associated with the development of the level of abstraction from which complex problems are tackled. Several authors (e.g., Jaques & Cason 1994; Dawson-Tunik et al. 2005) have described hierarchies of complexity handling within bounded tasks. These frameworks do not usually assume that a person functions within a particular phase of cognitive development. Remaining bound to clearly defined tasks formulated in a strictly logical fashion, they describe heuristics that people follow within specific tasks. Since they are based on written assessments, not recorded structured interviews in real time, they do not capture the total scope of human thinking but only slices of formal logical thinking demonstrated in task behavior.

According to these logic-based approaches, people evolve from concrete thinking to abstract and more principled thinking. Researchers try to show that at each subsequent step, a person will grow from the use of single to multiple concepts and will then proceed to handle ideas systematically. Concrete thinking about customer orientation is expressed in particular categories in which one thinks, e.g., speed, correctness, and completeness of the information provided. When one talks about friendliness, building a relationship of trust, or the customer experience, more abstract thinking is required. A principle such as "coherence of the total customer experience" is still more complex and thus ambiguous. According to the theorists named above, the level of abstraction in performing a task will determine how a team member contributes to team dialogue and follows up initiatives a team has decided on.

Otto Laske's approach (2008), which builds on the work of Basseches (1984) and Bhaskar (1993), takes a perspective on cognitive development that combines a "dialectical" and a "dialogical" point of view and is decidedly focused on dialogue in real-time, not abstract thinking in an armchair (Schwartz 2015). In his Dialectical Thought Form (DTF) Framework, he sees cognitive growth as having to do with following the CPRT Sequence (also referred to as "four moments of dialectic"). This sequence refers to cognitive development as becoming aware of thought *structures* of one's thinking in contrast to "what" one thinks about (or content of thinking). Simultaneously, Laske moves cognitive research from written assessments to structured interviews in real time, which allows him or her to broaden the scope of thinking one can theorize about decisively. According to DTF, cognitive development comprises four interrelated conceptual dimensions called CPRT, each of which comprises the same number (7) of different thought forms.

You can think of *thought forms* as fishing nets, and of the world as an ocean of complexity far transcending the reach of human thought. What one can catch from the sea depends on the form and structure of one's net. Our thinking is embedded in thought forms by a process very similar to that by which the fisherman's expectation of the shape of the fish he or she is after becomes embedded in the design of the net he or she casts out to sea.

According to DTF, we can distinguish four types of fishingnets that determine "how" we think about the contents (or "what") of our thinking. These are four trans-logical perspectives from which to view the real world and its generative mechanism. Laske (2008) defines them as thought form classes and refers to them as CPRT: *context, process, relationship, and transformation.* By becoming aware of the thought forms one is presently using, one becomes conscious that "what one thinks" and "how reality works" might be entirely different issues. As a result, thought forms strengthens the thinker's sense of how social and physical reality may deviate from how humans think (namely, mostly in a rational-logical way).

An awareness of the thought forms one uses in a conversation or writing text, especially in a dialogue with others, strengthens self-reflection, thus the quality of dialogue, for both parties. For instance, one can "think" of something like a static configuration, a process, a set of relationships, or something like an organism that is in the constant transformation to remain identical with itself. In each case, the term, concept, or notion used is part of a different field of meanings associated with it, and clarifying these fields is an important tool in "thinking deeply" rather than superficially in following established logical conventions.

What a person takes into account when understanding a task, interpreting a challenge, or dealing with areas of social tension strongly depends on how he or she conceptualizes the issue in question. The notion in DTF is that the greater the number and variety of thought forms (from the four classes of CPRT), a thinker can put to use in real-time dialogue, the more systemic and integrative is his or her view of the subject matter in question.

In this book, we essentially follow Laske's DTF. Below, we further illustrate the DTF perspective on complex thinking by using the theme of "customer orientation."

### 2.2.1 Thinking About the Real World in Terms of *Context*

Thinking in terms of "context" thought forms help us develop an understanding of the organized whole from which a chosen issue derives its meaning. The key idea is that nothing exists in isolation: everything is part of something bigger and contains components smaller than itself. Within each thought form class, we can distinguish three subcategories, namely, those that help us to recognize contexts, promote the elaboration of contexts, and achieve integration, not only thought contents but also of thought forms from different classes.

Context thought forms help to discern a part within a whole as well as the contribution of part(s) to a whole and vice versa. They focus the attention on what remains relatively stable throughout occurring changes. In terms of how the real world works, these are the structures that hold together things that are in motion, for example, enduring generative mechanisms. Relative to issues such as customer focus, these may be the processes through which products and services are delivered to customers. Smoothly running customer care processes can mask evolving customer expectations. Digital formats in which customers are invited to express their wishes often do not capture evolutions of these wishes because sometimes only a limited number of choices are envisioned.

Context thought forms are systemic and holistic; they enable the understanding of an entity as a system along with its layers, strata, structures, and functions that form the big picture. Like any concept in an organizational context, "customer focus," for example, is layered and many different perspectives can be taken. For example, the notion of "customer focus" can be defined based on:

- Individual tasks to be performed (e.g., speed and correctness)
- A team perspective (e.g., functions carried out by the customer service team in contrast to those of the sales team)
- A process perspective viewing interactions with different departments (e.g., the invoicing process, the logistics process)
- Viewing an organizational whole in which overarching considerations are paramount (e.g., the desire to be sustainable or a market leader)

**Table 2.1** Thinking in terms of context

| Context | Thought forms | Questions |
|---|---|---|
| Recognition (r) | Relationship between part(s) and whole | What contexts (isolated systems) are essential to this project?<br>What are their essential components or layers of the system?<br>What are subsystems of A no longer in equilibrium with each other, thereby threatening A's wholeness (systemic health)?<br>How does an imbalance of components or parts of A change A's relationship to B? |
| Elaboration (e) | Structure and stability of a system | What broader context, B, is system A embedded in, and how does this context influence A (e.g., virtualize or cripple it?)<br>What is the function of context A as a system component? Does its functionality change if it is found that A is embedded in B, and if so, how? |
| Integration (i) | Multiple contexts and frames of reference | How do we assess the stability/instability of context A?<br>What intellectually more realistic frames of reference override A's original significance for maintaining B?<br>What evaluation system(s)—once helpful in understanding A—no longer are, and why? |

Context-thinking also focuses on frames of reference, traditions, or paradigms from which individual theories, thoughts, and assumptions originate. A customer journey perspective, which focuses on specific moments of interaction with customers, will lead to a different interpretation of the notion of "customer service" than an ecosystem perspective, where the focus is on creating a supportive network through which customers can answer their questions by themselves.

When used by an individual thinker working in real time, each of the contextual thought structures generates a multitude of specific questions through which to examine reality critically. We can say, therefore, that questions deriving from the context class of thought structure have a *mind-opening* effect.

For the three classes of contextual thinking mentioned (recognition, elaboration, and integration), Table 2.1 presents a selection of questions that a thought form functioning as a mind-opener (e.g., in a team dialogue) might bring forth.

### 2.2.2 Thinking About the Real World in Terms of *Process*

Process is the aspect of thinking that focuses on what is in motion, either in thought itself or in the world that thought is constructing, regardless of whether the focus is on the past, present, or future. Process thought forms help to develop an understanding of emergence, including the emergence of the past and future into the present. One thinks of situations or frameworks as continuously evolving, of relevance to what one sees as happening next. The key idea is that stability or durability is temporary, not the rule, however much logical thinking tends to reduce motion to a sequence of fixed states, thereby denying that everything is in flux.

Importantly also, thinking in terms of the process focuses attention on what is presently missing (absence), whether not yet or no longer "there." The underlying idea in this class of thought forms is that all change is rooted in *absence*. The notion of absence enables one to think in terms of change: if everything were absolutely and forever in its place, change would be impossible. Absence—in the form of incompleteness, hidden dimensions, suppressed aspects of a subject matter, or lack of social fulfillment—drives the development of new options provided by the real world and of human thinking about them. In fact, absences punctuate reality and are as real as what is present (Bhaskar 1993). Consequently, change has to be viewed as emergence from a void, a coming-into-being of what was not there before and is without unitary origin.

Thinking in process thought forms starts with the ability to acknowledge and recognize changes as unceasingly occurring. In terms of customer service, for example, this means we can identify how customer needs change over different time horizons. Accordingly, we can make explicit next trends, reformulate them, make explicit what is presently overlooked in how change is conceptualized, and formulate new steps taking what was previously not accounted for into account.

A second process thought form class enables the elaboration of recognized change by detailing patterns of interaction between the process(es) that bring it

**Table 2.2** Thinking in terms of process

| | Thought forms | Questions |
|---|---|---|
| Recognition (r) | Emergence and inclusion of opposites | What is the nature of the process that drives A to B, and what subprocesses of A are of prime relevance in this motion?<br>In what way are the subprocesses composing A becoming constitutive elements of B, which A is tending to morph into?<br>Is there something we cannot recognize in A that, if transparent, would facilitate our understanding of A's motion toward B?<br>What is the structure (and function) of changes in A, and in what way do these changes account for instability in B? |
| Elaboration (e) | Pattern(s) of interaction in processes | Are there flows of influence? Originating from … toward … how?<br>What correlations and interdependencies do you see in the way in which developments unfold?<br>How would you describe the pattern of influence of one process on the other?<br>Which patterns in the mutual influence of processes on each other do you see evolving?<br>Which patterns emerge into new configurations?<br>How does an observed interaction stabilize form and identity of a protagonistic process? |
| Integration (i) | Embedding in the process(es) | Does the move from A to B give rise to other, even multiple, contexts?<br>What is changing in A and is about to perturb A's identity with itself?<br>Can A be viewed as codefined by B in real time, or vice versa? |

about. In customer service, this may, for example, relate to the cohesiveness of service delivery via digital channels and patterns in smartphone use.

The third process thought form class within process provides an integrated perspective on the changing nature of a system, and the embeddedness of issues in overarching processes. An example of this is the intertwining of evolving customer expectations with evolutions in general spending patterns, such as the evolutions in the subeconomy, or evolving customer wishes to reduce the ecological footprint.

The examples given above exemplify the many possible interpretations of the term "customer orientation." Just as one can become aware of contextual forms of thinking through mind-opening questions (say, in a team meeting), such questions can lead to thinking in terms of process thought forms. Table 2.2 presents some questions that help trigger process thinking.

### 2.2.3 Thinking About the Real World in Terms of *Relationship*

In contrast to contexts and processes, relationships are entirely invisible and thus often difficult to grasp. Relationship thought forms help the thinker to develop an understanding of connectedness and common ground. This is the aspect of thinking that focuses on the internal and external links that hold things together. The key idea is that the real world is a network of relationships of systems, and we disregard them at our peril. In fact, there are pieces of the real world that codefine each other, such as "house" and "roof," so that two or more elements imply each other and are intrinsically linked with each other. While this vantage point is pursued in conventional systems thinking, that thinking stops short at recognizing and tracing *intrinsic* relationships, a major deficiency since many codefined entities play a role in organizational thinking.

Thinking in terms of relationship focuses attention on internal and external links among various elements that compose a system. To understand a system, the thinker needs to bring conceptual elements into relationship with each other. If, for example, someone explains that you cannot dissociate customer focus from a particular manager's mandate and describes how the definition of role boundaries limits how customer focus is implemented in practice, he or she does so by invoking relationship thought forms. In this way, an unlimited number of relationships that define customer focus are recognized, named, and acted upon, whether the issue in focus is access to additional customer information, the impact of commercial campaigns for creating customer expectations, and interrelated elements that define customer expectations in the first place.

The second subclass of relationship thought forms supports the elaboration of relationships, making explicit the structure of the link(s) that bind constitutive elements together. Through using this class of thought forms, one brings into focus on how relationships are structured to understand relationships more deeply. For example, one may want to interpret connections between dimensions of customer-focused collaboration, whether they be fundamental beliefs (e.g., competition versus cooperation) or values (sustainability versus ease of use).

An integrative perspective taken on relationships supports surfacing the relational nature of a system, doing justice to it as a set of intrinsic, codefining relationships. This brings into view patterns of interaction and influence in relationships (i.e., the existence of "constitutive" relationships), and reciprocal interactions that may be changing over time.

There are salient connections between all classes of thought forms. Relationship thought forms are essential for a full understanding of context because they lay open internal relationships within whole systems. Such thought forms are also critical to understanding what is in progress since they provide insights into how related processes coevolve or dissolve. More generally, things are different only to the extent that they are also the same (e.g., apples and pears) since differences between things presuppose what they have in common (their common ground, such as being fruits).

Table 2.3 presents mind-opening questions deriving from relationship thought forms.

### 2.2.4 Thinking About the Real World in Terms of *Transformation*

Transformational thought forms support an understanding of unfolding developments that preserve the identity of a system, bring about its disequilibrium, allow

**Table 2.3** Thinking in terms of relationship

| | Thought form | Questions |
|---|---|---|
| Recognition (r) | Bringing elements into relationship | Up to what point is A separable from B?<br>What is the value of linking A to B and both of them to C?<br>What relationships might exist between A and B that typically go unnoticed?<br>What aspects of an external relationship between A and B might be intrinsic to A (accounting for its demise)?<br>What opportunities and/or risks might emerge should A turn out to be inseparable from B? |
| Elaboration (e) | Structure of the relationship | What precisely is the structure of the relationship between A and B, whether looked at as static or evolving?<br>Why might relationships between A and B be more relevant than others regarding B's link to C? |
| Integration (i) | Patterns of interaction and influence in the relationship | Is there a pattern in how A tends to relate to B?<br>Could the relationship between A and B be anchored in C?<br>Could A and B coevolve through their relationship to C? |

for its coordination and integration, and transform mere quantitative into qualitative changes. Using such thought forms, the thinker deepens his or her understanding of realities that remain identical with themselves only in constantly transforming themselves (as persons do), these being the most complex systems (called "organisms") that exist in the real world.

Thinking in terms of transformation reclaims the absences that are usually hidden in things and brings them into the focus of attention. For mastering transformational thought forms, mastering context, process, and relationship thought forms is a precondition. Only due to their synthesis, a multidimensional lens on complex realities can emerge. Transformational thinkers discern the presence and absence of equilibria, the limits of stability and durability, and can do justice to gradual or sudden shifts, reversals, collapse, breakdowns, and pain. They see emergence as an outcome of only incompletely understood transformations of intrinsic relationships and can point to hidden potentials, failures, and the gradual breakdown of what appeared to be stable. Such thinkers pay attention to the unfolding of possibilities, problems of coordination and mergers, and changes in developmental direction and acknowledge human agency as intentional causality in the cosmos complicit with social action. The critical question such thinkers ask is, "How might systems of systems come into being, and if coalescing, what new systems do they foreshadow?"

The first class of transformational thought forms addresses the limits of system stability. This class asserts that every kind of stability has limits and helps focus on the places where a system is dysfunctional, lacks essential ingredients, or starts to break down. For instance, when looking at a company's customer orientation as a system from a transformational perspective, one may bring into view instability that derives from shifts in the use of distribution channels (e.g., situations in which customers give up seeking personal contact and instead switch to options open to them for buying a product or service more quickly or via different channels. Limitations in safeguarding customer orientation may also regard the fact that customers need faster feedback on their complaints and in the absence of getting feedback to proceed to share their issues instantly on social media, to the detriment of the company concerned.

The second class of transformational thought forms generates a consciousness that movement in a developmental direction is important for creating higher levels of functioning and that conflict may be valuable because it helps break down dysfunctional forms and systems whose breakdown can be channeled in a developmental (transformational) direction. In the context of customer focus, provoking a conflict with a customer can be a starting point to rethinking specific operational processes heretofore unquestioned.

The third class of transformational thought forms focuses on evaluating system transformations based on a range of criteria of equilibrium, or processes merging two or more systems into a larger and more effective whole. Here, one starts to use evaluative measures such as practical value, conformance to an ideal, and potential for contribution to important novel outcomes. Users of this class of thought forms are enabled to make explicit how systems interact with each other and to grasp how their interactions are or could become mutually sustaining. They focus on the coordination of systems as a way for systems to become more inclusive, integrated, and unified while also more highly differentiated.

Table 2.4 presents mind-opening questions deriving from the class of transformational thought forms.

To the extent that an individual's thinking is transformational, his or her thinking is highly tuned to what in a specific situation needs to be done, for example, in terms of interventions. Such a person is like a surgeon who tunes his team to share the holistic view he or she embodies. Such a person achieves the highest degree of complexity handling conceivable. If in addition, the person is acting from a high level of social-emotional maturity, he will demonstrate a masterful grasp of situational proclivities and facets. Paradoxically, such an individual's thinking maybe "slower" (better paced) than a "clever" person's thinking because he or she avoids errors and thus protects projects from having to be revamped.

## 2.3 Stratification and Developmental Diversity: The Three We-Spaces

We live within social networks and are in constant interchange with each other. In our interactions, we negotiate with others the meaning we attach to our environment: what seems to be happening, how to interpret it, what remains hidden, what a situation seems to require in terms of actions, and what results such actions can be expected to have.

**Table 2.4** Thinking in terms of transformation

| | Thought forms | Questions |
|---|---|---|
| Recognition (r) | Limits of system stability | What subsystems of A expose it to instability?<br>What are subsystems of A under development that weaken or reinforce A's intrinsic relationship to B?<br>What do we gain in letting go of assuming that A is stable?<br>Which quantitative changes within A drive it into a qualitative transformation into A? |
| Elaboration (e) | Developmental movement of systems | How do we take advantage of instability in A to safeguard B to which it is closely linked?<br>What conflicts define A relative to its environment?<br>Are the conflicts in A intrinsic (due to its own constitution) or caused externally, e.g., by B?<br>Do conflicts in A set up antagonistic polarities we should harvest?<br>Which parts and aspects of A reveal developmental potential that will reinforce B's relationship to C? |
| Integration (i) | Comparison and coordination of systems, the emergence of new entities | What pattern characterizes A's unceasing transformation?<br>Does coordinating A and B strengthen B's transformation into C?<br>Would merging A and B heighten or diminish their link to C (or hinder the breakdown of C)?<br>What are the ingredients of C that receive the most robust transformational energy from A and B? |

In the way such negotiations unfold, developmental differences play an essential role. Such differences determine the breadth and depth with which people enter into, not just exchange but dialogue with each other. In their interactions, people develop shared meanings and develop ideological frameworks of a very local and specific nature. In our previous book (De Visch and Laske 2018), we called such interaction patterns "We-Spaces." Such spaces are defined by (mostly implicit) shared meanings and, following from them, rules of interaction.

We-Spaces are mental universes whose members interpret challenges, make choices, and act collaboratively in a commensurable way. For an onlooker, they have a "family similarity." How such spaces function is a consequence of the cognitive and social-emotional maturity levels that come into play within them. Such spaces are invisible but very real, like absences in the real world. When they are not perceived or acknowledged, they hinder transparency, stop the action in the wrong places, and promote activities prematurely or belatedly. They constitute organizations' "hidden dimensions." The fact that they do not coincide with existing (logical or pragmatic) classifications, such as hierarchical levels, departments, or teams, makes them invisible twice over. However, using developmental theory, one can discern them empirically and increase their optimal functioning.

In this book, based on empirical research, we distinguish three different We-Spaces: (1) the space of continuous improvement of existing organizational subprocesses, (2) the space of rethinking value streams and operational models, and (3) the space of rethinking and evolving business models. The problems occurring in each of these We-Spaces are quite different, and so is the universe of discourse team members located in such spaces engage with and dialog within.

Below, we briefly outline the salient characteristics of We-Spaces. We can characterize all of them by a specific quality of dialogue directly flowing from the level of cognitive development members are positioned on. They are "thought spaces" defined by the complexity of thinking their members are capable of, not only on account of their professional competences but of cognitive capabilities that enables a member to become critical of his or her competences and transcend them for the sake of supporting collaboration.

The three We-Spaces characterized

In the *continuous improvement space*, the dialogue focuses on the creation of customer satisfaction, or meeting evolving product and service requirements. In the *value streams space team*, the dialogue centers around the rethinking of operational flows. The dialogue often takes the form of exploring new and meaningful ways of engaging customers or ensuring that the end-to-end operational processes get organized efficiently and effectively.

In the *business modeling space*, the focus falls on making decisions about, and curating, alternative patterns visible in the evolving product/service-technology-market and associated risk-assessments—thus on deep thinking regarding novel business models required for keeping the company afloat.

The three We-spaces require three qualitatively different levels of human capability, not simply competences, thus imply that members collaborating in these spaces have increasingly more complex developmental profiles and world views. The members of these teams experience not only objectively different challenges but are able to to view them from higher maturity levels. Accordingly, the values undergirding their work are increasingly complex and differ for each type of team.

Not only the values but also the quality of thinking and dialogue is different in each of the three We-Spaces. In the continuous improvement space, dialogue regards the immediate and mundane challenges involved in answering a variety of customer-related questions, such as errors, upgrading of work, slow deliveries, and so on. Solutions must be found as quickly as possible by optimization and differentiation of approaches. Situations are very often examined based on accumulated technical expertise, and problems are analyzed by dividing them into manageable parts. The logical, analytical approach prevails.

In the value stream We-Space, a more systemic, and at times holistic, approach is followed. One investigates problems in their mutual relationship and in terms of the time horizons needed to solve them. Often, work in this space aims to broaden the flow of organization-wide information and collaboration. The aim is to integrate inputs from separate and different functional domains.

In the business modeling space, dialogue tends to be informed by transformational thinking since it focuses on the company or even market in its entirety, as well as on emerging changes and disappearances, complex relationships, and imbalances that define the totality of an organization's functioning, even future viability.

In general, how members of each We-Space perceive its challenges and set its priorities is a function of their developmental stage and phase of cognitive development. As we saw previously, the level of adult development from which people deliver work to a high degree determines what they have, or have not, an awareness of, which is something that dramatically transcends mere competences. For instance, if a team's challenge lies in the domain of organizational value streams and the team's dominant focus is to optimize its own work process (as in the continuous improvement We-Space), it is highly unlikely that the broader challenge will be addressed.

The prevailing notion that teams are developmentally homogeneous—in the sense that all team members function on the same level of maturity—can therefore safely be called *fictitious*. This insight receives extra weight when one considers that the degree of work complexity is increasingly higher as we move to business model We-Spaces. Hence the empirical question arises of whether a team is developmentally ready to deal with the complexity of the task it has taken on or has been assigned to.

Quite independently of the question of what degree of collaborative intelligence one wishes to achieve in a specific team, one needs to address the issue of how individuals think differently at different levels of social-emotional and cognitive maturity. Only then can one be realistic about the level of self-organization a team can achieve and can put in place interventions meant to raise that level. In doing so, one is going to discover—in teams of all types—a considerable gap between the complexity of the real world, on the one hand, and the quality of thinking teams bring to the task of addressing that reality, on the other.

Given the developmental diversity of most teams, it makes sense to view teams in terms of their developmental minority and majority. If a team's majority is developmentally less developed than its minority, it evidently will be characterized by a dynamics that is very different from that of the opposite case in which the majority is more highly developed than the minority. The potential for achieving collaborative intelligence is thus a function of a team's overall dynamics as determined by the convergence of its members' developmental levels. Also, the more we move into the business model space, the more is the importance of cognitive development ascendant over social-emotional development. Overall, we can hypothesize that the potential of effective collaboration, especially of the self-organizing kind, depends on how a team is developmentally structured, in one of two ways:

1. As a *downwardly divided* team whose more highly developed members are unable to cope with their less-developed colleagues, especially if the latter command more political power than their more developed colleagues

2. As an upwardly divided team whose more highly developed members are successful in securing followers among their less-developed colleagues

A team's social-emotional We-Space is vital for teamwork. It grounds not only members' interpersonal process (bonding), but also their task process (problem-solving through thinking). A team's We-Space is the result of the extent to which self-authoring prevails among team members which, in turn, determines how team members choose to respond to the complexity of the real world they are embedded in.

Although self-authoring team members are rarely able to discern the limitations of their own value system, they are, in most cases, cognitively sufficiently developed to envision the invisible, such as future configurations and markets. If a big gap separates a team's social-emotional and cognitive profiles, it is unlikely that the team will rise to a level of collaboration needed to do justice to the difficulties of the real world. In that case, even optimal bonding will remain ineffectual.

Table 2.5 summarizes the essential upward and downward dynamics occurring in the three different We-Spaces introduced above.

## 2.4 A Template for Understanding Individuals' Experiences of the Real World

The fundamental assumption made by the approach outlined above is that human minds establish what they view as "reality" in interaction with each other (i.e., dialogically) and, further, that there is no way to speak of "reality" without speaking about oneself. This entails that, contrary to conventional assumptions, language does not simply describe what "is," but creates new realities that are constructed by individuals engaged in dialogue. In assuming that language merely "describes" rather than also "creates" world, sight is lost of the fact that socioemotional meaning-making and cognitive sense-making together lead to the creation of worlds unique to each participant in the dialogue.

Starting from the philosophical vantage point outlined above, we are able to focus attention on critically reflecting on the interpretative meanings we create through verbal language. We then also have to acknowledge that distinct truths may coexist. We thereby enable ourselves to do three things simultaneously:

- Observe how in speaking people produce sense and reality simultaneously.
- Recognize which seemingly absolute truths or patterns are no longer valid or functional for a particular task or task environment.
- Break through fixed opinions and patterns previously relied on.

From a *social-emotional* perspective, the critical question seems to be: what can be done about the fact that people, based on their way of making-meaning of their experiences, "lock themselves into" thought configurations unhelpful to them since they only reproduce problems and solutions they are already familiar with.

**Table 2.5** Types of thinking, interpersonal process, and central issues in downwardly versus upwardly divided teams

| We-Space | Downwardly divided team | Upwardly divided team |
|---|---|---|
| **Continuous improvement**<br>(Examples: task forces sharing a selected isolated focus; communities of practice, advisory teams) | **Thinking [attention and knowledge]:** instrumental, primarily based on downloading predefined theories and models, using concrete, procedural frames of reference without critical inquiry into their origin and limitations<br>**Interpersonal process [personal relationships and management of emotions]**: team members have difficulties in setting their ego aside. A lot of energy is spent on developing common goals with an emphasis on (hidden) self-interests<br>**Main Issue**: "for Me" overshadows "for others." The team gets stuck in inconsistencies of leadership (trying to adapt to individual team members' biases); insufficient understanding of differences in styles, motivations, and mutual expectations | **Thinking:** based mainly on data gathering and logical analysis. Nascent thinking about *what is not (yet) there*—what emerges through change, or is believed to be required in the future<br>**Interpersonal process**: focused on signs of structural consensus<br>**Main issue**: Dialogue gets stuck in slow decision-making following a consensus-oriented dynamics, which results in efforts to persuade the nonfollowers, associated with a risk of regression to the lowest denominator |
| **Rethinking of value streams and operational flows**<br>(Examples: teams with bottom-line responsibility; collaborative networks with the client; cross-functional workgroups focused on selected end-to-end processes) | **Thinking**: mostly based on data gathering and logical analysis. Insufficient grasp of taking multiple perspectives transcending the differences between functional specializations<br>**Interpersonal process**: tuned to others' expectations; reputations are sacrosanct; one wants to do the least harm to others and one's standing<br>**Main issue**: Team dialogue gets stuck in trying to grasp and define a more comprehensive system as a playground for one's own decision-making | **Thinking**: based on adaptive systems approaches, giving rise to multiple feedback loops. Decision-making is grounded in doubting, probing, researching, and examining supposedly linear relationships<br>**Interpersonal process**: persuasion is based on members' values and the identification with a larger whole; purposes are inseparable from safeguarding one's integrity<br>**Main issue**: The dialogue gets stuck in the inability of the team, to define strategy beyond member consensus, risk of abdicating leadership |
| **Rethinking business models**<br>(Examples: collaborative innovation networks; program management offices; teams with a focus on future value creation such as capital efficiency methods) | **Thinking**: scenario based, and geared to testing alternative models and strategies. Notwithstanding the mandate to create breakthroughs, taking multiple perspectives is weak; uncritically espoused value systems hinder the team from transforming its status quo<br>**Interpersonal process**: the team is seen as a neutral terrain in which different positions compete for power. (At each moment, there is one dominant power coalition, and those not belonging to it are expected to remain loyal to the team)<br>**Main issue**: The dialogue gets stuck in different conflicting value systems for which members are building political scaffolding | **Thinking**: characterized by broad holistic, inclusive, and transformational thinking, with a high level of coordination of thought forms. High awareness of "how one thinks" in contrast to "what one thinks" that strengthens members' cognitive fluidity and critical realism<br>**Interpersonal process**: humble inquiry, privileging asking over telling and doing, in a high-quality dialogue. Desire to understand how conflict is generated relative to oneself; little demand for power. Members think of and treat, others as contributors to their own development, thereby modeling ongoing learning, self-inquiry, and risking self-exposure<br>**Main issue**: Dialogue gets stuck in conflict leading to a lack of consensus, questioning of agreements made |

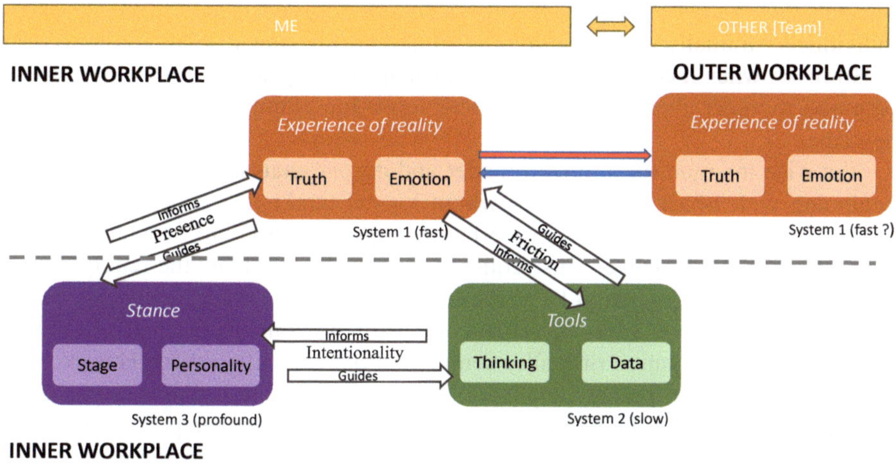


**Fig. 2.1** A template for understanding individuals' experience of the real world

From a *cognitive* perspective, the critical question seems to be: what can be done to raise individuals' awareness of their own way of thinking, in such a way that they recognize the thought structures they adopt; and further, how does the lack of complex thought structures reduce the degree to which they can gain transparency as to how the real world works. To do so, teams require a critical facilitator who can point out what thought forms are presently missing from a dialogue and conversely, which thought forms offer "fresh" perspectives on the subject matter under discussion.

In addition to the developmental stage a person is living at, his or her psychological profile ("personality") strongly influences how the social world shows up for them. Following Freud, Moris Aderman (Hawkins 1970) saw personality as a configuration of deeper *needs* constellated in relation to environmental *pressures* on a person. In his perspective, a person is continuously focused on fulfilling in-born needs, which are clashing with ethical ideals and are under pressure from society. Satisfying needs is made difficult by the social environment one is part of. Consequently, the person lives with tensions relative to need fulfillment, including the realization of personal and professional ideals. How efficiently he or she makes use of his or her own (limited) energy budget will determine his or her degree of suffering. From here, it is a small step toward explaining a person's intentionality based on how the real world shows up for him or her.

In Fig. 2.1, we propose a hypothesis as to the nature of the process by which individuals interpret their experiences of the world at large including their workplace. We start from the observation that perception of reality surfaces a set of "truths" and "emotions" that mark the individual's world as "real." Reactions to experiences are immediate and occur quickly; they are also taken for granted. In addition, rather than tracing experiences to an internal process, they are quickly made an object of description in communication with others.

Kahneman (2011) calls this *system 1 thinking* and describes a multitude of thought errors that are made in this fast-paced, first-step, experience of reality. In line with this, Kahneman argues for slow processing to eliminate the thinking errors individuals habitually make, for the sake of quickly arriving at what he calls *system 2*. However, when it comes to providing an analysis of system 2, Kahneman has no recourse to other than logical-analytical tools for eliminating the fallacies he describes.

It is wise to argue for a much broader and deeper analysis of thought fallacies beginning with Bhaskar (1993) for whom logical thinking is prone to a slew of reductions of how the real world works. He argues on account of what we have called the CPRT Sequence. This sequence honors the fact that "the reality is pervaded by absences" (as part of P), to the effect that what we superficially experience as "real" is far removed from the actual complexity we confront. Rather, it is simply a distinctive interpretation of reality sourced by our own life history. However we want to describe the "second step," or entrance into system 2, that is required for rational functioning in the world, we are dealing with a metaperspective based on reflection, removed from immediate experiences. Reflecting on the latter, what emerges for individuals is what we call their "internal dialogue," something we are going to explore in depth later in this book.

The diagram below describes our perspective on how individuals interpret their workplace. We make two fundamental distinctions, (1) that between inner and outer workplace and (2) that between "stance" and "tools." By distinguishing between an "inner" in contrast to an "outer" workplace, we point to the fact that contributors in an organization live and deliver work in their own internal world that is an interpreted version of the outer workplace they are part of and often has very little to do with the latter. The less highly they are developed, individuals are unaware of their interpretation of the workplace, their inner workplace, and therefore take it with them when they migrate to a different external workplace.

By distinguishing "stance" from "tools," we draw conclusions from our distinction between social-emotional meaning-making and cognitive sense-making. How an individual regulates and adapts himself or herself to the real world in the context of his or her stance and tools determines the effectiveness of the person's actions in the world as well as the degree of autonomy the person experiences.

As the figure makes clear, how individuals make meaning and sense of the world, even excluding psychological issues, is a highly complex affair.

In discussions of teams, it is often assumed that exchanging diverse personal perspectives on "the world" leads to a better understanding of reality. Figure 2.1 seems to indicate that this is a mistaken conclusion. People tend to exchange stories that are relevant to them without being aware of the emotional underpinning of their notions of truth, the cognitive tools they use and could use, and the fact that the fundamental perspectives they express are subject to their present stage of development. In short, people are, for the most part, anything but self-aware.

**Key Insights and Practice Reflections**

In this chapter, we have outlined an "adult-developmental" approach to work in organizations. We have shown the complexity of understanding individuals' and teams' work delivery by distinguishing three fundamental dimensions of individual functioning (We-Spaces), with extended conclusions for teams. We are now ready to consider what our developmental hypothesis regarding the nature of work gains us as we search for greater transparency in how organizational practices are constituted. Our main purpose in this is to make such practices more user-friendly as well as effective. Given what we said above about people's tendency to lock into organizational practices by way of inflexible ways of thinking, the issue for us becomes how to break open existing thought fixations when striving to deliver work in an effective and transparent way.

In each of the following chapters, we present different ways of looking at organizational practices. We show in detail how adopting an adult-developmental lens, briefly sketched above, gives new directions to dealing with stuckness in both downwardly and upwardly divided teams, thereby enhancing team member collaboration.

**Practice Reflections**

1. If you had to guess within what adult-developmental range of social-emotional maturity you presently make meaning of your life and work yourself, what stage would you decide on?
2. When you reflect on the development of your own thinking as an adult, can you describe episodes in your life where circumstances forced you to transcend formal logical thinking—not toward "irrational" or emotional behavior but toward a higher equilibrium?
3. In your work as a consultant or manager, have you noticed that clarity of thinking is not always a matter of thinking logically but rather of being able to grasp the bigger picture, emerging change, or essential relationships of reality?
4. If you consider that you operate in a number of different conversational spaces (We-Spaces), in which dialogue space do you feel most comfortable, and which signals do you receive that an upward dynamics characterizes the chosen dialogue space?
5. If you reflect on how you transition from Kahneman's "system 1" to "system 2" in your reflections on immediate experiences, what thought forms do you seem to employ to reach higher levels of reflection?

# Shared Intentionality and Coordinated Action in Meetings: How to Improve the Balance of Asking and Telling

# 3

*In meetings, the process of coordination, self-monitoring, and social monitoring take place side by side. Both monitoring processes find their expression in the mutual concern people have about what they and others can do, as well as what others think about what they should and should not do. Required is an understanding of others in terms of their different ways of paying attention and interpreting the real world based on their present level of emotional and cognitive maturity.*


**Abstract**

In this chapter, we focus on the function as well as the pitfalls of meetings. We emphasize that meeting participants are developmentally not cut from the same cloth. They are, in what they do and do not, limited by how they position themselves to others social-emotionally, as well as by the quality of their conceptual grasp of situations and topics of team discussion.

To lay bare the dialogical dynamics of meetings, we integrate findings from adult-developmental research with Tomasello's research (2014), which conceptualizes collaboration as based on shared intentionality. More specifically, we show that participants carry into meetings what we call their *internal workplace*—the mental space in which they construct their role identity and its interpretation. We see the internal workplace as the crucible of every meeting, whatever its topic, and discuss a range of meeting practices, suggesting how to improve the quality of dialogue in each of the three We-Spaces.


Meetings are essential for organizational functioning. People spend one-third of their professional time in meetings, and half of them complain about the quality of the session they attend. In this chapter, we focus on the function as well as the




J. De Visch, O. Laske, *Practices of Dynamic Collaboration*, Management for Professionals, https://doi.org/10.1007/978-3-030-42549-4_3

pitfalls of meetings. We emphasize that meeting participants are not all cut from the same cloth. They are, in what they do and do not, limited by how they position themselves to others social-emotionally, as well as by their conceptual grasp of situations and topics of discussion.

To better understand what happens in meetings, we integrate findings from adult-developmental research with Tomasello's research (2014), which conceptualizes collaboration as based on shared intentionality. More specifically, we show that participants carry into meetings what we call their *internal workplace*—the mental space they construct for themselves when interpreting their role. It is this workplace that is the crucible of every meeting, whatever its topic.

## 3.1 What Happens in Meetings

With the rise of self-organization, the meeting support industry is experiencing a revival. Almost every approach to self-organization (Holacracy, Sociocracy 3.0, Teal, Agile) has its associated variety of meeting formats. These formats vary from organizing work daily, to cocreating the future. Each of the proposed meeting approaches formulates an answer to the question of how to deal efficiently and effectively with time and with differences in the individual perspectives of participants. There is an underlying belief that one can improve the course of meetings through a set of principles (e.g., the Principles at Bridgewater (Dalio 2017)), organizational processes (e.g., the Holacracy Constitution (Robertson 2016)), and behavioral modules (e.g., Many Voices One Song (Rau and Koch-Gonzalez 2018)). These approaches all promise to facilitate alignment toward shared action. However, the efficiency and effectiveness of these approaches promise are not fulfilled in practice.

Despite the considerable investment in facilitating meetings (including with digital tools) and pieces of training in communication and execution, meeting inefficiency will continue to exist while the "How-to-Do" industry will continue to flourish. This is because the starting point for training in meeting practices is strictly behavioral, deriving from what one can see participants doing in real time and "logically" infer from it. It does not derive from insight into how participants internally experience the social reality around them to which they unceasingly contribute based on the level of adult development they are unconsciously subject to. In short, the scenario is one of the blind leading the blind.

Tomasello observes that children formulate individual objectives at an early stage. Often children fail in pursuing the goals based on the interpretations they make of others' intentions and assumptions about how others interpret their own objectives. Even if they succeeded, following their example would not suffice. Cooperation builds on shared intentions; however, it requires more than mutual knowledge of each other's goals. It also requires an understanding of others in terms of their different ways of paying attention and interpreting the real world based on their present level of emotional and cognitive maturity.

"Shared intentionality" by itself is not the solution but is instead the problem, even for children. While playing, they seem to provide each other with the information they find essential for taking action and are paying attention to one another. They do not always end up cooperating. This is because cooperation entails not only a shared focus of attention and intention but also a recognition of the social-emotional "stance" (world view) others are positioned in, and the resulting perspectives they are inclined to take, not to speak of understanding the thought-form structure of their perspective-taking seen as a mental process evolving in real time.

For the business community, the lesson seems to be that any formulation of objectives is weak if it is not supported by an understanding of differences in how different individuals pay attention to their own and others' functioning in collaborative processes.

In organizational work, an additional requirement of successful cooperation is to align assumptions concerning team members' specific roles and an accurate perception of how these roles are executed in dependence of individual actors' developmental resources. In short, the following is required: a mutual understanding of who can or will do what when. Agreeing on tasks per se is not enough. What is needed is the anticipation of differences between the quality of different actors' contributions. Given developmental—emotional and cognitive—differences between team members, such expectation is far from easy to obtain without the extensive practice of close listening to what is being said by team members. However, "listening closely" will not do either if one remains fixated on the notion that by speaking people are merely describing the world, rather than recreating it in their own interpretation.

Tomasello (2014) argues that all collective action presupposes an understanding of a team's division of labor in the sense of the organically unfolding give-and-take between team members (rather than a fixed template such as a job description). His research shows that in the process of coordination, self-monitoring and social monitoring take place side by side. Self-monitoring consists of evaluating one's capabilities as well as ascertaining how these may influence the team's work. Social monitoring consists of evaluating the collaborative quality of a specific team member for the sake of achieving objectives. Both monitoring processes find expression in the mutual concern people have about what they and others can and cannot do. They also have to do with what others think about what they themselves should and should not do.

In Chap. 2, we sketched the three systems involved in team members' evaluation of each other: System 1 (fast), System 2 (slow), and System 3 (profound). Since team members' mutual adjustment engages the entire mental processing of participants—psychological, social-emotional, and cognitive—obviously, the attempt to formulate common objectives, conclude work agreements, and aligning the focus of attention will be a struggle. The reason for this is simple: a "bird's-eye-view" of the possible course collaboration can take never becomes available to participants.

Figure 3.1 visualizes the dynamics of collaboration as we see it from an adult-developmental vantage point.

The figure focuses on the core of the social, psychological, and developmental exchange process between people, i.e., that of aligning the focus of attention,

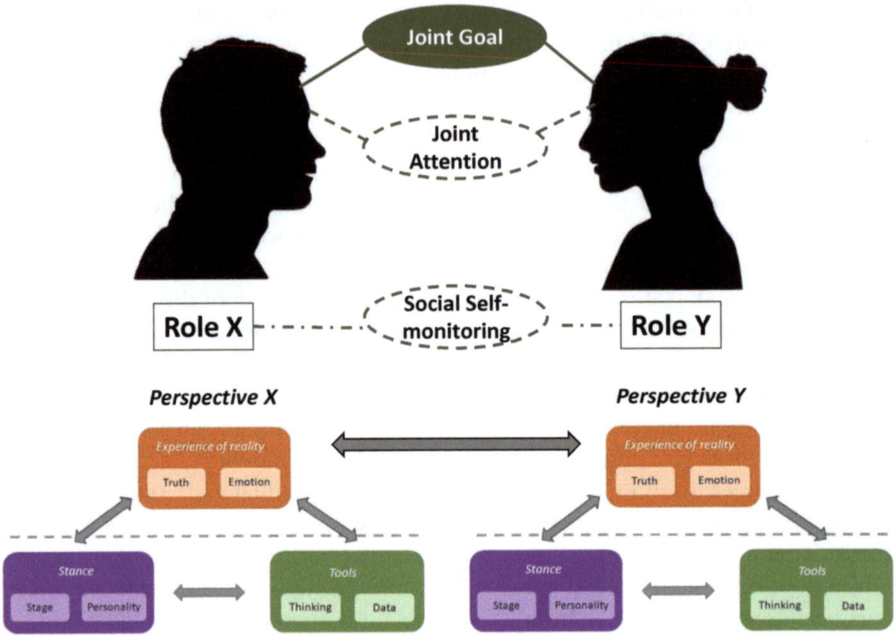


**Fig. 3.1** Essential elements of cooperation at work

formulating mutual intentions and interpretations, and arriving at a division of labor agreements. As seen, any two people's attention and social self-monitoring processes are different from each other. Each of them operates in his or her distinctive internal workplace and thus holds a specific perspective on the social world around them. Actually, cooperation is more complicated still than conveyed above: our figure only focuses on the variety of *interpretative processes* that come into play without clarifying the process of self-observation.

The function of meetings

Business meetings are an ideal venue for coordinating individuals' attention, intentions, and contributions to the division of labor required for delivering complex work. There have been many attempts to develop standard formats that assist in creating pathways of success in a meeting. Over the years, various meeting formats, kinds of information exchange, problem handling procedures, and decision-making processes have emerged (Keith 2018). Keith puts forward three ingredients as essential for the smooth running of a meeting: making explicit (1) meeting purpose, (2) meeting format, and (3) participants' profiles. In the present context, these ingredients of good meetings are necessary but in no way sufficient for achieving coordination. We discuss their deficiencies below.

The majority of existing meeting guidelines are strictly behavioral. They consider meetings "from the outside in," as an object, not as a process that has a psychological and developmental dimension. Such guidelines are only procedural. They look at goals and outcomes, but not at the processes to achieve them. Since there exists a multitude of observable and inferable aspects of business meetings looked at from the outside—preparing agendas, timing discussions of specific items, drawing up reports, distinguishing roles, asking for clarification, questioning assumptions, etc.—there are also endlessly many "clever" behavioral suggestions one can come up with about how an ideal meeting should unfold. All of these suggestions lack an understanding of the structure of mental processing that unfolds in meetings.

Among the dimensions that forcefully come into play in business meetings is that of the differences between participants' emotional and cognitive maturity profiles. Each meeting participant is a "world to itself" that, to a large extent, remains opaque not only to others but to the person himself or herself. This is so since people are not in control of, but rather are *subject to*, their own developmental position and associated emotional and cognitive processes and therefore have no way of spelling them out for others in a way others can understand. Participants are "islands floating in the ocean," monads of the social world, trying to do their best to adhere to externally outlined agendas even if they have created these agendas themselves.

We are speaking of the influence of adult-developmental diversity on meetings. This influence shows up in how people pay attention to shared goals, share intentions, and they coordinate their activities in meetings. Below, we focus on the patterns of interpretation that unfold in a developmentally mixed group of people holding a meeting. Our discussion focuses on three meeting objectives:

1. Getting work done
2. Learning
3. Innovation

In making these distinctions, we are quite aware that they are often intertwined.

## 3.2 Getting Work Done: Daily Stand-Up Meetings

Daily Stand-Up Meetings (DSMs) were created in response to the limitations of highly planned, long-term approaches to projects. They are a core practice in doing work referred to as "agile." DSMs entails that team members have frequent short meetings and exchange what they have contributed the day (or period) before to the team objective, what they are planning to do in the short term, and what obstacles they see in doing so. It is a working method in which participants share insights and experiences to make decisions quickly.

A planned approach is based on clearly defined issues regarding which all participants have the same information and a shared understanding of the consequences of choices they make, along with possible solutions.

In contrast to conventional meetings, DSMs are of short duration. They provide a template for starting a workday, stimulate exchanges of recent learnings and perspectives, and allow colleagues to get to know each other and ensure they agree with the results envisioned.

DSM meetings come in various forms: scrum meetings, morning report meetings, daily huddle meetings, and action meetings. To limit the duration of the meeting (20 min), participants often hold meetings in a stand-up position.

### 3.2.1 Some Drawbacks of DSMs

In most companies, DSMs have been held for several years now. Stray (2009) notes that in practice, the focus of such meetings is on information exchange, which leaves a discussion of existing problems in the background. They are about "doing," not "thinking about doing." Through a 4-year longitudinal study, Stray found that in such meetings, participants develop focused attention only to a limited degree. They mainly deal with the highest priorities on the table, but either do not follow them or deviate from them.

Another deficiency of DSMs' Stray found is that team members tend to select tasks that suit their primary interests or strength. The selection process leads to unintentional and unwanted specializations and further reduces team members' awareness of the totality of scheduled work. When members connect their piece of the work to the broader plan, they often experience the latter as unrealistic. With increasing specialization, interest in what colleagues are doing declines, and the promise of mutual learning evaporates. The indirect consequence of these tendencies is that conflicts between team members fester, remaining opaque and unresolved.

Overall, Stray concludes that DSMs contribute to problem escalation. Such meetings do not seem to foster a culture in which one can arrive at joint intentions and coordinated action any more efficiently than conventional assemblies.

Although the feeling that DSM is the "right" framework prevails, this feeling is unrealistic. Negative feedback given in DSMs tends to lead to excessive justification of the correctness of choices made. People develop an emotional attachment to their work, so that accountability issues require interventions from team leads (Scrum Masters and Product Owners). Although the dialogue format of DSMs is focused around labels such as "common objectives," "shared attention," "roles," and "self-monitoring," in practice, there is little time for in-depth dialogue about any of these issues.

Other drawbacks of DSMs given realizing a common intention through coordinated action abound.

Dialogue on common objectives is being pushed into the background by the frequency of exchanges about what was done. Therefore, DSM meetings need to be interspersed with sessions reminding participants of the overall planning framework followed and connections with work happening in other teams, thus an outline of the essential interdependency with other projects, as well as drawing attention to areas of tension existing within and beyond the group. Otherwise, employees will fall back on their issues. They find it challenging to take a bird's eye view of the whole they are a part of. Often, such a holistic view is taken only by the "team leader" (very often the Scrum Master or the Product Owner in agile contexts), or else an external facilitator. In practice, the latter chooses a *solution-oriented communication method* to facilitate a meeting.

The core of solution-oriented communication is rooted in focusing attention on the future, visualizing the desired outcome, and making successive small steps to bring it about. However, working in a solution-oriented way often follows a process of purely linear, logical thinking. Logical thinking does not guarantee that the storylines built by the team realistically address the complexity of the situation they are facing. Solution-oriented working also neglects to consider the adult-developmental issues that pervade team meetings. A debate often arises about the correctness of analysis or completed step, in which a team member or a subgroup of members seek to prove they are "right." This dynamic has its origin in the instrumental and/or other-dependent stage of adult-developmental functioning that characterizes a subset of participants or even an entire team, especially at the work level of continuous improvement where most people work.

In *Dynamic Collaboration*, De Visch and Laske (2018) view Stray's findings as an exemplification of what they call *the dynamics of downwardly divided teams*. The essence of this dynamic is that a subgroup of emotionally and cognitively less mature individuals has sufficient clout to monopolize a team's conversation, both in terms of content and time available, and thus achieves factual dominance, undeterred by, or subverting, a more highly developed subgroup. This dynamic has severe consequences for what the team, despite its best intentions, can achieve.

In general, DSM teams reduce the scope of what is discussable, thereby narrowing the mental space of the team. Instead of focusing on a common agenda, discussions in such a group tend to focus on selected individuals' intentions or accomplishments. As a result, they aim to reach consensus for a narrowed-down, ego-centric agenda. Feedback on this agenda by others is not discussed. Instead, attention is paid to procedural frames of reference (simple step-by-step plans), and rules that are in line with what participants already know. Risk-taking is diminished. Emotionally charged unilateral statements characterize conversations. As a result, the team's interpersonal process overshadows the task process. Relevant fields of tension remain opaque, and the most influential individual settles conflicts in terms of power and persuasiveness. Quality listening vanishes and is replaced by information processing.

### 3.2.2 Interventions Leading to More Considerable Shared Attention and Intentionality

We have found that three distinctly different interventions can be helpful in such a situation.

The first approach consists of focusing on interactions between team members. Doing this entails intervening in a group's attention process by challenging specific individuals to embrace new ways of relating to others in the team. This reorientation can be achieved by splitting up meeting participants (e.g., into smaller DSMs) and selectively bringing individuals back together in a broader meeting. In this way, attention gets focused on particular transactions ("I'm doing this, and therefore expect you to do that"), and new agreements are created in each subgroup around very concrete deliverables. As a result, individual contributions are increasingly coordinated.

When pursuing this strategy, it becomes easier to enforce new working methods in small subgroups, one by one. Based on the experience engendered in participants, that the newly chosen approach works, their emotional commitment to their previous method of coordination is broken. In this case, it is advisable not to discuss task conflicts that emerge from the new way of working. Addressing such conflicts only leads to a justification of what one is already doing without strengthening shared intentions.

A second intervention requires a strong leader who focuses on harmonizing personal intentions. Such a leader is advised not to restrict conversations to common objectives and working arrangements. Rather, he or she must be prepared to play with individual team members' specific intentions. She can do so by ensuring that everyone is treated equitably, inviting participants to share feelings (the nonviolent communication method is very suitable for this), stimulating them to ask mutually clarifying questions, expressing objections, and coming up with solutions. In practice, this amounts to choosing for discussion a single (sub)topic to be discussed in detail in a specific meeting, instead of allowing team members to bring forward a multitude of issues.

A third approach requires a team member or outside party to play the role of a *critical facilitator*. Critical facilitation entails that in addition to the content of discussions, attention is drawn to the quality of the team's ongoing thought process. In our work, this is done by using tools provided by Laske's *Dialectical Thought Form Framework* (Laske 2015b). When used in DSMs, an intervention based on this tool leads to a deeper questioning of otherwise overlooked topics, such as (1) the specific intention behind prioritization proposals, (2) assumptions made in analytical interpretations, (3) expressions of uncertainties, and (4) the disconnect between feelings evoked by a formulated solution and the logistic specifics of the solution. In such conceptual and critical work, the facilitator simultaneously intervenes in the team's dialogue and the inner dialogue of individual team members' external dialogue is based on. We will return to this topic in the chapter seven on the development dialogue.

While the three approaches outlined above cause a delay in coordinating action, they also lead to an increase in shared attention and intention. In DTF-based conversations, a different balance is created between telling each other about problems and solutions and questioning the team's ongoing thought process. Although the combination of these three practices often leads to more strongly coordinated action, they do not necessarily generate experiences that have a developmental potential for participants. The time available in DSMs or related types of progress meetings is too limited for achieving higher levels of cognitive and socioemotional development.

More than DSMs, meetings aimed at improving practices and developing new approaches or products offer many more opportunities to discuss the dynamics flowing from teams' adult-developmental diversity, which are discussed below.

## 3.3 Improving Existing Practices: No-Objection Decision-Making

Few companies have not embraced continuous improvement initiatives, often under the misleading name of "innovation." The range of practices is wide: Retros, Lean, Six Sigma, No-Objection Decision-making, Kaizen, and the Toyota Production System are just a few of them. Although the methodologies differ, the underlying ideas are similar, namely a focus on the step-by-step improvement of products, services, and processes. They are all bottom-up approaches. The input and initiative of employees are central to them: employees are the ones who identify, analyze, and propose solutions to improvement opportunities.

Below, we take a closer look at *no-objection decision-making*. It is an approach in which managers are encouraged not only to provide solutions to problems but also to test these solutions with employees. The person requesting advice estimates on how beneficial integrating employees' input into the original proposal might be. The revised proposal is submitted to a core group that formulates objections and possible solutions.

Figure 3.2 summarizes the no-objection decision-making process.

The model rightfully assumes that rarely anyone in an organization has all the knowledge and information necessary for making quality decisions. Advice and input are always required. The input is collected from people who know more about the subject matter than others, as well as those affected by the decisions these experts make. The importance and scope of a decision together determine which people to ask for input and advice. The central notion is that if a round of

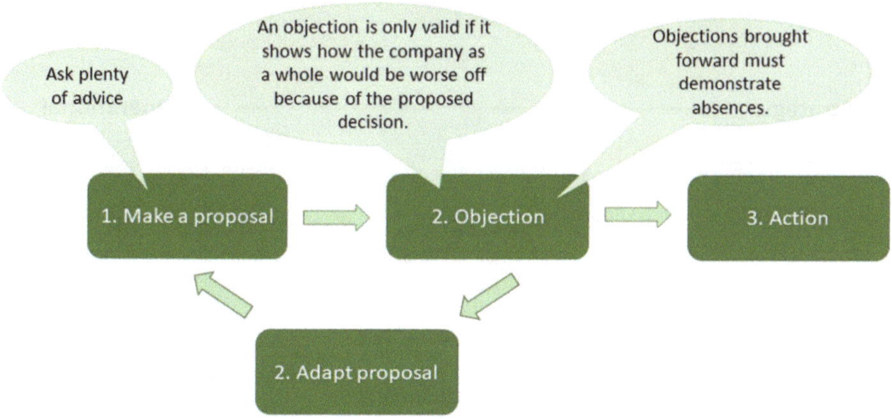


**Fig. 3.2** No-objection decision-making

consultation is not carefully carried out, the chance that valid objections arise will grow. In this way, team members learn to prepare their proposals more thoughtfully than they would typically do. Objections during meetings stop being free test proposals.

### 3.3.1 Two Cases

#### 3.3.1.1 Case 1: HCC

Our practice has shown that using no-objection decision-making process is not easy. We observed this ourselves in a health care company (HCC). The company specialized in supporting networks of independent nurses. The support took the form of training and refresher courses, the provision of IT tools to make nurses' administration more manageable, and facilitating growth. When regulations changed, the company experienced a lot of pressure. Several projects were launched to support nurses as customers. The Managing Director applied the Six Batteries of Change model (De Prins et al. 2017) as the starting point.

The model hypothesizes that a successful change project requires balancing a formal with an informal approach and a strategic with an operational plan. Figure 3.3 visualizes six possible practices, namely, the batteries' (1) "clear strategic direction," (2) "robust management infrastructure," (3) "action planning and implementation," (4) "ambitious top team," (5) "healthy culture," and (6) "strong connection with employees." Each battery consists of three parts: a quick scan of the existing

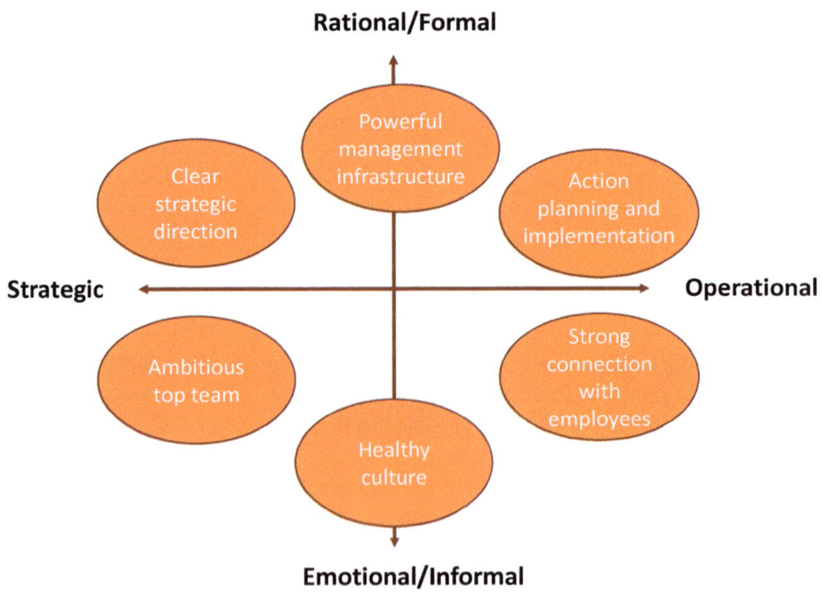


**Fig. 3.3** Case 1—the six batteries of change categories

situation, a simple model providing solutions, and several inspiring one-page examples from other organizations.

In our client organization, based on the model depicted, a variety of project options was considered within a small management group, resulting in establishing a set of projects. This step gave rise to a formulation of corporate values, a customer segmentation project, and a project on performance management. Around each of the projects, 24 in all, small subteams were formed and given 3 months to define an improvement proposal around the project challenge. The teams were provided with a definition of the project and its desired outcomes. They were asked to come up with elaborations and provide a solution within 3 months.

Soon most of the projects got delayed. The teams got stuck in irreconcilable interpretations of the project definitions, and doubts arose as to decisions they wanted to make, with tensions between them rising. There were regular interim joint status meetings through which the teams exchanged results and formulated objections to each other's proposals. Formulating objections turned out to be complicated. Teams barely managed to get the status updates ready, building a story about their work the night before the status meetings.

The customer segmentation project is representative of what happened. In spite of the difficulties project members experienced in identifying clear-cut customer segments, they chose a third-party template suggesting to divide customers into platinum, gold, silver, and bronze groups. Within the project team, there were heated discussions not only about the criteria to use in classifying customers in terms of these four groups but also about the usefulness of the resulting segmentation. In the eyes of employees, all customers deserved the same high-quality service. The collection of objections and feedback from colleagues intensified mutual irritations. In the interim reporting meetings, the focus (of blame) was placed on the person who had the most influence within the team at that time, which meant that collaborators no longer recognized themselves in the project and relinquished it internally. If someone was on leave, the approach changed. In short, few good ideas found their way into practice. We would say that project teams moved on a downward spiral.

#### 3.3.1.2 Case 2: OWCP

We encountered a no-objection decision-making approach in a second company that was putting in place an organization-wide change program (CWCP). The company felt confronted with the evolution of technologies that put existing working methods in doubt. Project teams formed around these technologies. One project member identified as challenge anchoring results of ongoing projects more optimally. He decided to discuss with members of different project teams on how to approach the challenge posed.

The OWCP program comprised 18 projects. External parties from different supplier organizations cooperated. Teams were working on the integration of artificial intelligence into providing services to customers; other groups looked at integrating chatbots into customer service, while still others interwove blockchain applications in administrative applications. Additional teams worked to adapt service/product specifications to new regulatory quality requirements and to change performance dashboards into flexibly prioritizable customer requests.

In this organization, each project was associated with a different time horizon ranging from several months to 5 years. In addition to their ordinary function, employees were assigned specific project roles, for example, expert roles, control roles, script roles, and others. Each project had a lead role, and leading roles formed a program circle. The program aimed to identify all those standard operating procedures (SOPs) on which technological changes were anticipated to have an impact.

Foreseeably, managing the interdependencies between all of these projects proved difficult because the scope of subprojects changed, technology evolved, and the timing of projects was a function of budget and employee availability. Despite detailed project monitoring, it was unclear how the projects could be anchored.

The project initiator, therefore, decided to sit down with staff and create a working method allowing projects to be anchored in the organization. Instead of choosing an existing template to discuss anchoring, he or she and project leaders decided to create a *canvas* by which the future was to be drawn into the present. The starting hypothesis was that operational risks could be controlled only if project results were incorporated into day-to-day operations. The initiator formulated a hypothesis as to which company procedures might be able to manage operational risks.

The canvas started with the question about what was necessary to guarantee project anchoring. It developed iteratively. The project initiator developed the first canvas. Participants voiced objections to the canvas based on their own subprojects. This procedure shed light on what was missing in the canvas, which, based on a new set of objections, was adapted accordingly. Working iteratively helped the members of various project teams to develop a broader view of their project environment, the project's development, and the existing interdependencies between projects. Iterative work also engendered an understanding of what needed to be coordinated to guarantee anchoring project results. After three iterations, a *definitive canvas* was created. Only a few employees had small objections to it.

The definitive canvas comprised three parts:

- In the first section, project members were asked to clarify achieved objectives and take a "bird's eye view" of the result of employing the various methods and frames of reference in play. This amounted to a multidisciplinary recalibration of project contributions resulting in role clarity ("I do").
- In a second section, participants stated which SOPs they followed in each project, and the role each project contributor would take on in the anchoring process. The section comprised an overview of all commitments made to the anchoring. Contributors spelled out results foreseen. A distinction was made between enablers and quick wins, as well as between results expected (output) and their measurement. This exercise enabled members to refine the first section; it resulted in a closing checklist of shared critical points in the handover process ("We do").
- In the third section ("Thinking Differently: Conscious Decision Making"), project members were asked to place themselves into the shoes of employees of the

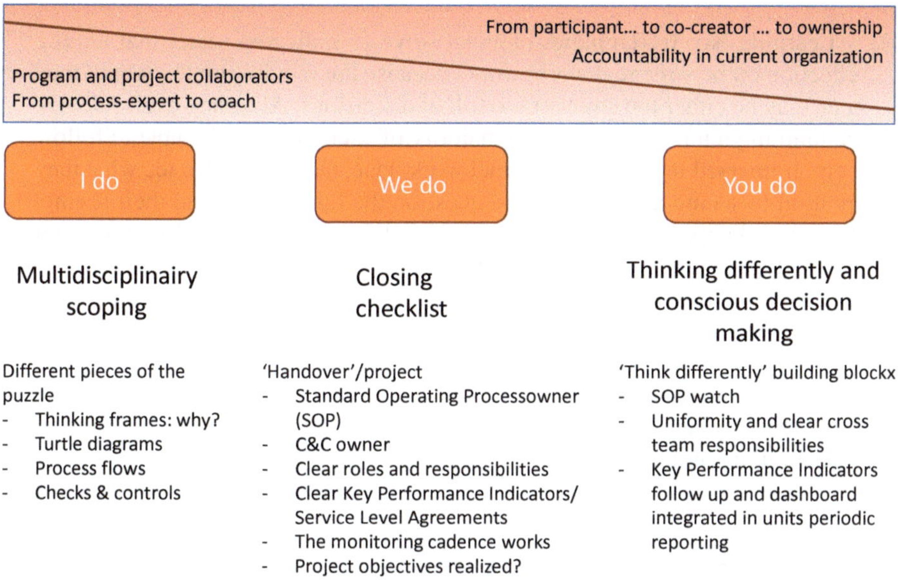


**Fig. 3.4** Case 2—the three parts of the CWCP anchoring canvas

existing organization and ask themselves what would make them redundant, freeing them up to take on other roles. They stated what they thought anchoring ownership in the organization (from the participant to cocreator and owner) would require. In this way, they mainly made explicit to the rest of the organization what the involved employees, who were on the receiving side of the changes, should do ("You do").

Figure 3.4 visualizes the three parts of the OWCP.

### 3.3.2 Four Learnings

The comparison of the two cases reported above teaches four lessons. The overall insight engendered is that the use of templates crucially affects the balance between telling (instruction) and asking in project teams. Templates that lead to putting telling over asking, thus over contributors' reflection, lead to inferior results.

Learning No. 1: Templates may not solve complicated issues that require reflection on how the real world works because the window on the reality they open may be either too small or too full of distortions. Also, however, "clever" the thinking templates embody, a majority of users may not be able to follow them. Immersed in their own internal workplace, template users see what they are used to seeing and often fail to question the thinking behind their seeing. When that happens, templates turn into containers of anecdotal findings and narrow logical thinking, rather than mind openers. In that case, users fail to enrich templates with critical thought, and no complex thinking is realized. As well, objections to templates themselves or their use lack critical depth may remain purely operational rather becoming of structural importance. The way out of this situation takes work: template users must be made aware of what they take for granted which equates to making them aware of the structure of their thinking, nothing less.

Learning No. 2: Absence of objections by itself does not guarantee a template's goodness of fit. Rather, one must ask *why* no objection was raised, and if there were objections, their implications have to be unfolded to understand their implications and ramifications. Questions must be raised as to what may have been overlooked, what related matters are implicated by objections, and whether the objections themselves may be shallow or deep relative to what they are aiming for.

Learning No. 3: "Objection" is a very general term indeed and may entail important hidden messages. Upon hearing an objection raised, it is important to keep listening to understand and follow up on their hidden meaning and implications. The way an objection has also been formulated matters. For instance, the objection might have been raised to convey that "the other party has never taken responsibility for the project" or that "the project is no longer meaningful." The objections' implicit or hidden messages need to be explored. Very often, the way objections are raised says more about the person raising them than about the subject matter they refer to. They may, for instance, convey a contributor's need for an opportunity to converse about what is "really" important to him or her, which was not previously communicated.

More deeply hidden and far-reaching objections may also occur. They may be of a nature to deny or minimize future problems, in the sense of "this will probably not be that difficult." Alternatively, objections can be a cover-up of doubting colleagues' expertise. Positively, coming from the project initiator himself or herself, they can have the function of creating an appreciation for previously neglected insights leading that may lead to the need for reexamining a project. In short, objections can have a negative, subversive, as well as a positive (team-gathering) function. They are carriers of cultural and political meaning-making in an organization, not just indicators of how a project may be going.

Learning No. 4: In the OWCP case, it is noticeable that the project leader interwove the various sense and meaning-making processes appropriately. The multidisciplinary scoping he adopted was a dialogical tool for getting joint attention. The closing checklist was the result of a process in which respective roles were clarified. The "thinking and acting differently" element was an invitation for all those involved, to take part both in a self-reflection and in exchanges about how participants judged each other. Making it possible to discuss connections between these three cornerstones of collaboration led to a well-orchestrated set of interactions in which incipient positional attitudes were disrupted, and project staff eventually came to collaborate intelligently.

In the third type of meetings, discussed below, the need for developing critical thinking to promote coordinated action becomes even more evident than in the two cases discussed above.

## 3.4 Meetings for Preparing for the Future: Strategy and Innovation

Issues of innovation are more in the foreground of companies' thinking than ever: what playing field are we betting on? What should we be able to offer? How can we win? These three questions are the starting point for many strategic exercises and for "reinventing the future." Team members try to build a deep understanding of a project's context, of associated evolving technologies, competitive approaches, customer expectations, and essential relationships between the latter. Based on this, challenges are defined, investment themes are chosen, innovation projects are initiated, and processes and working methods are adapted.

Most strategic dialogues are prepared by defining templates. We only mention a few of them: The Ten Types of Innovation Framework, Mission–Vision–Strategy alignment, Initial Opportunity Mapping, Competitors–Complementors Mapping, SWOT analyses, Persona definitions, User Journey Mapping, Foresight Scenario ideation sessions, Strategy Roadmapping. Each template invites its users to look at reality in "different" ways, but often the differences are purely logistic and thus shallow. Therefore, the dangers discussed in the previous section beckon here, too. Templates may function as collections of fragmented ideas with no common ground relative to how the real world works, as distinguished from how humans tend to think (namely logically).

### 3.4.1 The Ten Types of Innovation Experience

In general, few managers are aware of the narrow interpretations they make of templates. We illustrate this below by using the "Ten Types of Innovation" (TTI) framework (Keely et al. 2013). This template is intended to function as methodological support for understanding the context of an organization and environmental trends associated with it.

The TTI template suggests that, independently of any specific industry, innovations are developing in four areas: *finance, process, offerings, and delivery*. In these four broad domains, ten innovation patterns have been identified. All of the concepts used to convey these patterns are abstractions built upon abstractions, each of which can have many different meanings. Thus, rather than securing consensus, they disperse it, often in a self-destructing way.

This becomes clearer from the many meanings attached to the abstract term of "evolution" none of which is like the other. In the financial field, there are evolutions in business models and networks. In the process domain, developments in core processes differ from those in enabling processes that relate to how customers receive products and services. Innovations in the offerings domain are grouped into product performance, product systems, and service. The delivery domain includes changes in the channels, brand development, and customer experience. In calling this concept salad a "framework" for viewing the future, the reduction of the real world to how people think has begun!

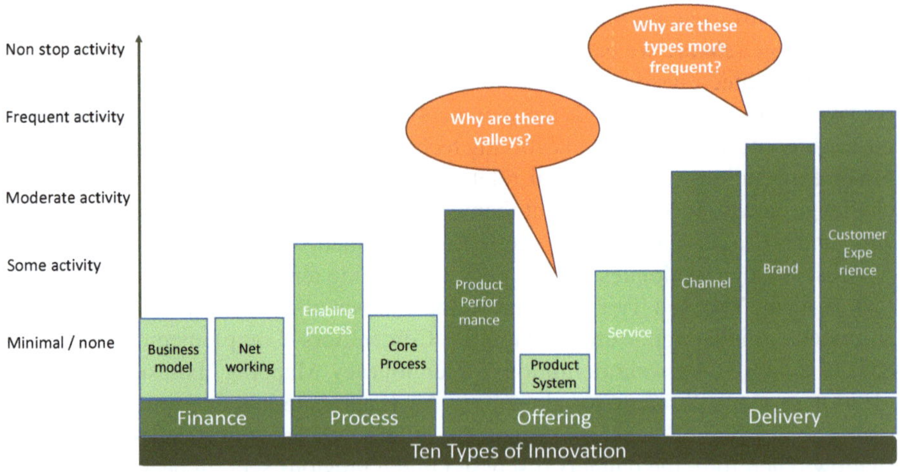


**Fig. 3.5** Data collected for the use of the "Ten Types of Innovation" Framework

Applying the *Ten Types of Innovation Framework* starts with identifying the key players in the industrial and business environment and collecting available information from the four domains selected. The flavor of "best practices" is hard not to notice as is the flatness of the questions asked.

- *Finance*: How do most successful organizations generate revenue through business model innovation? How are they effectively networking with partners?
- *Process*: What are the successful (operational) core processes for making offerings associated with a competitive advantage? How do companies innovate in enabling processes providing support for employees and operations?
- *Offering*: What are the innovations in product performance that offer distinctiveness relative to other players? How do companies successfully link their offerings as product systems? What are the service innovations that assist prospects and customers?
- *Delivery*: What are the industry's innovations in managing channels of distribution and getting offerings into the hands of end-users? What are the industry's notable brand innovations? What are the most distinctive experiences in the industry?

Rather than clarifying interrelationships between these concepts and their associated themes first, in the following step, each of these sets of questions is "concretized" by qualitatively very different data. The data collected are plotted in a graph (see Fig. 3.5) that is taken as the starting point for fostering a higher-level dialogue about why these divergent developments may be occurring.

We were able to attend a series of meetings using this model. This is what happened.

Within each *type of innovation*, several one-page sheets focused on the most important developments were drawn up by an external consultant. Managers filled in one-page notes regarding developments that were already evident to them. The initial enthusiasm for this work was great; however, many externally provided observations were dismissed as either too futuristic, only partially relevant to the organization (whose attention was focused on a small part of the innovation), or not yet feasible. No profound connections between the data points used were being paid attention to. Instead, the notion was that the data collected spoke for itself and precisely told what was happening in the real world, even though data never exhausts the depth of the real world which is, in addition, constructed differently by different participants meaning and functioning of concepts in different individuals' thinking were completely ignored. Both of these incidents are good examples of the fallacies logical thinking is prone to.

Expectedly, the lack of reflection on the concepts in play and their associated data led to a great deal of frustration on the part of the CEO. He saw that valuable time was being lost in quasiphilosophical discussions never leading to action planning, not to speak of coordinated action. When asked to join the exploratory meetings using the TTI template, we introduced four remedial steps. All of these steps were oriented to participants' thinking in real time that occurs unbeknownst to them but can be explicated by listening to speakers based on "mind openers" deriving from "thought forms" contained in Laske's DTF:

- Step 1: We introduced the notion that every participant follows their own peculiar perspective of the real world (called "internal workplace" in organizational settings), and this perspective is biased and emotionally charged (System 1—Chap. 2).
- Step 2: We introduced the notion that all participants were purely logical thinkers unaware of the thought forms that fed their logic and, therefore, well advised to experiment with different ways of questioning collected data (System 2—Chap. 2). The invitation was to deconstruct the team's train of thought in real time and thereby find alternative ways of understanding an observation made or argument formulated. This created a focus on what had so far been missing in the conversation—its *absences*.
- Step 3: We invited participants to enter into an internal dialogue with themselves. This term refers to a self-examination of what you are thinking in real time, the distinction between what you see or hear and how you interpret it, how you feel about it on account of your interpretation, and what the interpretations you privilege say about your personal needs.
- Step 4: We stated that our task would be to take a holistic view of the concepts and data in question and make self-reflective, critical statements about them with an emphasis on their core sense, following our own internal dialogue about that core, and using the DTF thought forms we are experts in using. In short, we acted as critical facilitators of team meetings.

In this role, we made the following observations.

Participants mainly saw the real world as a static configuration of events or situations (what in Chap. 2, we called "Context"). Even "evolutions" were not presented by them as such but were contextualized as "facts" and thus frozen. For instance, the shift from telephone calls from customers to the use of social media applications was positioned as a "fact," without questioning (a) the broader social environment within which the increased use of social media took place, (b) customers' shifting expectations, or (c) how shifts observed might evolve further under the influence of technologies still unknown.

We found, moreover, that essential relationship between concepts or data went unnoticed, such as the common ground between (1) the evolving business model and changes in the customer experience and (2) the structural links between process enablers and product performance.

By introducing mind-opening questions, we were able to prompt a discussion about the fragility of the organization's approach to serving customers. We were also able to formulate where the development potential in the organization might be located, and what new dynamic collaborations could be vested in them.

### 3.4.2 Three Critical Facilitator Insights

As critical facilitators, the cases discussed above led us to three main insights.

*Insight 1:* Team members' understanding of verbal language and of speaking it does not match their mandate. Their notion that language "describes" misses that it "creates" new realities with every word spoken. As a consequence, speakers take what they see as being "out there" as given, as an object, neglecting that they construct it in real time. They thrive on the subject/object split they are introducing unbeknownst to them. As a result, they do not realize that people create reality together and cannot speak about "reality" without talking about themselves at the same time.

What seems to be needed is to begin speaking from a different level of awareness. The reality, rather than being something "out there," is, in fact, right "in here," created from everybody's internal dialogue access to which, in logical thinking, is highly limited. By reflecting on how one uses concepts, everybody can find out about his or her own "in here," one's own internal dialogue and workplace that is the basis of communicating with others.

Once a speaker is more aware of his or her speaking and use of concepts, restructuring one's thought processes becomes possible, followed by a more refined way of problem formulation and choice of potential solutions, as well as the manner of speaking. This attunement presupposes listening to oneself speaking, seeing and acting from a bigger picture, aware of emerging changes, and the sharing of common grounds between concepts referring to different objects, dimensions, and perspectives. We will describe this way of proceeding in Chap. 7 as *double listening* as a path to complex thinking.

The core issue, then, is the restructuring of thought processes by which information is processed, problems are identified, and directions for finding a solution are chosen. It becomes "strategic" to let go of current thinking to connect with a larger whole, emerging change, the common ground opposing realities share, as well as the pervasive shift of things of the real world toward ceasing to exist and undergoing transformations in real time.

*Insight 2*: Team members presently lack a way of entering into their own dialogue before they enter into communication with others. They are inexpert in listening to themselves and, therefore, cannot separate what they put out from what they receive. In terms of "systems of interpretation," they fail to build a third system on top of Kahnemann's two systems, namely, that of adult-developmentally anchored discrepancies between their own way of making meaning and sense and that of others. In short, a lack of self-aware self-monitoring and listening to others.

*Insight 3*: Although unable to predict the future, team members need to craft forward-looking dialogues. To have to do so is part of their human predicament. They need to take coordinated action by "thinking through" next steps in close connection with what they understand of real-world functioning in the way they presently construct it, to find meaningful next steps to act out. Without questioning the structure of their own thinking, all of this remains impossible for them.

**Key Insights and Practice Reflections**

We started this chapter from the observation that few participants in meetings are satisfied with the course of meetings and frustrated by the waste of time they lead to. In self-organizing contexts, meetings are increasingly important as vehicles of becoming collaborative than was previously the case, and wasting time is even more damaging.

We argued for the necessity of becoming aware of the nexus between paying attention, making interpretations, self-monitoring and social monitoring processes, and division of labor agreements for the sake of coping with developmental diversity in teams. We demonstrated that complex thinking shifts the balance of "telling and arguing" to "asking and questioning."

In the following chapters, we will examine other essential organizational practices and the dialogues they are grounded in from the vantage point of the insights shared in this chapter.

**Practice Reflections**

1. How is human thinking energized and broadened when one switches from the belief that language merely describes to the assumption that it creates new realities in real-time?
2. What happens to people's thinking if they become aware that no concept has any meaning in isolation from other concepts together with which they form a network?
3. How would you shift the meeting dialogue from arguing to asking?
4. What would be your way as a critical facilitator to align self-monitoring and social monitoring with creating shared intentions?
5. What is your experience with people's difficulties of becoming aware of their own internal workplace as it derives from how they interpret their role, and how would you proceed in being of assistance to them?

# The "Common Ground" Dialogue: Working with Upwardly and Downwardly Divided Teams

# 4

*Team cohesion is a function of two nonbehavioral factors: (1) differences in the way in which team members together build knowledge (cognitive dimension; "tools") and (2) differences in how they relate to themselves and others (social-emotional dimension; "stance").*

**Abstract**

In this chapter, we introduce the cognitive and social-emotional team cohesion (CSTC) triangle which aids understanding how a team is developmentally constituted in terms of its majority and minority. Adopting a bird's-eye view of teams in general, we distinguish between two fundamentally different forms of collaboration: one that we call "upwardly," and the other that we call "downwardly," divided, where by "divided" we imply "between team majority and minority." We demonstrate that these two dynamics assume a different form in each of the three We-Spaces we distinguish. Throughout, we offer advice on how to deal with the two contrasting dynamics in each of the three We-Spaces.

In this chapter, we discuss teamwork as a generator as well as an ingredient of corporate culture—in the sense that it creates, as well as is subject to the influence of such a culture. For us, the reciprocity of these two aspects is the core issue of any corporate culture. More specifically, this reciprocity is the backbone of the "common ground" that contributors reach to collaborate. As we show in this chapter, the extent to which team culture constitutes, or fails to constitute, a company's "common ground" in large measure derives from the quality of dialogue established in and by its teams.



J. De Visch, O. Laske, *Practices of Dynamic Collaboration*, Management for Professionals, https://doi.org/10.1007/978-3-030-42549-4_4

To shed light on how teams establish *common ground* within themselves, to begin with, we suggest paying close attention to three critical aspects of teamwork:

- Understanding oneself in relation to other team members inside and outside of one's role
- Taking a perspective on one's team's mandate and functioning relative to outcomes aimed for
- Experiencing oneself as sharing thoughts and feelings with colleagues to create common ground for one's team's decision-making.

In this book, these three aspects of self-awareness are thought to define "role identity" in the broader sense of the term.

Arguing based on empirical findings of research in adult development over the life span, we propose that creating common ground in teams is difficult on account of the diversity of *frames of reference* anchored in different social-emotional levels of meaning-making, and thus of "world views." The variety of world views quickly leads to unwilfully misinterpreting the intentions of others from one's own worldview. It also triggers second thoughts about sharing oneself freely. How far reluctance to do so plays a role in a team's functioning varies with the degree of developmental diversity present in it, which, in turn, depends on how a team is developmentally constituted in terms of its majority and minority.

Adopting a bird's-eye view of teams in general, we distinguish between two fundamentally different outcomes of working together: one that we call "upwardly" and the other that we call "downwardly" divided, that is, "divided" between team majority and minority. Expectedly, these two dynamics assume a different form in each of the three We-Spaces we distinguish, as shown in detail below. We show that while highly developed team members know that they are ceaselessly thinking and have internal access to their thinking, lower developed team members either do not or defend against it, for various reasons.

Ultimately, what matters in collaboration is how far a team, or even a network of teams, can establish "common ground," that is, a common culture. It is the extent of common ground between team members and teams that determines team cohesion and, based on it, the potential of realizing collaborative intelligence.

## 4.1 Commentary on Contemporary Approaches to Culture

In their book *Firms of Endearment*, Sisodia et al. (2007) describe the importance of a robust, coherent, and shared corporate culture. Companies that succeed in reconciling the interests of all stakeholders (society, investors, customers, employees, and partners) have been found to do about eight times better than their competitors over 10 years. It is a valid assumption that these findings also reflect the culture of collaboration in such companies. Many studies support the hypothesis that a strong culture is essential for successful collaboration.

Developing a cohesive culture is easier to write about than to execute—70% of efforts to transform an organizational culture fail. Employees often do not commit to the design of a new culture, whatever the different levers and methodologies put in place for such a purpose may be.

The first enabler of culture change is to make explicit the mission, vision, strategy, and values that support a new culture. Rethinking daily workflows is a second ingredient of anchoring cultural changes. Thirdly, attention needs to be paid to forms that self-reflection takes among employees and to find ways of transcending limiting beliefs or hidden commitments they are identified with. A fourth enabler consists of developing managerial skills the workforce is currently lacking.

The dominant idea usually followed in attempts to change corporate cultures is that by taking "the right steps," all employees can be brought to a consensus about desired cultural values. We know from findings of adult-developmental research that this idea is not cogent since it drastically simplifies what it entails to reach consensus among individuals of different maturity levels who, in addition, pursue different psychological agendas they are mostly unaware of. Also, drawing up charts of abstract values has little to do with how individuals experience their own and others' values in a way reflecting their developmentally rooted frame of reference.

Recently, the concept of "agility" has been turned into a value of high importance and has been included in many fashionable charters, with the result that is meaning has been diversified in uncommon ways. In addition, a great deal of effort has been made to realize what this concept is supposed to entail in practice. In this chapter, we raise questions about not only the possibilities but also the limits of connecting employees to their organization via postulating abstract values such as agility. In this section, we choose the term "agile" from a multitude of other possible concepts—such as transparency, effectiveness, or customer focus—because it is presently thought by many to be an essential ingredient of a self-directed organization.

We have learned from the first three chapters of this book that each individual's mindset is idiosyncratic, although undergirded by broad commonalities of adult development over the life span. The reader has also been alerted to the fact that individuals' mindset is hard, if not impossible, to understand on strictly behavioral grounds since it is the product of life-long adult development extending into the future, and is moreover multidimensional, comprising social-emotional, cognitive, and psychological elements connected by close, intrinsic relationships to each other. This evident complexity stands in stark contrast to the "terrible" simplification imposed on the concept of a human being by all types of Taylorism, to the detriment even of knowing what could be the meaning of "integrating" human and algorithmic intelligence.

Confronted with the multidimensionality of "mind" and "mindset," it makes sense to stipulate that both of these concepts integrate two opposing but interrelated aspects: (social-emotional) "stance" and (cognitive) "tools." By stating this bifurcation, we are doing justice to the empirical finding that both strands of development, although unfolding alongside each other, are in no way similar or reducible to each other, nor are they linearly connected or parallel.

According to what is empirically known about meaning-making in relationship to sense-making (stance to tools) today, they are simultaneously different from and intrinsically related to each other. Even today, how exactly they become distinct in evolution and intertwined over an individual's life span is largely unknown, giving us reason to suggest that they may stand in variable relationships to each other in different periods of an individual's life. One finding, assured through developmental assessment studies, though, is that these two developmental strands are rarely in equilibrium with each other within an individual. For this reason, we find individuals who are more highly developed in their stance rather than their tools, as well as vice versa.

It is essential for understanding the nature of human work that work is embedded in life and is shaped by it as much as, according to different configurations of society, it shapes life. As a result, work is always delivered based on a particular stance associated with particular cognitive tools which exist in interaction with each other. From the togetherness of both of these aspects derives the reality that work is always delivered as an expression of a specific and temporary frame of reference of an individual—a frame of reference that will change as the individual "moves on" in the level of maturity. There is no difference in this between CEO, managers, and employees simply because they are all on a life-long developmental journey toward mature adulthood. All categories introduced by human resource departments that define different organizational roles are based on this common ground between organizational contributors.

Importantly also, what we call a particular developmental position—and positioning of individuals toward each other—is not simply an abstract category or behavioral "trait," but defines how the real world, including the social world, daily and demonstrably shows up for individuals. Their developmental position is neither a set of competencies nor a set of traits, but rather the anchor of both. Such a frame of reference gives rise to explicit or inexplicit hypotheses as to what the "real world" looks like, what should be done, what can be done at a certain point in time, and what are the capabilities of collaborators with whom to interface.

In light of the term "agility," one could say that it is understood and interpreted in a way entirely determined by how an individual currently interprets what is "real" for him or her in the world he or she presently constructs. "Agility" is a fine value but assessing how "agile" a person is or can be is like chasing an abstraction, since it is not a matter of behavior alone but regards how an individual's behavior is shaped by the breadth and depth of his or her present level of meaning-making and associated cognitive tools. Depending on an individual's developmental level, the concept of "agility," therefore, assumes an entirely different meaning which equally holds for other abstractions that come into vogue.

For these reasons, a concept such as "agility" has little to contribute to understanding how the social world works and how human work is carried in real time. It means something entirely different for someone who does, or does not, incorporate a perspective on technological evolutions or customer expectations in his or her approach to work.

For instance, if an account manager is social-emotionally other-dependent (rather than self-authoring), and a group of colleagues interprets "cross-selling" as an aspect of agility, rolling out this practice across the entire sales team can be successful only to the extent that the manager can comfortably link himself or herself to the practice seen as "agile" by others, thereby following others' definition of what is required of him or her. To what extent colleagues view contributors as agile, however, is a function of the complexity theme to which an employee is thought to contribute. As well, "agility" means something entirely different if work is focused on very concrete tasks compared to work that requires close collaboration. In short, the concept of agility has no unitary meaning and is, as an abstraction, divisive rather than productive for realizing high-quality collaborations.

## 4.2 The Cognitive and Social-Emotional Team Cohesion (CSTC) Triangle

To illuminate the stark limitations of existing approaches to agility, we developed the *Cognitive and Social-emotional Team Cohesion (CSTC) Triangle* shown in Fig. 4.1. The triangle sheds light on the specific type of dialogue that unfolds in situations of team disagreement and tension as a function of differences between team members' adult-developmental frames of reference, both cognitive and social-emotional.

It draws attention to areas of tension arising from developmental differences between team members.

The figure embodies the assumption that sharing conceptual abstractions in a team is subject to the me–other dynamics grounded in differences between individual perspectives and that these differences are determined by individuals' level of adult development over the life span. As a result, degree of team cohesion

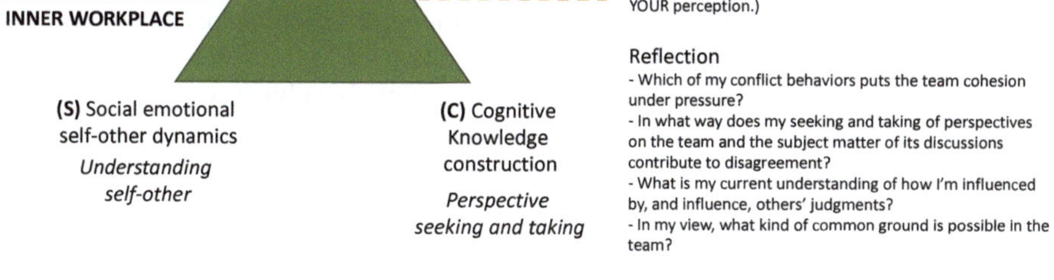


**Fig. 4.1** The Cognitive and Social-emotional Team Cohesion (CSTCT) Triangle: Making sense of We-Space dynamics cognitively and social-emotionally

(coherence and common ground) is a function of two nonbehavioral factors: (1) differences in the way in which team members together build knowledge (cognitive dimension; "tools") and (2) differences in how they relate to themselves and others (social-emotional dimension; "stance").

As shown in our critique of using terms like "agility" for the sake of supporting collaboration, abstract concepts have the property of being open to a large number of different interpretations but also subject to horrendous reductions of their complexity by cognitively undeveloped minds—a fact that template-builders (who thrive on distributing highly abstract concepts destined to become buzzwords) rarely consider. Reducing real-world complexity to templates based on mere logical abstractions indeed tends to reduce a concept's meaning to a fraction of what it entails and implies. For instance, if the dominant majority of a team is in agreement about what activities guarantee quality service, there is a good chance that team members at the instrumental level of development will interpret "agile" as a set of procedures for adapting to the customer. In such a case, the team's dialogue process will be narrowed to the common logical denominator of evaluations such as "right" and "wrong." Should there exist a cognitively more highly developed subgroup that experiences such an approach as overly instrumental or even fragmented and instead senses a need for addressing, say, the interplay of operations involved in a particular concept, it will most likely not be given a chance to constructively question the rock-solid, logic-based beliefs of the less developed colleagues without having the latter suffer from a hurt ego.

It is to alert to the possibility of such a sad fate suffered by complex concepts that we have introduced the CSTC triangle. The triangle hypothesizes that team cohesion is large an adult-developmental, not a behavioral, issue.

When working with actual teams, the CSTC triangle is relevant in regard to any individual who influences the behavior of a team. In the presence of subject matter on which there is no agreement, participants will experience the pressure a specific issue puts on team coherence. To investigate members "point of view statements" in greater depth, a deeper questioning of the concepts involved in an issue is needed, so that everybody's thinking may be made explicit and broadened. Such a reflection step permits a team leader or manager to formulate a hypothesis as to how "ego" plays a role in team discussions and to make the ego-centrism involved visible to all for the sake of their own learning. As a result, participants may be led to reflect on the dynamics they unconsciously engender.

Each component of the CSTC triangle poses a puzzle as to how its components are going to shape each other within each team member's mental space and process, and thereby contribute to the total dynamics of the team. Since each team member is co-defined by all three components and unconsciously subject to their influence, based on empirical research one can predict how far a specific team member, X, can realize his or her developmental potential within a given zone of adult maturity in a particular context of a team.

For instance, a social-emotionally speaking other-dependent person—who defines himself or herself by the expectations of others—will be unable to transcend certain constraints defining his present developmental position and therefore can be predicted to take a specific position toward the team as a whole. Such an individual's participation in a team will have cognitive limitations that a more highly developed person would not experience, both in terms of thought fluidity and adequacy of complexity handling. This being true for each team member, it is clear that predictions of what the team as a whole may agree on and commit to are going to be inaccurate and unrealistic as long as the adult-developmental dimension of teamwork remains unknown or is considered irrelevant.

Below, we investigate what kind of sharing and consensual decision-making is possible in the three different We-Spaces described in Chap. 2. We start the discussion of We-Spaces in the continuous improvement domain of organizational work, followed by that of rethinking value streams (cross-functional departmental interplay) and concluding with the domain of business model transformation. We briefly describe the essential characteristics of each of the three We-Spaces, put forward an hypothesis regarding downwardly and upwardly divided dynamics in each of them, and finally consider what a critical facilitator might do in each of the three spaces to improve the quality of team dialogues, assuming that this quality is based on strengthening each team member's internal dialogue with himself or herself. All this will be done in reference to the notion of "agility."

## 4.3 The Continuous Improvement We-Space

In the continuous improvement We-Space, the work focus is mainly on discussing adjustments to existing work methods. Discussions in this space are not typically experienced as "dialogue," but instead as talk on "getting things done." After all, employees working in this space do not question their own developmental level or the tools they are using. They are outer-directed and, thus, rather take these for granted when providing client services. They unquestioningly use procedures and quality standards associated with their specific professional level, this being their "competence" and, in their view, their professional identity. These procedures impose on their users' strict limits of what can be effortlessly thought about, and more or less directly tell them how to proceed. Team members, therefore, usually do not "think twice" about the procedures they use but accept them uncritically. As a result, they experience their activities almost as something "out there" and as no more than either "right" or "wrong." Only customer feedback, not their own reflection, gives employees a chance to adjust their work to customer needs, but this adjustment rarely leads to individual enlightenment.

In this We-Space, the dialogue on values is also quite limited. Very often, it starts with the notion of "measuring" a value. The questionnaires used to assess work quality and outcomes include a variety of behavioral or other indicators. By discussing questionnaire outcomes, one hopes to arrive at a consistent understanding of the meaning of "agile" in one's specific dialogue space.

Figure 4.2 shows an example of a typical questionnaire. The higher the number of points in a team, the higher the agility of the team is thought to be. In a very

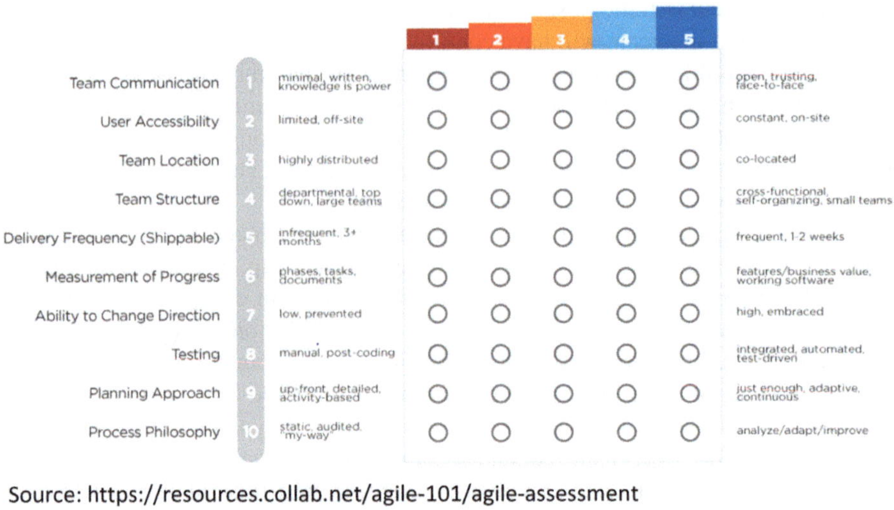


**Fig. 4.2** An example of an "agile" assessment questionnaire. (Source: https://resources.collab.net/agile-101/agile-assessment)

restricted meaning of the term, "agility" in this case could refer to the speed at which a team adjusts its activities to customer needs.

In practice, discussions of questionnaire results are not straightforward because the way the team builds knowledge in this space is never entirely transparent, given that how people deal with each other is opaque and rarely itself becomes a topic of discussion. Nevertheless, one can usefully distinguish two very different dynamics that arise in conversations in this We-Space, which we name "downwardly" and "upwardly" *divided*, respectively. This distinction refers to the specific team dynamics found in continuous improvement teams when they are considered as comprising a developmental subgroup that accounts for team division in adult-developmental terms. We are evaluating a team adult-developmentally by asking: do highly developed people in this team form a majority or minority, and in what proportion to these two groups relate to each other?

We speak of a team being "downwardly divided" when a developmental subgroup of a team tends to diminish or weaken the functioning of those team members who are more developed both emotionally and cognitively, but as a subgroup cannot obtain a voice in the team. In the opposite case, where a developmentally higher developed subgroup calls the shots and can persuade less developed members of the team to follow it, we speak of an "upwardly divided" team. As we will show, team dynamics in each case are entirely different, often dramatically so.

### 4.3.1 The Downward Dynamics in the Continuous Improvement We-Spaces

When a team makes meaning of its mandate in the context of a downward dynamics (where less developed team members dominate over more highly developed ones), discussions often revolve around the appropriateness of indicators or of underlying definitions, as well as the reliability of the measuring instrument used. Focusing on 'right' versus 'wrong' stems from an apparent consensus around the notion of "correctness" in task execution. Team members are often unaware that they are acting from a belief in a single truth and are thus holding a minimally complex perspective on reality. As a result, they do not address differences in individual interpretations of notions they subscribe to or bring into play. Colleagues who take a different view of subject matter keep their distance from the majority of participants. We take these dynamics to lead to a "downward" division of the team since it ultimately reduces the breadth and depths of the team's understanding of its mandate. The cause for that is the limited degree of team members' self-authoring in how they make meaning and, related to that, the limited fluidity of thinking team members can or feel prompted to realize.

Subject to these dynamics, those team members tend to dominate the discussion who have already slightly adjusted adopted procedures. These are team members focused on profiling themselves in the context of others, and in need of strengthening their position. Their interface with colleagues is determined by what they surmise helps them to appear as experts, thus undermining an equilibrated task process in favor of personalized interventions. As a consequence, their dealings with colleagues are merely transactional (not reflective) and by nature, manipulative. As a result, team cohesion is significantly weakened, amounting to nothing more than the belief that people will help each other achieve individual goals. The team's world then becomes a jungle where the stronger eat the weaker. The interpersonal team process overwhelms the team's agenda and its task process.

Remarkably, in such dynamics, neither the customer nor the procedures adopted are the direct focus of attention. What reigns supreme is blind confidence in one's personal approach. Since the level of maturity from which team members act is instrumental, customers' are reduced to being a set of needs. The notion underlying teamwork is one of collegial competition: that whoever can "best" meet these needs "wins." The analysis of customer needs remains superficial, especially since the pressure of responding immediately to customers or the required efficiency of service keep reflection in abeyance. Task implementation usually starts from prescribed procedures, and it is these procedures that determine the speed, form, and content of information exchange in the team.

What saps the vigor of the self-organization of such a team is a clash between two kinds of logic: their own unconsciously held logic of other-dependence—which lets them act according to others' presumed expectations, either of team members or clients—clashes with the logic of personal competition among team members. The first logic goes along with internalizing conventions as to how team activities should be carried out, also to stay on course with one's team. The second logic pits one experience of success against another one, thereby deviating energy from the task at hand to personal goals. Since team members are not aware of the clash, they will accept new ways of working together only upon receiving clear instructions and when asked to focus on role models other than their own. Even then, there will be many different understandings of such instructions, depending on developmental level, and little chance for consensus.

An additional deficiency of collaboration in this dialogue space lies in the absence of a strong connection with the broader environment in which the team works. Team members follow an inside-out logic—in that rather than starting from the interaction process with the customer itself, they start from abstract dimensions thought relevant to them in providing services. As a consequence, their feeling for the greater whole in which they are embedded is woefully limited. It is based on a collection of data points (in whose "reality" they believe) rather than a deeper reflection on the broader context they are working within.

No wonder, then, that discussions of "agility" (and other culturally prescribed values) are limited by preconceptions of team members regarding what is essential and that exchanges of diverse opinions have no structural impact. The team focus is restricted to questions about the relevance of chosen measurements, and the correctness of definitions adopted within the narrow confines of a reduced team agenda. Since preconceptions of what is essential, that is, *abstractions*, prevail, team members' experience is that translating these conceptions into action is challenging. (So-called business software makes their task more difficult by the day since it is based on an absolute belief in abstractions severed from all context.) As a result, team members tend to keep a distance from the conceptual information provided them, identifying only with what momentarily becomes a problem for them, which is quickly replaced by another issue, and so ad infinitum.

In a context defined by a downward dynamics of meaning-making, the main challenge of improving the quality of team dialogue lies in breaking through firmly established ideas of "correctness" and the disbelief in the truth that humans are unceasingly thinking. Considering that it is not very difficult to give reasons for why one does something in a certain way or should not do it, Toyota developed a practice referred to as "asking five times why?", to break the belief in the absence of thinking. By persisting in asking why-questions, one hopes to move closer to the essence of what should be done before it is too late.

If, for example, people keep arguing for a detailed rather than a broad approach to a goal, one can deal with contradictions that arise by asking Why-questions. To do so helps make explicit heretofore neglected aspects of a subject matter and integrate all kinds of relevant information previously considered as a side-issue or not at all. Working with "five times why" questions is a fruitful step toward bringing a diversity of opinions to awareness and also to ask which practices and ideas stand in the way, as well as facilitate, the implementation of "agility," however conceived of. It is an indirect way of avoiding and reducing the impact of people's ego, which is notoriously difficult to discuss in immature groups if not entirely taboo and thus "unthinkable."

The core of downwardly directed team dynamics in the continuous improvement space is determined by the worldview of the dominating subgroup. Employees functioning from an instrumental stage world view do not quickly feel invited to question themselves. Their contribution to common ground is thus near nil. This is masked by maintaining bias in favor of the abstraction of "correctness," which implies and "cements" the true or false distinction of formal logic. To break this binary bias (by which the real world shrinks to isolated entities without context) is most successful if one can show concretely that fixed opinions limit curiosity and openness since they make one blind to disconfirming evidence as well as other members' better thinking and the existence of a real world at large. Starting to discuss mind traps can be a starting point for instrumental meaning-makers to begin questioning fixed ideas, thus themselves as nonthinkers. The social-emotional fixation on one's own world "in here" makes it likely that an individual at this developmental position will focus on those aspects of a subject matter that are in line with his or her limited understanding of their role identity. Openness to questions of

**Table 4.1** The CSTC-interplay highlighting downwardly and upwardly divided dynamics in the continuous improvement space

| | Downwardly divided dynamics | Upwardly divided dynamics |
|---|---|---|
| | Instrumental (majority) > Other-dependant (minority) | Other-dependant (majority) > Instrumental (minority) |
| Team cohesion dynamics | Team members stick together and move toward becoming a team only when seeing a promise of being helped by others in reaching their own goals. | The team coheres based on socialization processes. Mindtrap of 'we agree'. |
| Cognitive knowledge construction | Limited contextual awareness (following of conventions if in line with self-interest). Mindtrap of 'being right'. | Daily practice of hypothesizing, testing, and verification. Contextual awareness (clarifying how to meet expectations) and incipient thinking about 'what is not there', what emerges through change, or is needed to realize the future. |
| Social-emotional self-other dynamics | Tension between functioning based on ego and as a team member. Attention is focused on aligning team members' self-interest. | Tension between functioning based on ego and as a team member. Attention is focused on conforming to templates offered by third parties (experts, authorities, …). |
| Improving dialogue quality in teams | The practice of the five 'why's. Focus on bringing the diversity of opinions to the surface. | Explore how meanings change/evolve in different contexts. Establish multiple levels of inquiry (= working daily to break the belief that 'truth' is something that exists independently of oneself). |
| Improving the quality of tean members' internal dialogue | Organize explicit confrontation with one's own ego by confronting biases, such as the 'being-right' mindtrap. | Suspend judgement and question assumptions underlying observations. |

"how the real world works," made complicated by the unawareness of having reduced the real world to "data," then becomes impossible to achieve.

Table 4.1 shows the dynamics of downward and upward dynamics in the continuous improvement We-Space.

The first three rows in the table are derived from the CSTC triangle while the remaining two rows suggest remedies. The left column of the table spells out instrumental teams' downwardly oriented team dynamics. In reality, there is little chance in instrumental groups that a fruitful dialogue process can be developed. Rather than attempting to remediate thought fixation caused by a fixation on data per se, a strategy for changing the developmental structure of such groups will be needed which is likely to materialize only with strong, developmentally aware, leadership.

### 4.3.2 The Upward Dynamics in the Continuous Improvement We-Spaces

The right column of Table 4.1 summarizes the upward dynamics in the continuous improvement We-Space. Here, the meaning of "agility" is a function of consensus around the way one pays attention to, and interacts with, different evolving contexts in which a customer finds himself or herself.

The team's dialogue consists of an exchange of ideas about how to create a broader context of the team's work and increase the awareness of ongoing real-world processes that threaten yesterday's truths. This dialogue is more fruitful if the team can make clear agreements about who will facilitate the exchange. Facilitating here relates to the promotion of context and process interpretations of the team's work, the postponement of forming fixed opinions due to lack of reflection, and the monitoring of equitable inputs to decision-making. Nevertheless, the pressure to reach a consensus, in the sense of team members' compliance with what the group agrees on, is inevitable. In practice, however, different team members will engage with consensus to varying degrees due to a large number of factors, and this will limit the feeling of belonging and connecting with the whole.

If we assume that the quality of a team's dynamics becomes apparent from the quality of its dialogue, what is decisive for guiding those dynamics in an upward direction? In our experience, such a turnaround derives from how team members perceive the entity initiating team conversations, whether it be the institute that developed a chosen questionnaire, the track record of the authority supervising the team's work process, or the senior manager who explicitly supports the team's work.

In the present We-Space, group members operate on the level of other-dependence, defining themselves by others' expectations of them. There is thus a tendency to conform to interpretations, definitions, and indicators provided from outside one's thinking. As a result, employees tend to agree with important analysis results quickly and equally quickly commit themselves to the most obvious solutions. When questionnaires are used, different sections are often mistaken for being dimensions of the real world "out there," rather than specific, possibly narrow, ways of thinking about that world in the team. This then leads to a rather pedantic approach to agility, which, instead of being seen as an inner attitude, is translated into behavioral platitudes such as "needing to adapt better," "consult more or more frequently," "play the ball for a shorter period," etc. However, committing to such behavioral directives, abstract as they are, is often confusing and challenging for employees since it complicates adherence to expectations of others (which is difficult enough).

In this We-Space, it becomes vital that team members "listen" to customers' wishes and receive their lasting respect. To do so, team members need an acute awareness not only of context but also of changes over time, thus also of what is missing or not yet in evidence for customers. Contextual awareness shows itself in simple ways, such as distinguishing customer wishes and optimizing work methods to meet them. Fulfilling client requirements happens by isolating requests, collecting data on their relevance, and making adjustments in line with them.

Downwardly divided teams most frequently follow an approach that puts a premium on strictly logical procedures such as testing assumptions, either through experiments or decision-making based on falsification. (This is much easier than sharing one's untrammeled thinking with others.) But understanding a context is only one piece of the puzzle, the other being an understanding that the real world is unceasingly changing and that concepts one has chosen to work with have many interpretations or are thus ambiguous. (For instance, in simplistic thinking, "agile" easily comes to mean providing quick solutions. As a result, one remains unaware that "fast" is an entirely relative term: if a parcel distributor delivers within the day after delivery, the delivery is slow compared to a courier service that delivers within 5 h, while it is fast compared to the postal service, which takes 2 or more days. Often, the way team members perceive customers is strongly linked to how customers themselves tend to view changes in their environment. In other words, independent thinking is hindered further by identifying with customers uncritically.)

By contrast, in teams characterized by an upward developmental dynamic, common ground is easier to come by, not only because team members can question their own thinking but also because there is a minimal awareness of changes over time and things missing. Such awareness is apparent in the conviction that there are always unfulfilled customer wishes and that the most exceptional opportunities in customer service lie in identifying what is emerging and what to do to help it unfold.

In this setting, team cohesion has to do with collective agreement on the methods of formulating hypotheses, and testing and verifying them. The team glows in its empiricism of associating a consensual agenda with methods of daily hypothesis formulation, testing, and verification of what needs to get done. "Agility" comes to mean following agreed-upon decision-making procedures for the sake of trying out new ways of working.

Despite the empirical ideology it follows, however, the team remains unaware that its strictly logical thinking bars it from understanding change. Strictly linear, logical thinking also hinders team members from understanding that outwardly "different" entities are different only because they share common ground, thus different only in a specific context and not absolutely. For the team, it is therefore difficult to see that thinking is as unceasing as breathing, being present without fail all the time but still going unnoticed. As a result, thoughts remain objects "out there" whose link with one's thinking remains hidden. It is as if the concepts used in team discussions had an independent existence relative to one's mental activity and could be quantitatively measured as aspects of the real world itself, rather than as giving rise to individual perspectives on that world.

What can be done to instill an upwardly directed dynamics in teams stuck in empiristic ideologies and strictly linear logical thinking? If this were known, there would be no need to speak of downwardly directed team dynamics. Having team members realize that reality is continuously in motion and thus requires a critical view of one's assumptions is difficult and requires a mental effort. Developing a critical practice requires, first, building an understanding of different contexts and, second, understanding that contexts are never stable, are sets of relationships, and may be transforming in their identity. As an example, take the notion speed: there is no single, logically correct, analytical way of defining speed. Instead, when dialoguing about customers, employees' need to examine the diversity of perspectives from which speed may matter to customers.

A second practice consists of questioning the concepts team members are using at different levels of reality. Team members can investigate what increasing speed could concretely mean for a customer and can learn to interpret fields of tension relative to quality, safety, or costs in dealing with customers. At Honda, for instance, rather than trying to solve tensions by addressing them directly at the operational level, employees ask concept-focused questions such as what is the meaning of the term "speed" for the customer in question and, more generally, what specific procedures are needed to acquire or strengthen a particular customer relationship? In this way, team members do not merely think *about* what is important to customers, but put themselves in customers' shoes and thus think *like* them, fully empathizing with them. This is an embryonic form of *internal dialogue* which we address below in detail as "double listening."

Also, when failing to resolve contradictions (tensions) either at an operational or conceptual level, one can ask about the overarching purpose of a specific customer-oriented team activity or even the ultimate "why" question. Why, for example, is it essential to invest in this customer relationship? At first sight, such questions may appear to be out of touch with the business at hand. However, genuinely new solutions often arise due to a change in perspective, such as asking higher-level questions beyond the immediate operational context. It is this kind of flexibility and holism of thinking in a team that, if it existed, would truly connect team members. It would do so by showing them that they all "continuously thinking," rather than only having emotions about each other. In short, it would promote the team's task process, not just its interpersonal process.

A significant limitation of practices in this We-Space nevertheless remains.

The limitation has to do with the absence of one might call an employee's *inner dialogue*, that is, their ability to listen critically and with a detachment from their own thoughts as emerging, both unconsciously and through interchange with others. **This ability requires the awareness that one is unceasingly thinking and**

**that due to one's unconscious thought process, one's thoughts are not replicas of something out in the world, but one's own interpretations of what one receives from one's observations as well as from others in the form of comments, questions, or data**. Awareness of one's internal dialogue is an awareness of one's own always ongoing mental activity—one's unceasing movements-in-thought—which is sourced from the constant interchange with virtual and physical others, *including oneself*. The reality of individuals' internal dialogue becomes irrefutable when one considers that one's thoughts and opinions derive from internalized others presented within oneself in a modified form as one's own. (The latter realization is crucial for transitioning from other-dependence to self-authoring as empirical research has amply shown.)

The risks encountered when skipping one's internal dialogue becomes glaringly apparent, especially when there is quick agreement among coworkers. Nobody then thinks "twice." One is focused on receiving recognition of having identified with others' opinions, often to improve one's standing in the team. To avoid such silent "grandstanding," an interrupt is needed, and such an interrupt can be generated by testing one's observations and underlying assumptions (e.g., in the sense of Argyris "double-loop" or even "triple-loop" learning) which can be greatly enhanced by learning to identify and use what in this book we refer to as "thought forms" or "thought structures."

For instance, decision-making in the absence of objections (see Chap. 3) requires team members to think for themselves rather than to listen to colleagues thinking alike. One is required to take the time needed for researching one's assumptions. If this "reflective" step is skipped, contexts related to an issue but not immediately visible will be neglected, relationships between contexts will be skipped, and relevant but absent contexts will be bypassed. As a result, team members will practice a parody of the "no-objection" method simply because they cannot think of any objection. In such a case, there is a good chance that the team will act based on what its members have internalized by listening to others, without a creative thought of their own. Splitting the team into "us" versus "them" then becomes almost automatic, especially in team members unquestioned "logical," that is, identity thinking.

## 4.4 The Value Stream We-Space

As before, we view what we call a "We-Space" as a dialogue space, in this case, a space centered on understanding and recoordinating value streams. Value streams are model-based representations of inputs and outputs between different teams or departments. Examples include the logistic value stream, the development value stream, the market approach value stream, and the financial value stream. In thinking about value streams, the focus is on the entire work systems and the cross-functional collaboration it gives rise to and requires. The notion of "value stream" implies that organization-wide partnerships are a crucial determinant of a company's bottom-line results. When the term "agility" is applied to the value stream

We-Space, it points to a coordinated response to changes in the organizational, social, and market environments of contributors and teams.

The fundamental question raised within this dialogue space regards the extent to which the working methods presently in use remain suitable under changing circumstances. Evolutions in customer expectations, technological possibilities, new products, or services or in the competitive environment put existing methods, the processes they trigger, and the choices they lead to in question, thereby forcing new thinking to emerge about the speed and depth with which one needs to respond to occurring changes, especially regarding the need for alternative products and services for customers. And linked to this, discussion arises about whether a further financial and time investment in existing work methods or rather the development of entirely new methods is in order.

### 4.4.1 Mapping Value Streams

The dialogue in this We-Space is strongly based on issues having to do with mapping value streams onto each other. Value streams are pictures of the flow of resources and activities identified with a specific organizational effort. Mappings involve process definitions questioned as to their relationship. How limited such mappings are becomes evident when considering that linear representations rarely correspond to how reality works. Organizational workflows and value streams are more like spaghetti dishes, especially in nonhierarchical organizations.

For one thing, processes in the real world often occur in parallel and intermittently, something mappings obscure. As a result, visual mappings falsely suggest demarcations of responsibilities as lying within the boxes they comprise rather than showing that they exist *between* boxes composing the diagram. Such mappings also falsify that the organizationally higher hierarchical level subsumes lower-level relationships, thus flatten hierarchies. Despite these drawbacks, value stream mappings bring to light three important issues: (1) disconnected flows, (2) wasted resources, and (3) potential system breakdowns.

Discussions in the value stream We-Space are problematic in most companies because they are often simple- and single-minded. This is because each of the teams involved tends to have its own vision of its participation in a specific value stream and also because this vision rarely corresponds to how other groups view the team's participation. In short, a consensual big picture even of a single value stream rarely exists. This is so since dividing operations into value streams overlooks that separating operations is simultaneously a way of linking them within a common ground, which, however, remains hidden.

For example, highlighting the limits of one's team's agility relative to other groups often creates tensions between groups. If not understood or accepted by other teams, it may lead to a duplication of effort. An example of such a waste of resources is the tracking of project progress by different parties in different spreadsheets or the splitting-up of partial services to customers across various departments. To avoid such waste, contributors search for an overarching model of coherence of current practices or at least a set of principles regarding who is responsible for what operational process.

The main limitations of value stream mapping do not lie in the concept itself but in the incomplete understanding its users have of what a "mapping" entails and what it obscures. The notion of mappings theoretically derives from the theory of complex adaptive systems. It involves principles such as emergence, interconnectivity, feedback, equilibrium, coevolution, path-dependence. To improve contributors' understanding of mappings, Middleton-Keller (2011) developed the EMK methodology which helps clarify what happens in different value streams mapped in terms of the principles just mentioned. The principle of "interconnectivity," for example, focuses on the interactivity of elements of a system. The principle entails that each initiative has an impact on the integrated whole it is part of, which impact is of course shaped by the reciprocal influence and level of integration of initiatives reached since all of them modify the characteristics, and even the meaning, of individual initiatives.

Consultative interventions within the value stream space presuppose complex and systemic thinking, both on the part of the facilitator and participants. Interpretations of what is happening in a mapping depend on the quality of systemic reflection that operates with concepts such as "agility," "innovativeness," "transparency," and "effectiveness." How far contributors can understand initiatives as part of a larger whole will determine what rules of collaboration they develop. These rules must make contributors understand situations as parts of a larger whole. Contributors must also be sensitive to constant changes over time, as well as imbalances affecting structural relationships between mappings. With regard to how well teams are able to accomplish successful mappings, again, we distinguish two different team dynamics: a downward and an upward one.

Table 4.2 outlines the two dynamics of value stream dialogues based on the CSTC triangle.

## 4.4.2 The Downward Dynamics in the Value Stream We-Spaces

In downwardly distributed dynamics, tensions emerge between very detailed analyses of activities, on the one hand, and abstractions such as models, on the other. Pertinent models are based on empirical studies of value streams employing root-cause methods, which give an overview of situations by way of Ven (or fishbone) diagrams. These diagrams (Blokdyk 2018; Campbell 2019) assume that a core question or problem can be split up into several parts. As each part is amplified by gathering more facts, the root causes of subproblems and the desired end goal are formulated, a procedure that eventually leads to a step-by-step plan.

High-level value stream mappings establish a bird's eye view of a value stream related problem for the sake of sketching a broad-perspective solution. Such mapping points to necessary coordination to be realized and thus stimulates thinking in terms of sequences and dependencies of activities. Usually, a mapping produces "aha" experiences followed by interpretations that are best characterized by

**Table 4.2** The CSTC-interplay highlighting downwardly and upwardly divided dynamics in the value stream space

| | Downwardly divided dynamics | Upwardly divided dynamics |
|---|---|---|
| | Other-dependant (majority) > Self-Authoring (minority) | Self-Authoring (majority) > Other-dependant (minority) |
| Team cohesion | Team cohesion derives from engaging with abstractions regarding a group's vision of the future and associated coordination needs. However, these abstractions are interpreted in view of specific situations so that status quo is preserved. | Team cohesion derives from engaging with abstractions regarding a group's vision of the future and associated coordination needs. The group critically questions them and builds enthusiasm around possible solution strategies. Decision making focused on contributing to the greater whole. |
| Cognitive knowledge contruction | Predominance of logical-analytical systemic thinking.<br>Some process and relationship thinking (= emerging systemic thinking). Growing awareness that unforeseeable events could have been foreseen if only one had paid attention to relationships. | Incipient complex system thinking. Maturation of process thinking and strengthening of relational thinking (= fully systemic thinking) |
| Social-emotional self-other dynamic | Tensions between pragmatism geared to meeting expectations and principled thinking which are settled by searching for consensus about models and templates to be used. | Tensions between pragmatism to meet expectations and principled thinking which are settled by searching for absence of objections and adjusting best practices as much as possible. |
| Improving the quality of the dialogue between team members | Systems that support switching dialogue from 'what' to think to 'how' to think, e.g., by exploring topics by using complex systems principles. Scheduling of reflect-back meetings. | Shifting attention from coordination to the integration of perspectives, by scrutinizing the CPRT-dimensions of focal concepts. |
| Improving the quality of the inner dialogue | Increasing self-reflection, mainly aimed at determining one's own point of view in light of divergent opinions. | Initiation of peer-to-peer dialogues about identity landscapes. |

expressions such as "we could have foreseen this, 'and' now that we see it, we can do something about it."

In a team characterized by a downward-directed team dynamics caused by low complexity of thinking, follow-up discussions revolve around the interpretation of diagram boxes and associated activities but not complex interrelationships inside of, and between, boxes (activities). As a result, team members fail to grasp the systemic features of the situation they are facing. Specifically, functioning on a plateau of low thought fluidity, the team majority remains deaf to being told about what carried out analyses are hiding or fail to view partial initiatives taken in their totality when efforts have been scattered across different workgroups. In that situation, a team's task process—focused on solving the problem at hand—gets hijacked by the interpersonal process triggered by team members' seeking an audience for expressions of their ego-centric needs, and trying to play persuasion games with colleagues based on a less than comprehensive understanding of the situation at hand.

Another striking feature of teams following a downward dynamics is the exaggerated importance attached to specific value streams in contrast to focusing attention on the whole of value-creating activities of which a particular value stream is an integral part. In that case, values are mapped (translated) into rules for cooperation within a specific value stream, not in terms of an overarching whole but rather logistic detail. As a result, how one shares information, plans together, gives each other feedback, and deals with areas of tension is misconstrued since chances of translating abstract concepts such as "agility" into effective cooperation rules are slim.

An example of this snag is the collaboration rule about "noticing" employed in Seven Eleven Japan Co., one of the largest retail companies in Japan where it forms the basis of dialogues aiming at the integration of value streams. The "noticing" approach requires every employee to personally visit a colleague from another team or department in the company and listen to him or her without prejudice, focused on how this colleague carries out his or her activities. In such "lateral" conversations, employees are asked not to judge but focus on understanding a contributor's perspective regarding workflow. The manner and frequency of conducting such interviews with colleagues are an integral part of periodic performance reviews. In this case, "agility" translates into taking colleagues' perspectives into account when making work proposals. The inclusion of others' perspectives in one's own work planning facilitates and speeds up orchestrated action of larger groups of contributors. Also, it schools employees' awareness of their own bias regarding how to deliver work and may even push them into their internal dialogue that has been lying dormant since it went unchallenged.

The characteristic tension that arises in a downwardly oriented dialogue space is that between two parties, the first, larger one, whose members act from established practices and are open to new practices only out of fear of losing respect or recognition, and a second, smaller group, whose members act from their value system and fluidity of thinking. These two parties are developmental opposites. For this reason, their dialogue, which is mediated by templates aimed at creating consensus, often comes to a halt because it is restricted to dimensions referenced by the template which are mistaken as representing "reality itself," rather than being part of a simplistic model of reality that is missing crucial insights into how the real world works. A model is mistaken for what it models, and concepts derived from the model are isolated and fetishized. As a result, the team's engagement with the real world is lost through team members' uncritical fixation on pure abstractions, including desired outcomes, all based on lack of awareness that one is "always thinking."

What might be an optimal way of strengthening the quality of team dialogue in the case described above? In our experience, it consists of introducing a holistic and systemic perspective to team members on account of which they can shift the way they think about a specific subject matter. This amounts to *interrupting* conversations to highlight the conceptual structure of the team's reflective process manifest in its dialogue. Also, one can raise awareness of common biases prevailing in team discussions, as exemplified below (Box 4.1).

**Box 4.1 The Most Common Logical Thinking Biases, first named by Francis Bacon in the sixteenth century (Anderson 1978)**

- Confirmation Bias: favoring information that confirms previously existing beliefs.
- Authority Bias: attributing greater accuracy and importance to the opinion of an authority figure (unrelated to subject matter content).
- Ambiguity Bias: choosing options with known probabilities over (potentially better) options with unknown probability.
- Halo Effect/Horns Effect: being influenced in one's evaluation of something or someone, either by a positive (Halo) or negative (Horns), but unrelated, trait.
- Action Bias: doing something to avoid doing nothing and feeling helpless.
- Representativeness Neglect: assuming that something is more (e.g., anecdotal evidence) or less (e.g., standardized tests) representative than it probably is.

Courtesy of Possert and Possert's (2019) "Mindopening Game."

An even more impactful way of proceeding would be to instruct team members in the basics of thinking in terms of complex systems. Mitleton-Keller (2011) describes examples of such instruction at Rolls-Royce, Shell, BT, Humberside Training & Enterprise Council, the World Bank, and Citibank. The core of her approach consists of increasing the awareness that one cannot fully control behavior in complex systems, and therefore must continuously pay attention to the impact of parts on the whole, coevolution, mutual dependencies, system imbalances, and tipping points—all situations requiring complex thinking. Beyond focusing on mere contexts, one must point to from where in team members' thinking their neglect of systemic issues derives, that is, whether it is habitual or due to unreflected linear logical thinking.

In her interventions, Mitleton-Keller starts from an inventory of how different parties experience a specific set of problems. She then proceeds to a deeper questioning of essential themes that play a role in generating meaning, existing interdependencies (patterns), assumptions made, and conditions through which complex interdependencies can be influenced. All of these aspects become the subject of a "reflect-back" meeting. The reflect-back workshop sets up a process in which team members' thinking about an issue per se, in terms of the structure of thinking, becomes thematic. The essential learning point of such an exercise is that the real world is too complex for applying universal, even nonlinear models. Focusing on subject matter complexity helps team members avoid concept fetishization, thus enabling them to dissociate themselves from purely logic-analytical thinking (where such fetishization is rampant) and so arrive at a richer understanding of subject matter.

Mitleton-Keller's approach is meant to counteract the tendency of dialogue partners, to become identified with what is relevant to them and thus fail to detach from it. Her approach makes team members aware that terms such as "agility" have a wide range of meanings, from purely contextual ones to those focusing on process and relationship or even transformation. As a result, it becomes obvious to workshop participants, that, in practical terms, some aspects of agility relate to defining coordination roles, while others have to do with ways of restructuring what has taken place in the past, the allocation of budgets, systems of information exchange, and so forth.

It is precisely the developmentally sourced diversity of possible concept interpretations that creates a need for in-depth dialogue, not only between team members but within each team member (internal dialogue). The most significant step in learning to honor complexity is, therefore, to examine one's thought process (not just point of view) in situations where participants formulate divergent opinions or options. Various methods are now available for heightening complexity awareness: Laske's three-houses method and moments of dialectic (2008), Hopkinson's Landscape of the Mind method (2019), Possert and Possert's Mindopeners (2019), and the multitude of cognitive bias awareness workshops that arose in the wake of Kahneman's work.

The CSTC triangle introduced above supports self-reflection based on the following questions:

- Which of my conflict behaviors puts team cohesion under pressure?
- In what way does my taking perspectives on (and evaluating) the team and the subject matter of its discussions contribute to disagreement?
- What is my current understanding of how I am influenced by, and influence, others' judgments?
- In my view, what kind of common ground is possible in the team?

Again, these are all "templates" which by themselves cannot substitute for self-aware and complex thinking. They only work when such thinking is already in place. They cannot by themselves produce such thinking as they often advertised to be doing. Rather, the thought forms underlying the asking of the questions above must already be in place since it is these forms of thought (such as contained in Laske's DTF) that act as sources of deep questioning.

In sum, in a value stream environment, a downwardly directed team dynamics originates in a narrowing of perspective-taking on the part of less developed adults compared to a more highly developed subgroup. Such team dynamics issues in problem interpretations that lack a systemic character, in large part because of an absence of explicit sharing of movements-in-thought among participants and, of course, ignorance of thought forms. This failure is easily avoided by teams whose members can make patterns of their thinking process explicit in exchange with colleagues, as shown below.

### 4.4.3 The Upward Dynamics in the Value Stream We-Spaces

Although in upwardly oriented teams, tensions caused by a clash of concrete situations with high-level conceptual abstractions such as scenarios cannot be ruled out, team members deal with such tensions differently than in the previously described environment. The subgroup directing discussions do so with a deep conviction that outcomes are going to evolve according to choices the team has previously made. These choices are rooted in knowledge about the systemic limitations of value stream mappings. From their experience of waste, disconnections, and tensions, team members have formed a notion of where their working methods risk leading to stuckness and therefore need to be retuned. In short, their approach to reality is characterized by a more integrative systems perspective that is closer to how the real world works.

There are two ways to promote this more complex thinking. The first consists of outlining a broader view of the value stream picture and entering into discussions on how to do justice to this broader view. A second way is to broaden the scope of the dialogue in which initiatives are jointly set up. In this scenario, decision-making in the absence of objections has a chance of success because developmentally more mature members practice holistic thinking and are also familiar with the reality that individuals differ in their thinking. A well-founded objection is one that refers to how it affects the operation of the company as a whole; it stimulates participants to think in terms of the bigger picture, at the same time placing personal ambitions on the backburner. The higher quality approach followed in upwardly divided teams also shifts the focus of attention to future possibilities and unforeseen rhythmics of situations discussed.

As a consequence, a more significant number of options for reconciling conflicting positions exists as well. Overall, team coherence develops by expressing and justifying objections, and by making transparent how one chooses solutions. Team members are comfortable with making choices between different agility experiments whose added value they assess based on their practical experience.

However, even when so proceeding, conversations tend to remain focused on subject matter content, in contrast to developing an awareness of what kind of thinking gives rise to such content. To make a turnaround to approaching complex situations with a deeper kind of thinking, one needs to make participants aware of what we call the "four moments of dialectic" engaged with when discussing a subject matter. Awareness of these moments of both thought and reality entails that the real world is not a set of static contexts as postulated and reinforced by linear, logical thinking (also referred to as "identity thinking"). Instead, complex thinking requires the acknowledgement that, in addition to recognizing the contextual dimension, the real world also exists as an ongoing process, a dense set of relationships, and functions as an organism under unceasing transformation. We have already introduced these four dimensions of reality to readers as CPRT: context, process, relationship, and transformation (see also Chap. 2).

Below, we illustrate the four moments of dialectic using the concept of "agility," highlight the importance of weaving the internal and external dialogue together, and add two processes enabling members in the value stream We-Space to deepen their reflective practice.

#### 4.4.3.1 Each Concept Has Four Dimensions: Laske's DTF

The abstract term "agility" has a plethora of meanings and is therefore often overstretched and watered-down, to the point of becoming a synonym of "change." Viewed in terms of the CPRT dimensions of team dialogue, introduced above, the term can refer to static contexts, ongoing processes, explicit or hidden relationships, or transformations, none of which are usually distinguished which gives rise to a great deal of confusion and ideological thinking about how the real world works.

*Contextual meanings* of the term "agility" typically refer to functional frameworks in which things are thought to exist. However, most often such meanings are not contexts but rather processes that have been reduced to contexts by linear thinking, and thus "contextualized," such as interpretations of waste, disconnections, and tensions. Real-world settings comprise a multiplicity of dimensions. Therefore, they are stratified. They have different meanings from different points of view and are interconnected.

At the level of activities, the term "agility" is often used to point to interchangeability between employees or to indicate that existing skills and competencies do not require further development. At the level of subprocesses, "agility" might be related to the existence of different views of how to execute a set specific of activities or changes that frameworks undergo (e.g., a consideration of the growing importance of "sustainability" or of "circular approaches"). To achieve implementation of end-to-end processes in an agile way is often taken to mean that there is more than one way to implement agility, such as from a dashboard or in terms of relationships between boundaries or roles.

To make the confusion worse, meanings referring to the *process dimension* of the term "agility" highlight that each of several aspects of the concept coevolve. From a process perspective, what is called "agility" often has to do with "uncontrollability," which then becomes a breeding ground for still other interpretations of "agility." Or else the term 'agility' is used to identify trends, such as digital evolutions, which implies a focus on unforeseen challenges. Also, an "agile" company may not respond to customer expectations, as a result of which it will not be seen as agile by specific customer segments.

The *relational meaning* of the concept of "agility" refers to issues it is intrinsically linked to and cannot be separated from. This holds true not only for value stream design but also for matters such as strategic choices, investment opportunities, and technological possibilities or limitations. After all, "agility" cannot be understood by way of reduction; it is not an absolute term but rather a concept that derives its meaning from the network of conceptual relationships it is built upon, and these relationships show patterns one needs to be aware of and take into account.

This is borne out by the literature. For instance, Holbeche, in his book *The Agile Organization* (2015), discusses the structural relationships associated with "Resilient Agility," an issue referred to by Arora (2019) in a different way under the name of "Requisite Agility." Still, others talk about "Deep Agility." While these approaches differ in their choice of the terms addressing agility issues, they all conceive of "agility" conceptually as being embedded in, and giving rise to, structural relationships.

Rightfully, agility is equally seen in a *transformational light*, namely wherever its meaning is understood as referencing limits of stability and durability, or the developmental potential it may unleash. References to transformation point to fields of social tension, potential stresses caused by implementing agility in organizational wholes, as well as coordinating systemic dimensions of agility as intrinsically related. Some transformational notions of "agility" also imply, for good reasons, that a company's identity is nothing purely contextual but can be preserved only on account of the unceasing transformation of its own systemic identity.

In short, "agility" is an ideological as well as an inflationary term whose unreflected and undialectical use causes an enormous amount of confusion among purely logical thinkers (who make up a determined majority in our society). As any abstraction well used, the concept requires complex thinking, which, in most cases, is absent from discussions of this term, to the detriment of implementing what the concept stands for.

#### 4.4.3.2 Weaving the Internal into the External Dialogue

These semantic and epistemological considerations of the term "agility" directly bear on its real-time implementation as well as the team discussions required to bring it about. By exploring the multidimensionality of the same concept, team members shift their focus of attention and stop taking the meaning of ideas they are using for granted. Regarding the concept of "agility," they can ask, "what are the implications of a concept such as 'agile platform architecture'?" Team members who engage in such reflections learn not to use a concept like a piece of mental furniture that can be moved around arbitrarily, realizing that one needs to explore what a concept entails, what dynamics it implies, how it relates to other concepts and existing metrics, and what potential it has to transform the meaning of parameters involved in its implementation. In short, by reflecting on crucial concepts together, team members enhance their thought fluidity to the limits of their present cognitive resources.

Such reflective questioning is based on what we call *internal dialogue*, a way of consciously listening to one's own movements-in-thought as well as in response to others' communication, which we refer to as "external dialogue." It is the feedback loop between internal and external dialogue that determines the quality of exchange between individuals such that the latter is rooted in the former. A simple way of rendering this feedback loop would be to call the internal dialogue "reflective listening," a form of listening "with eyes closed" to what others are saying in one's own stillness. When such a feedback loop is realized in a team, team members become aware of "how others think" in contrast to themselves and perhaps become able to point out subtle differences in thinking about one and the same concept. When schooled to do so by a critical facilitator, team members can also begin to discern the thought form structures of others' way of thinking, although such an "interviewing" ability takes time and practice.

When team members are poised to "hear" (understand) each other in this critical way, based on teachable thought forms, they learn to discern not only single thought forms (TFs) but also entire TF-constellations—variously appropriate or inappropriate ways of attending to a specific subject matter before them. One can say, therefore, that TFs, once absorbed, function as a *discovery procedure* or a set of "mind openers" that shifts people's attention to what was previously left unattended by them, individually or as a group. The result of shifting conceptual focus on a subject matter held constant is to set up a stretching of what is being thought about into what could be thought about (Laske 2015a, b, 2019k, 2018a).

Just about every concept used in a management environment is open to the four thought form classes (concept dimensions) referred to as CPRT. Since logical thinking is overwhelmingly focused on C, context, engaging with the CPRT method amounts to enriching logical thinking by introducing the additional dimensions of P (process), R (relationship), and T (transformation), and thereby transcending logical thinking proper in the direction of complex, transformational thinking while keeping logical thinking fully intact.

#### 4.4.3.3 A Playful Way to Deepen the Reflection: De Visch's Re-Thinking Game

Working with DTF (i.e., the CPRT method), say, in the value stream domain, is rather straightforward. In general terms, one examines the underlying themes (aspects) that compose a particular value stream in a more productive and more integrative way than purely logical thinking allows for. This process can take the form of a game made possible by De Visch's "Re-Thinking Game" (2019a). The game entails using—asking and answering—a series of questions (written on cards) from each of the (four) classes of thought forms (CPRT) in light of which one can reflectively "open up" any concept, such as the CPRT-aspects of the term "value stream." Applied to a real-time team discussion, the CPRT method amounts to playing a game. In the game, one switches between "reifying" and "fluid" thinking. In *reifying* thinking, a concept, its assumptions, and implications are simply taken for granted, while in *fluid* thinking, the concept itself becomes the topic of discussion since it is systematically taken apart into its C, P, R, and T aspects. (See further examples given in Chap. 2 of this book.)

Essentially, what discussions modeled after the Re-Thinking Game achieve is creating a broader and deeper mental space for one's own and others' movements-in-thought in real time. The game can be said to develop an awareness of the concepts an individual or group is using, which amounts to the discovery of "I am constantly thinking." How deeply the game can bring its users to that discovery is directly responsible for the quality of the internal dialogue they subsequently conduct with themselves and others. Simultaneously with the experience of oneself as "thinking," an individual also becomes aware of others as thinkers and begins to listen to them, relating concepts embedded in his or her movements-in-thought to those inferred from the interlocutor. The depth of internal dialogue that ensues can be measured by the extent to which a thinker succeeds in becoming aware of his or her emotional and cognitive ego-centrism and gains enough detachment to distance himself or herself from it, thus changing attitude. Typically, this ego-centrism is either something one remains subject to (because unconscious of), or something one intentionally and defensively keeps from oneself and others. In using the Re-Thinking Game, hiding behind one's ego-centrism or denying it becomes a more difficult undertaking.

#### 4.4.3.4 The Identity Landscape Methodology

With the help of thought forms used in the Re-Thinking Game outlined above, we developed the "Identity Landscape Methodology" (De Visch 2019b). The methodology inquires into contributors' social-emotional meaning-making. It can be used both one-on-one and in groups.

Employees start their discussion on topics of tensions that have emerged in their cooperation with others; they choose two or three themes related to their topic to deepen their mutual understanding (and thus personal relationship). Each person is given the mental space to reflect on each of the themes chosen to nourish participants' internal dialogue. Unbeknownst to them, participants' developmental stage of maturity strongly determines what is important to them, how that importance is articulated through speech, and why what is being said causes social tensions. Characteristically, themes such as "communication" and "feedback" are more frequently selected by those who function from an other-dependent position, while themes such as "opportunities" are more attractive to employees who operate from an instrumental stage. Issues of planning and strategy most often emerge for self-authoring individuals. Teams being developmentally mixed it naturally occurs that participants are drawn to topics not of their choosing, and thus get to know their colleagues' way of thinking and socially relating. They also learn to anticipate developmentally more advanced topics they would not themselves have come up with.

Box 4.2 lists some questions generated by the methodology explained above.

**Box 4.2 An Example of the "Identity Landscape Methodology" Meant to Strengthen an Understanding of One's Own Role Identity and Its Impact on Others**

The Identity Landscape Methodology raises questions regarding one's role identity and social stance toward others when pursuing a team mandate or goal. It comprises 25 social-emotional and psychological *themes* spelled out in the form of pertinent questions to team members. Questions appear in three different formulations: for a group discussion, for a one-to-one conversation, and personal reflection. Team members and individual employees choose one or two themes they find relevant regarding a field of tension they find themselves in. Six of the 25 themes the methodology comprises appear below. **All of them bear the imprint of a contributor's adult-developmental level**.

**Table 4.3** Example Questions from the "Identity Landscape Methodology"

| | | |
|---|---|---|
| *Questions for use in a group conversation within a team* | | |
| **Assertiveness**<br>How do we cope with people that stand up and speak out or sit still and keep quiet? | **Conflict**<br>How could we handle disagreement more creatively and resolve disputes? | **Feedback**<br>How could we become more open to constructive feedback? |
| **Openness**<br>How could we be more open to other people's ideas, and in what specific way? | **Planning**<br>How could we build more flexibility into our planning? | **Transparency**<br>How and what do we need to change in our communication to be more transparent for each other? |
| *Questions to explore in a one-to-one discussion* | | |
| **Assertiveness**<br>Under what circumstances do you feel reluctant to be assertive? When and with whom is it easier for you to be trusting? What could help you become more assertive? | **Conflict**<br>What do you need to move through or beyond this conflict? How can you respond to this conflict as constructively as possible? | **Feedback**<br>What feedback would be helpful to the other person? |
| **Openness**<br>What would help you to be more open-minded on a particular topic? How could you increase your comfort in incorporating ideas from people with different backgrounds? | **Planning**<br>What limitations do you experience in how you are currently planning? What options do you have to improve your planning? | **Transparency**<br>What does transparent communication mean to you? What topics are you inclined to share with others, and what beliefs do you need to share more than you presently do? |
| *Questions for self-coaching and personal reflection* | | |
| **Assertiveness**<br>How is my assertiveness experienced by others? What makes knowing how I come across to others important to me, and how can I become more assertive? | **Conflict**<br>When do I experience conflict as productive, and where am I avoiding conflict outside of me? What am I gaining with my present stance toward others, and where would I be prepared to take more of a risk in being frank? | **Feedback**<br>What if I were to hear more suggestions from others? How can I better understand other people's thoughts and feelings? |
| **Openness**<br>Under what circumstances might I ask more open questions to see where they lead? | **Planning**<br>Where might I stay too attached to a single plan at the exclusion of other opportunities? | **Transparency**<br>Am I transparent regarding my values and integrity? Is what others see (of me and in me) close to my notion of myself? |

The outer right column in Table 4.3 (feedback and transparency) indicates aspects of an upwardly distributed dynamics in teams working in the value stream We-Space. In this field of discussion, setting time limits is crucial. The exercise can be geared to specific moments of tension (as in "Reflect-Back Workshops") or may regard an entire organizational process.

## 4.5 The Business Model We-Space

For us, contrary to conventional wisdom, designing the future has more to do with transformations humans undergo and are capable of than mere technical innovation. The reason is that ultimately, technologies are used by humans and have little value in themselves but in their effect depend on their use. The future to be designed is, by definition, absent from the real world as it presently appears, although complex thinking has a fair chance to anticipate relevant aspects of it, even though there is no chance that it will emerge in a linear, "logical" way (as hoped). Essentially, any future can be envisioned only to the extent to which past and present have been deeply understood and become interrelated in one's thinking.

In the present context, the specific meaning of "inventing the future" is focused on creating value through decisions team members make about mission, vision, strategy, innovation, and technology within a specific organizational model. In comparison to previously discussed We-Spaces, in this dialogue space, the conversations shift from *alignment* (the essence of working in the continuous improvement space) and *integration* (the core of work in the value stream space) to *design.* Decisions are made about capital investments, competitive position, development of product and service portfolios, the channel mix for connecting with customers, and the technologies needed to innovate the present mission and its associated procedures and processes.

When designing a future (in the sense of an organizational "next stage"), ideas need to be tested in the context of a multitude of different stakeholders whose understanding of each others' needs and interests is limited. The search for shared understandings and resulting common ground (e.g., between investors, owners, social groups, customers, and employees) therefore occupies a prominent place. Relationships between diverse factors that have an impact on the future move into the foreground. Since futures are virtual and invisible and there are many factors by which they may declare themselves, differences in convictions about what is presently "real" and how they will shift over time, both through foreseeable and unforeseen changes, are becoming more pronounced and relevant than ever.

The business model We-Space is often explored through "Future Labs" attended by a diverse set of stakeholders bent on conceptualizing the future through complex models which are abstractions considerably, if not entirely, out of touch with how the real world works (since the latter issue is neither linear nor logical but transformational). Through such models, the core question is often that of strengthening a company's competitive position, thus relational concerns more than process concerns. Given that the teams functioning in this space are no less developmentally

**Table 4.4** The CSTC-interplay highlighting downwardly and upwardly divided team dynamics in the business model space

| | Downwardly divided dynamic | Upwardly divided dynamic |
|---|---|---|
| | Self-authoring (majority) > Self-aware (minority) | Self-aware (majority) > Self-authoring (minority) |
| Team cohesion | Consensus based on recognizing the legitimacy of conflicts supported by tolerance of personal differences. Clear understanding of the limits of purely logical thinking. | The interpersonal processes are held in check by shared values and goals of political, ecological or common good importance despite often unresolvable conflicts of interest. |
| Cognitive knowledge contruction | Some transformational thinking (thinking based on insight into relationships between contexts seen as undergoing constant change). | Full transformational thinking. |
| Social-emotional self-other dynamic | Tensions between finding the common ground of differing value systems and searching for a more highly inclusive value system are resolved in terms of a dominant ideology. | Tensions between finding the common ground of differing value systems and searching for a more highly inclusive value system are resolved in terms of a dominant ideology are resolved for the sake of achieving a long-term legacy. |
| Improving the quality of the dialogue between team members | Switch from 'what' to 'how' to think, with a focus on building integrated perspectives on the dynamic and relational nature of systems, with a focus on ecosystemic collaboration and future value creation. | Switch from 'what' to 'how' to think, with a focus on building integrated perspectives on the dynamic and relational nature of systems, with a focus on creating an environment enabling deep transformational thinking, by focusing on societal value creation. |
| Improving the quality of the inner dialogue | Recognizing the limits of one's own value system and ideology by sharing accountability for group dynamics. Engaging with humble inquiry permitting to risk one's own standing in the team. | Spiritual practice. |

mixed than in the previous two We-Spaces discussed above, here, too, we distinguish two dynamics, a downwardly and an upwardly directed one, as partly explicated in Table 4.4.

Again, the first three rows of the table refer to the CSTC triangle, while the subsequent two rows contain improvement suggestions or descriptions of team capabilities. As well, the table is applicable to work with individuals as well as teams, as in Tables 4.1 and 4.2.

### 4.5.1 The Downward Dynamics in the Business Model We-Spaces

In downwardly divided teams (where the less developed subgroup is dominant), team cohesion is fragile due to tensions between stakeholder's different value systems, on one hand, and the fact that a more highly developed subgroup resolutely wants to go for a new, often more inclusive, approach not followed by the majority, on the other. The latter group's bend toward innovation usually involves choices as to whether or not to discontinue or sell organizational subactivities to develop a distinct focus on the future. Typically, dialogues in this space are strongly fed by a large quantity of known or stipulated data, such as the evolution of regulatory frameworks, results of environmental analyses, trend reports, relative capacity estimates, risk analyses, and more. As in previous We-Spaces, an extensive range of templates is used to capture the essence of available data.

A widely used tool in this space is the business model canvas (Osterwalder and Pigneur 2010; Laske 2017b).

A business model canvas dialogue usually begins with filling the canvas with a whole range of "post-its," followed by general groupings of problems and issues that can be envisaged and expressed in terms of logical "if-then" chains (if this, then that; if that, then the other). In downwardly oriented team dynamics, the focus of attention is limited to the awareness of dialogue content, not the quality of reasoning that creates that content in the first place. To alleviate the bias favoring content over the structure of a team's movements-in-thought, Laske's *Dialectical Thinking Framework* (DTF) offers procedures for identifying what might be missing in an individual's or team's thinking in terms of options and possibilities one could ascertain. DTF provides a broad set of mind openers, based on what we have called the CPRT method. It invites people to investigate the "thought forms" (TFs) they use—unbeknownst to themselves—when trying to make sense of reality. In the mental process of envisioning the future, these thought forms matter significantly since it is crucial to transcend thinking purely logically and in terms of content, aspects that frequently coincide—logic being used as the great objectifier that turns the real world into a set of abstractions (and thus opens the gap between "how the real world works" and "how humans think").

A DTF-based business model dialogue starts with capturing the canvas' hidden dimensions by questioning the different post-its found on the canvas. For instance, in the customer segment (CS), team members may realize that they have failed to account for multiple contexts, underlying processes, their relationships, and thus transformations CS would undergo over time. The questions below serve as mind openers for recognizing the context, process, relationship, and transformational dimension of a CS:

- Context (the big picture and its layers and dimensions): what might set our CS apart from similar CSs; what might be the parts of CS we are overfocusing on; are these parts further differentiated into layers we need to observe, or do they overlap; how does the total CS influence each part?

- Process (opposite realities; emerging changes): what internal evolutions in a specific CS are we excluding; are there parts we are disregarding but should be including; to what extent are elements different from, or antithetical to, each other, and in what way?
- Relationship (common ground; intrinsic relatedness): what do the components of different CS share; how solid or fuzzy are the lines of separation between them; what is the value of bringing elements of CS that appear as distinct into a relationship with each other, searching out their common ground?
- Transformation (preserving identity by way of unceasing motion): how stable are the parts we distinguish within a CS, either conceptually (in terms of our definition of them) or in terms of real-world trends; do some parts compete or develop akin to each other over time, in a way that logical categorization does not capture?

The above questions are examples of a "breadth-first knowledge creation strategy," a procedure favoring scope over depth. The strategy helps participants to become conscious of all those aspects of their topic they might have missed and makes them aware of an issue's complexity. In this dialogue step, participants deconstruct a problem into its four thought form and real-world dimensions (CPRT) and explore the bigger picture that gives meaning to the concepts they use, as well as the transformations the big picture is subject to. They also explore the structural dependencies and path dependencies of discussion topics and strengthen their awareness of transformational opportunities so far missed.

For best effect, a breadth-first knowledge creation strategy needs to be backed-up by a "depth-first knowledge creation strategy." In the latter, attention shifts away from working with the four classes of TFs themselves, to how exactly to use different TFs (thought forms) in each of these classes (i.e., C, P, R, T). This entails learning individual TFs rather than simply deriving questions from learned classes of TFs.

When exploring the *process dimension* of CS, for example, the following questions help build a more profound understanding of the real-world changes a CS is subject to:

- Recognition of changes in CS: outlining emergence and inclusion of opposites:
  - What consequences might choosing this specific CS have when looked at long-term developments?
  - Can we trace the current CS back to the process from which it emerged?
  - Looking at how our CS is evolving, which of its elements need further integration?
- Elaboration of changes in CS: detailing patterns of interaction in the ongoing process(es):
  - What social processes interact to determine how our CS is evolving?
  - Does thinking about interactions between a specific CS and other social groups aid us in developing our understanding of that CS?

- An integrated perspective on the dynamically changing nature of CS as a system: the embeddedness of issues in the overarching process(es):
  - Looking at CS evolution within a broader time horizon, what dynamics become evident or harder to discern?
  - What broader social process or psychological predilections influence the development of a specific CS? What does taking a broader perspective on a particular CS teach us?

Whatever meanings may be given to the term "agility" in this context, these meanings are rather insubstantial if, in the domain of collaboration, the term does not reference the shared thinking employees are capable of. Such shared thinking can be measured by Laske's DTF in terms of "fluidity of thinking" which refers to the complexity of thought forms used in real-time team dialogues.

In our consulting experience, it makes good sense and is productive to reduce all meanings given to the term "agility" to the human capability for thinking in thought forms, for the simple reason that that capability is not something one can decide not to use, or a tool "out there," but is rather a human capability "in here" that can be awakened, if not through education in early life, then through critical facilitation in adulthood. While in no way encouraged by present educational systems (public or private), this capability is rooted in the human condition that one is "always thinking," thus always philosophizing, whether one is aware of it or not. Thinking, or sense-making is like breathing. It only ends with death.

Why is becoming aware of the unceasing activity of one's mind so important? In a constructivist view of the real world, there is nothing outside of us that could be called "real" if it were not simultaneously "constructed" by conceptual thinking, so that what is "real" emerges as a co-construction between the subject and the object of knowing. Due to the fallacy promoted by logical thinking, that there are either objects without subjects constructing them or subjects that are mere derivatives of objects existing as facts, this capability has suffered a long-term decline during the last 200 years.

However, at the point of history where you find ourselves today, the personal and societal denial of the reality of unceasing thinking in every individual has become a very risky proposition. Although knowledge creation requires a conceptual effort no emotional handwaving can provide, it is entirely "worth the effort" since awareness of one's thinking capability leads to a larger "world" to live in, a deeper truth about that world, and a higher quality of dialogue than can otherwise obtain, whether in life or at work. In fact, what is called "freedom" is found in this very direction. By comparison, putting "post-it" blocks on a virtual canvas can be a mindless undertaking that does not even scratch the surface of the complexities the canvas is awkwardly and incompletely trying to model.

Successfully transforming a business model requires the collaboration of team members of high social-emotional as well cognitive standing who have a grasp of the totality of their organization as well as of its function and functioning in the broader social environment, joined to a sure grasp of how the real world works in contradistinction to "how people (typically) think," namely logically. If a team does not satisfy these adult-developmental preconditions of quality dialogue in which colleagues see each other as midwives of their personal development and co-stewards of their company, we refer to such team as a "downwardly" rather than "upwardly" divided.

A downwardly divided team is thus a team composed of a highly developed minority overwhelmed by a less developed majority (often with political clout), and unable to sway the majority in the direction of what one might call "critical realism": a holistic and systemic perception of the company's future that integrates a balanced view of its human and algorithmic resources with a holistic perception of its social and societal surround.

In the business model space, the downward tendency of teams shows up in the form of a lack of a sense of the greater whole of one's organization which, in our experience, translates into lack of competitive strength relative to other organizational or institutional entities. The most visible and audible predicament of such a team is a lack of awareness of the thought form structure of its dialogue, thus the conceptual flatness of the latter. There is a lack of metalevel thinking that could override the prevailing fixation on mere subject matter content without self-critical reflection.

Listening to a downwardly divided team, one makes the experience of conceptually impoverished dialogue fixated on unshakable and cherished contexts, preferred processes, unquestioned relationships, and a mistaking of mere change for transformation that results in a task process that is constantly overwhelmed by the team's interpersonal process. There is also a lack of humility in carrying forward one's own strengths without compassion for others' challenges or weaknesses due to a frail perception of the team as deeply engaged in learning and transformation.

The cognitive requirement in this We-Space is equitable to the social-emotional one. It is that of *integration*. Integration is not simply a matter of content (or what needs to be integrated), but more essentially, a way of thinking in which cognitive-structural elements such as context, process, and relationship *thought forms* are themselves integrated in the effort to understand real-world transformations. There simply is no way to transform a business model if team members are unable to synthesize in their thinking all four classes of thought forms introduced above. This is so since transformation far exceeds change in momentum and multidimensional complexity both of which in unaccessible to purely logical thinking.

Putting this into more pragmatic terms, one could say that a downwardly divided team in the business model space fails to build an integrated perspective vis-à-vis competitors and therefore endangers or reduces the likelihood that customers will respond to the future company's offerings positively rather than hesitatingly or critically.

To make the cognitive preconditions of designing critical realist business models for an envisioned future more transparent, let us review the CPRT Sequence that guides adult-cognitive development in more detail.

#### 4.5.1.1 Context Awareness

The key to building new business models lies in the ability to think through and combine different frames of reference. There is a need to maintain a multidimensional context perspective that focuses on broad ideological, political, or philosophical issues. Such a view helps generate, as well as understand, value systems real-world and reference frameworks expressed by notions such as *sustainability*, *ecological footprint*, *social transformation*, *inequality*, all of which invite evaluative comparisons.

For this reason, it is not enough to recognize the importance of context per se, but also the process and relationship issues contexts entail. It is, therefore, important for a team working in this We-Space, to honor a plurality of ideas about a company's future whose investigation is likely to enable high-quality design choices to be made. Most of the mental frames of reference of importance are multidimensional, comprising distinctly different knowledge and activity domains. Political issues are also involved: companies increasingly need to take a position on how they view the dominant free-market model, its associated social inequities, and how to deal with them.

#### 4.5.1.2 Process Awareness

Process thinking about business model transformation requires a focus on patterns of interaction defining coevolutions. Rather than being a static entity, a business model is a set of adaptable moves that both influence the competitive environment and are influenced by it. Integrated process thinking focuses on the embeddedness of business model choices in broader, overarching social evolutions. In the design domain, for example, decisions on product characteristics need to be embedded in a perspective on entire product life cycles, circular or not.

#### 4.5.1.3 Relationship Awareness

Relationship thinking focuses on intrinsic, not just external, relationships of business model components. While extrinsic relationships can be inferred from the post-its of a canvas, intrinsic relationships are invisible. They are hidden relationships that bind together (co-define) business model components. For example, a "marriage" is an intrinsic relationship that co-defines what it entails to be a spouse or partner, thus also the options they have for living their life. The same holds for an enterprise architecture or governance structure that, by definition, determines existing options for transacting business.

When we invest effort in developing an integrated context, process, and relationship perspective on a particular theme, we are being political. For example, team members are called upon to address tensions between a dominant self-authoring subgroup and a less powerful self-aware subgroup within a team. In the ideal case, team members would act as critical facilitators of each other, to clarify disagreements regarding values and ideologies (including those embedded in templates).

#### 4.5.1.4 Awareness of Transformation

Transformational ways of thinking are absent from logical thinking where A is always A and remains A in the face of an oppositional B which is simply declared "false." That is not how the real world works, however. To do justice to real-world functioning, transformational thinking is integrative; it brings together movements-in-thought focused on context (C), process (P), and relationship (R) as happens in the real world.

Consequently, to think of a specific CS transformationally, such as in terms of its limited durability and fragility, requires to have already understood that a CS is a context undergoing constant change and is co-defined by many different social factors that determine customer attitudes toward products and services. Such an understanding is, unfortunately, not widespread. The practical question that arises is how to persuade participants in this dialogue to enter into an inner dialogue with themselves that allows them to explore the limits of their own logically limited thinking. This is a pathway for them to question the boundaries of their value system as well.

One of the possibilities for team members to proceed is suggested by E. Schein and P. Schein (2018), who advocate that group members share responsibility for the dynamics developing in their groups. Shared responsibility for group dynamics means that each group member enters into a dialogue with himself or herself about the stance and the role they are taking (in real time) that influences the group process, such as building a systemic understanding, exploring possibilities, comparing options, and testing consensus. What is required is to take personal responsibility for how the group's dynamic develops rather than leaving that issue to specialist facilitators. Playing a leadership role and being responsible for group dynamics becomes the same thing.

Practically, this requires asking oneself questions such as: "why am I here with others?"; "how can I contribute to this group's development?"; "how can I create a safe space in which to discuss hidden agendas (or the elephants in the room)?" Opening up to one's internal dialogue around one's own contribution to the dynamics of one's group reduces defense mechanisms and augments the quality of questioning in the group. Ultimately, personal transformation leads to greater modesty and less dogmatic defenses of one's points of view. It entails moving away from the focus on efficiency in meetings as a priority and letting go of strict time limits and prepared agendas in favor of a constructive critical dialogue.

In contrast to E. Schein's view on this, our suggestion here is not simply a behavioral "good advice" since we know about the adult-developmental preconditions of what Schein suggests. In short, we are aware that many group members will be developmentally unprepared to follow Schein's suggestion (which is exactly what happens in downwardly divided teams.)

### 4.5.2 The Upward Dynamics in the Business Model We-Spaces

In the upwardly distributed dynamics of the business model We-Space, the social tension in focus is that between the value systems of a self-authoring subgroup and a self-aware subgroup of team members. Because individuals in these groups have left behind other-dependent behavior, they naturally establish a stronger balance between interpersonal and task process. Team members succeed in postponing judgment and (after a thorough debate) abandoning personal judgments in favor of a broader, more inclusive, and more principled solution. One's reputation and one's social legacy are seen as intrinsically connected.

In such a team configuration, we can speak of what is happening as transformational knowledge creation. Team members share their value systems not only among themselves but also with a multitude of reference groups. Typical of these dialogues is the creation of new abstractions and language (e.g., green design, twilight zone, industry 4.0, digital healthcare, sharing economy, platforms). The language developed in this way covers many areas of human activity and takes the form of broad aggregations of value systems from different social groups. Members question the relevance of high-level abstractions and choose the networks to which they want to belong. These networks may be think tanks, government-related circles preparing future regulation, and other high-level vision exchanges (e.g., Davos, Bilderberg group).

An essential feature of a self-aware approach to business model transformation is the awareness that one is rarely in a position in which to make decisions in isolation from others and also that one is oneself only a tiny speck within a social and physical universe. For this reason, the quality of dialogue is high. New perspectives are engendered. Attention goes to ways of bringing people together (e.g., deep dives, learning journeys, open innovation network collaboration, living labs). It is not only subject matter content that is investigated. It is rather the issue of where does a particular subject matter comes from, who thought it up, what was that person's/group's way of thinking, and can we follow that thinking fruitfully here and now. In other words, the dominant groups in such a team should act as its critical facilitator.

A *critical facilitator* can make complex issues transparent without losing their complexity by way of accommodating to momentary team dynamics, and to do so without "losing the team." To achieve this, he or she dialectically questions points of view, shows how to transcend existing perspectives, and keeps differences and tensions among discussants on the table productively for as long as possible. He or she guides participants in making increasingly nuanced conceptual choices and relates these choices to real-world configurations without reducing the latter by purely analytical objects "out there." He or she does so by constantly questioning the subject–object split logical thinking invariably imposes on dialogue and thereby frees up participants' inner dialogue about their reflection in the present moment.

The limitations of the critical facilitator's work do not lie in his tools but in his audience whose members' fluidity of thinking is determined by both social-emotional meaning-making and level of conceptual acuity. How these preconditions work out in real time decides how far participants feel in need of defending their role identity rather than opening up new thought horizons. That is the reason why facilitators pay a great deal of attention to momentary team dynamics which is as vital as body temperature. Insight into team dynamics derives from an assessment of the degree of openness and cognitive resources of participants as to their degree of holistic thinking, and in light of a topic in its totality, how a team's thought process affects the organization as a whole.

The critical facilitator is guided in his choices by the following convictions:

- The social world is full of conflict and tension that contributes to a feeling of alienation on the part of specific individuals and groups.
- Problem analysis and the development of problem-solving approaches need to be aimed at identifying opportunities in areas of tension and opportunities for improving the social status of individuals and groups involved.
- Possible interventions need to be weighed against each other in terms of their contribution to the larger social whole, and in terms of the opportunities, they offer individuals and groups for taking responsibility for their own future.
- Transformations tend to be successful if attention is paid to whether they strengthen the core quality of participating parties for the sake of the whole they compose.

In a self-aware group, a strong motivation to promote change goes hand in hand with a certain detachment. Detachment creates distance from personal beliefs and suspends unreflected certainties. In such a context, it is unlikely that people identify with abstractions such as "agility." Instead, they will critically question the meaning of such abstractions in specific contexts and their relationship to each other, and will focus on the systemic tensions apparent in the team, and the opportunities and required steps that makes agility possible. Strikingly, often such detachment goes hand in hand with engagement with spiritual practice and personal questing for the deeper essence of things. (Many players in this field are looking for a spiritual master. These spiritual masters rarely formulate answers, but use their questions to stimulate the internal reflection process of their students.)

**Key Insight and Practice Reflections**

In this chapter, we have provided a *phenomenology of team thinking* in real time for the three different We-Spaces we introduced in this book. We have done so with a focus on how organizational cultures are created, not based on mission statements but in real time. For this purpose, we have explored in what way culture, viewed as a "common ground" that both undergirds and is created by work in teams, is a function of how far unconscious individual commitments across an entire organization, when not brought into the open through ways of transformational thinking, tend to cripple a corporate culture's openness. We have shown that the way this happens by discussing downwardly divided teams. In addition, we have demonstrated that the way culture-crippling tendencies take over is decidedly different in each of the three dialogue-spaces (We-Spaces). Specifically, we have shown that the specific structure of a We-Space not only defines the central issues of discussion (their "what") but also determines the degree of openness and fluidity of thinking available to a team, and the risks taken if team members cannot transcend the present limits of their own personal development that they are subject to regardless of how human resources happen to be viewed in their company.

We have wanted to make it evident that the more decidedly team goals regard the future, the more transparency of team members' movements-in-thought is required for successful collaboration. Throughout the chapter, we have demonstrated how difficult it is to achieve a common ground on account of the developmental diversity of team members that puts team cohesion at risk in ways that are specific to a particular We-Space, and moreover are often covered up by using behavioristic lingo to describe team issues or define remedies for them.

In the following chapter, we discuss the design of work systems and the roles that constitute them. Again, the cognitive-developmental approach implemented in Laske's DTF, the Dialectical Thought Form Framework, is shown to shed new light on this topic.

**Practice Reflections**

1. What, in your experience with teams, are the roots of team cohesion outside of behavior, which is rather a result of it?
2. How do the developmental parameters—especially those of cognitive development outlined in this chapter—shed light on a recent difficulty you encountered in establishing "common ground" in a team, department, or entire organization?
3. What dimension(s) would you add to the CSTC triangle introduced near the beginning of this chapter to explain the difficulty of creating common ground in teams, and how do they relate to the three dimensions of CSTC?
4. What are your criteria for judging the quality of team dialogues outside of their mere content, or of "what" is being said, that bear on how content is conceptually conceived of and articulated through language?
5. What demands are being made on you as a critical facilitator of team dialogue? Have these demands become transparent for you in this chapter? If not, what was missing for you?

# 5 The Commitment Dialogue: How We Agree on What Needs to Be Done

*Managers assume that employees will execute their role as agreed upon, without noticing that this agreement is flawed to the extent that the employee's developmental size of person may be incommensurate with the complexity of his or her role.*

**Abstract**

In this chapter, we explore the building blocks of commitment. We see commitment shaped by the way in which individual contributors conceive of their role functioning in real time both emotionally and conceptually, rather than in terms of timeless abstractions as pervasively found in conventional role definitions. We make use of findings from adult-developmental research for recasting roles as co-constructed by role owners' interpretive process and thus as "made" (mentally constructed) rather than simply "taken."

In the first section, we show why a conventional role-making model cuts down on the complexity and ensuing ambiguity of role definitions. In the second section, we explore four dialogue practices for exploring work commitments: (1) the dialogue on the framework within which to deliver work, (2) the dialogue on priorities for the sake of transcending the short-term focus on output quality, (3) the group-focused organization of performance feedback aiming for achieving broader role fulfillment, and (4) the role integration dialogue held in terms of the scaled agile framework (SAFe).

In this chapter, we explore the building blocks of commitment. We see them as shaped by how individual contributors conceive of their role both emotionally and conceptually in real time, rather than in terms of organizational abstractions beyond time found in typical role definitions. We make use of findings from



J. De Visch, O. Laske, *Practices of Dynamic Collaboration*, Management for Professionals, https://doi.org/10.1007/978-3-030-42549-4_5

adult-developmental research for recasting roles seen as co-constructed by interpretive processes. An approach of this kind, of which we think as developmentally grounded and thus focused on employees' internal rather than external workplace, is increasingly required in organizations striving to be self-organizing.

The chapter is in three parts, as follows:

1. Section 1: we show why a *role-making* model cuts down on the ambiguity of role definitions.
2. Section 2: we explore four dialogue practices for exploring work commitments.
3. Section 3: we summarize key insights and provide practice reflections.

Commitments are made in an *internal workplace* where individuals mentally construct their approach to work in the external workplace by interpreting organizational givens. The relationship between the two workplaces is such that when they leave their outer workplace, they take their internal one with them, it being the grounding of "how they work." This internal workplace is adult-developmentally determined and in complexity far exceeds organizational role definitions. This has to be kept in mind when speaking of commitments to a role and commitments not measuring up to the definition of a role. Both of the latter are abstractions that have little to do with how roles are executed by people in real time on a particular workday.

For the same reason, separating role definitions from team dialogue in real time, both in and about roles, makes only limited sense. Roles are not abstractions but are the casing into which contributors pour the energies of their internal workplace. Only commitments arrived at through dialogue in real time can connect the two workplaces. The bridge that connects them is constructed not from the external but the internal workplace. The rest is what can be read on paper.

Also, roles do not "speak for themselves"; rather, they are a gateway to the thinking and interpretations of those who "hold" and act in them. Their core is not assigned but dialogically constructed. It is the dialogical component of making commitments that moves to center when we conceive of "role" not merely as something linked to specific challenges of a temporary character or a specialization but rather as centered around the personal identity of the individual "in" a role.

This becomes clear when we see Individuals as living at a discernible position of adult development over the life span at each of which they hold a specific world view, including a view of what "work" is and what "role" means to them. Taken out of this developmental grounding, an individual, as well as a role, is a pure abstraction ready to be committed to paper.

From this perspective, four major questions arise:

1. What is the relationship between an individual's developmental "size of person," or capability, and his or her "complexity of role"?
2. How can team dialogue become a tool for clarifying to what extent the complexity of a role exceeds the suggested role holder's developmental size of person in which his or her commitment is grounded?

3. What are specific dialogue practices that assure that role commitments envisioned by members of a team are commensurate with a prospective role holder's (team member's) present developmental size of person (which is unknown to the team)?
4. Pragmatically, this question addresses the issue of dealing with the ambiguity that arises when role holders interpret a role unaware of the fact that they are subject to their adult development rather than in control of it and thus misconceive of their own capabilities?

These questions highlight that role ambiguity has at least two aspects: first, the open interpretability of any role definition provided "from the outside" to an individual meaning maker and second, the incomplete knowledge available to team members about how a provided role definition is interpreted, unconsciously as well as consciously, by the holder of the role in question.

## 5.1 How Role Ambiguity Arises

The main aspect of role ambiguity derives from how employees, unbeknownst to them, understand agreements from the perspective of their present emotional and cognitive maturity level (which is unknown to them by nature) and thus unaware of their present adult-developmental limits. In this developmental perspective on role interpretation, the difference between a role-taking and a role-making model becomes crucial since it decides between organizational success and failure.

Most managers, eschewing knowledge of adult development, follow a "role-taking," not a "role-making," approach. Uninformed about developmental theory, they naturally leave the interpretive multiplicity pointed out throughout this book of the account, thus operating in terms of "the blind leading the blind" maxim. As a consequence, managers assume that employees will execute (or even "fulfill") their role as agreed upon, without noticing that this agreement is flawed to the extent that the employee's developmental size of person may be incommensurate to the size—or complexity—of his or her role.

To counter this naivete on the managers' side, in this chapter, we propose a *role-making*, rather than *role-taking*, model. The advantage of this model, to be demonstrated, is that it opens collaborators to the many different interpretations any role is subject to and open to as a topic of team dialogue. One of the advantages of this switch from taking to making roles is the movement from a SMART to a FAST conversation about roles.

Contemporary role agreements often are nothing but lists of activities. Lists are insufficient for coping with interpretive issues they are sure to raise. For instance, as a training coordinator, you may be expected to develop training modules, organize concrete training courses, and follow up on their transfer. Working from roles as lists of activities, however, does not make clear which specific contribution is linked to which individual activities. Activities have very different functions and purposes. For a training coordinator, these may be aimed at personal growth support, supporting the transition to a new way of working, or addressing the impact of new technology developments on specific ways of collaborative work. In short, role agreements reduced to activities of diverse functionality make no sense.

Another limitation of thinking of roles as lists of activities is the inherent reductionism of it. Reductionism makes questions such as "how do role agreements link to the organizational culture as a whole?" impossible to ask. What is lacking is holistic as well as real-time thinking. This can be repaired by adopting a storyline methodology instead. A storyline methodology helps grasp the essence of a role by opening it up to team dialogue. With this methodology, team members can to co-construct their role and thus "make," rather than simply "take," it.

Once one begins to think about roles dialogically, as something not merely given but emerging in team members' consciousness over time, it becomes clear that they are open to a slew of interpretations. Dialoguing about a specific role holder's complexity handling (which is left implicit in a mere list) is a natural outcome. This approach not only creates a bird's eye view of a role, such as making explicit issues of target customers, innovation issues, resources, and planning, but also, by making explicit specific dimensions of role responsibility, allows for a precise formulation of expected contributions and thus increases room for discussing role holder's decision-making as more or less appropriate and commensurate with the complexity of the role in question at a particular time. In short, it brings the role into the real world.

Once team dialogue about roles is the accepted way of proceeding for creating work commitments, it becomes possible to view any dialogue about a role dynamically, that is, in light of the tension existing between what needs to be done (the complexity of the role) and the means available for getting it done (the size of person). Addressing this tension means to think developmentally, as was modeled by Jaques (1989), Laske (2008, 2015a), and De Visch (2010).

Role agreements are, by nature, mutual and are thus intrinsically linked. "My" role makes no sense without "yours" and vice versa. To bring this to light, team dialogue is needed, and team dialogue requires learning dialogue practices that are commensurate with the level of work and thus commitment, complexity. A new "real" world arises.

Immediately below, we explore three dialogue practices within the continuous improvement We-Space. We look at the dialogue around the scope of decision-making by employees, as well as the boundaries to which they must adhere. Since what formerly was an important aspect of a manager role is increasingly replaced by group decisions, we pay attention to how team members give each other feedback on their role and arrive at modified and renewed role agreements. Finally, we consider how to dialogue about integration of roles might be conducted—a process of great importance within the value stream dialogue space.

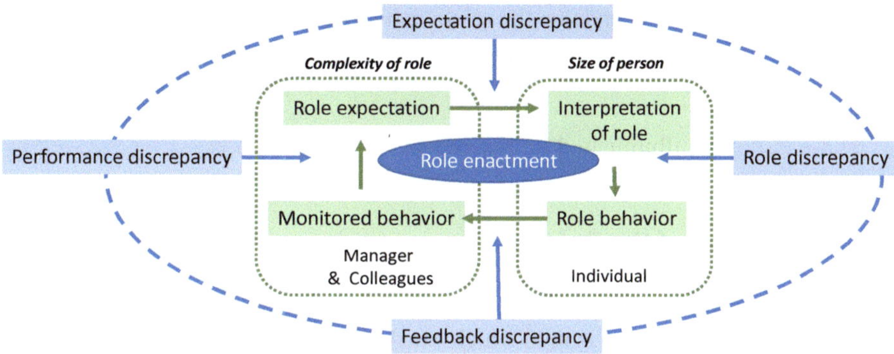


**Fig. 5.1** A model of role-making focusing on the ambiguity of role definitions. (Adapted from Roos and Starke 1981)

### 5.1.1 Role-Taking Versus Role-Making

Roles might be equated with "things that need to happen." Such things often get abstracted from, thereby turning them into objectives, responsibilities, contributions, and activities that exist as list items as if they were independent of a specific person and his or her level of adult development. This abstraction process creates a hindrance to having a clear notion of a role. In addition, the idea that it has isolated individuals who take up a role is a substantial simplification of reality. Rather, the content of agreements results from the structure and environment in which the parties involved find themselves and, to a much lesser extent, from the free decision of individual employees. For this reason, it is more realistic to view effective role fulfillment as a result of social construction, an interpretation process that is related to how employees interact with each other. In this view, employees consciously or unconsciously, as well as continuously, create their own role as an essential ingredient of their performance and work delivery. Individuals undergo mental growth, at least some. This being so, it is the quality of their dialogue that will determine outcomes of bilateral coordination and calibration of agreements (Fig. 5.1).

In a strictly behavioral fashion, the role-making model above centrally focuses on the issue of the definitional ambiguity of a role, pointing to four kinds of discrepancies: discrepancies between (a) expectations, (b) performances, (c) roles, and (d) required feedback. The ambiguities highlighted all derive from employees' and managers'/colleagues' meaning- and sense-making processes, that is, ultimately, from the way they construct their internal workplace at a particular juncture of their lifelong development toward maturity.

The model assumes that how a person daily shapes his or her role results from how he or she interprets others' role expectations, whether or not he or she demonstrates consistent behavior in line with such expectations, and whether his or her behavior is, or is not, in line with the initial expectations raised by the role. By putting in relationship aspects of defined roles (or role definitions) and individual performance, the model predicts that the degree of ambiguity of a role definition (in the mind of participants) depends on the relationship between an employee's *complexity interpretation of role* and *size of person*, thus the issue of whether a contributor's developmental level is commensurate with the role assigned to, or chosen by, him or her.

These issues are illuminated further below.

### 5.1.2 The Size of the Role

"Size of Role," a measure of role complexity, is an informal measure having to do especially with the time horizon in which a task is carried out, and secondarily with the complexity of the task itself, especially in cognitive terms (Jaques 1989). The broader the time horizon associated with a role, the more obstacles to pursuing a task successfully are likely to surface, the more ambiguous are the functions making up the role, and the more interpretive leeway exists for conceiving of the role in the first place.

Relative to the role holder, size of role has to do with the developmental resources required for perspective-taking and fluidity of thinking when acting in the role. The latter abilities correspond to the work level on which the role is situated. Perspective-taking needed in a role is a function of the work complexity a role holder is settled with. Evidently, in the case of ongoing improvement initiatives, the breadth of perspective-taking required in a role is smaller compared to tasks such as rethinking operational flows and collaborative processes, which, in turn, is more modest than where the integration of new products, service, technology, and market developments is at issue. Integration usually requires either project-oriented or program-based work, taking place within several different, often staggered, even interrelated, time horizons.

Size of Role and role ambiguity are correlated: the larger the factual size of a role, the greater is the ambiguity of the role's meaning for the person in the role and his or her associates. The size of role is generally smaller when it results from standards, procedures, and guidelines that determine the interpretation of product and service delivery. It is more significant in complex settings where the size of the roles comprises contributions from employees from various disciplines working together and where continuous collaboration is required. Role ambiguity is usually more relevant for managers or employees with in-depth specialist expertise than for ordinary employees.

### 5.1.3 The Size of the Person

Irrespective of the size of a role, employees, being meaning and sense makers as meaning makers and thinkers inevitably interpret their role (which is really what they are paid for). Their interpretation is a function of their ability to handle complexity, their social-emotional maturity, and psychological profile—in short, a function *of their internal workplace* (as described in Chap. 2). This holds for all professionals.

Roos and Starke (1981) refer to several studies that show that nurses interpret care guidelines due to how secure or insecure they feel in terms of their identity. Laske's work (2008), as well as Need/Press studies (Hawkins 1970), would suggest that they interpret instructions differently depending on whether they are other-dependent or self-authoring in conjunction with their psychological profile. Some nurses firmly adhere to guidelines, while others increase task complexity for themselves by involving a multitude of stakeholders from the patient's environment (e.g., the primary care physician, other healthcare professionals, family, etc.) in the care process.

Teachers interpret prescribed curricula, procedures, and codes of ethics in two ways: behaviorally based on their conviction that they may or may not be able to improve a learning situation or adapt it to the diversity of pupils in the classroom and developmentally based on the maturity of their value system. In temporary project teams, team members redefine critical steps, relevant indicators, and delivery times of project charters in the function of advancing insight around the multitude of overarching objectives that can be achieved simultaneously, that is, in function of their level of cognitive development.

### 5.1.4 Four Discrepant Dynamics

Role is a high-level abstraction that is beyond time. However, how an employee fills in a role evolves. In this real-time evolution, four kinds of interwoven dynamics play a major role in how a role is seen, evaluated, and given feedback.

*Expectation Discrepancy*: This type of discrepancy has to do with the correspondence between the person's own and others' expectations of actions to be taken in the role. The higher the expectation discrepancy, the higher the chance that employees operating from instrumental, self-authoring, and self-aware stages will interpret the role from their developmental boundaries (their optimal capability). Not even employees who function from an other-dependent stage can be expected to have a smaller discrepancy in their expectations since the expectations they define themselves by are not identical to those that actually exist in others.

*Role Discrepancy*: The second type of discrepancy has to do with the difference between employees' interpretation of a role and how they act in the role in practice. This discrepancy depends both on whether or not the role holder has the necessary skills and competences and on the extent to which he or she is aware of their carrying out their role. The fluidity of thinking and the extent to which contributors are in touch with their strengths and developmental potential play an essential role here. Those who are not aware of the limitations of their role interpretations (for instance, by adhering to the perspective acquired through professional training) can strongly influence the quality of a role interpretation.

*Feedback Discrepancy*: The third type of discrepancy has to do with the kind of feedback an employee may or may not receive. Such feedback can focus on a small aspect of the role or can be extensive and include what the employee has overlooked, or employee's work attitude in general. Even in the successful delivery of work in a role, a small adverse reaction of a customer may get magnified and then undermines the overall positive impression of role execution. Or else feedback may be confrontational and thus unhelpful to the role holder.

*Performance Discrepancy*: The fourth type of discrepancy has to do with the correspondence, or lack thereof, between useful feedback given and initially formulated expectations. This gap is related to the fact that there is a time difference between the formulated expectations and the actual moment at which feedback is given. Since roles unfold over time, progressive insight may change often implicit role expectations.

On account of these discrepancies unfolding over time, we cannot reduce the issue of dialoguing about a role to momentary clarifications at the moment that a role is taken on. This means that we not only should focus on the specific, measurable, achievable, relevant, and timed aspects of a role (SMART) but also will have to pay attention to discussing the process of role collaboration.

### 5.1.5 From SMART to FAST

Over the past two decades, trying to understand organizational roles anew has given rise to the notion that working agreements must be specific, measurable, achievable, relevant, and timed—in short SMART. The approach is thought to increase the

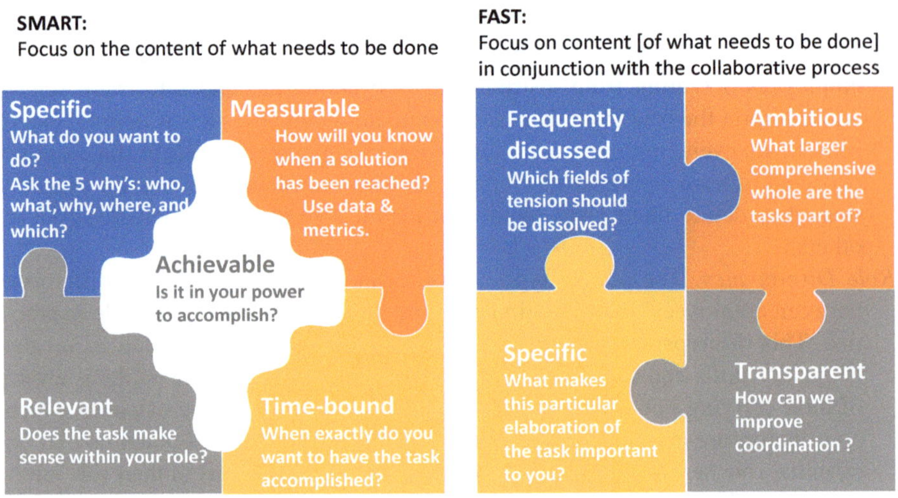


**Fig. 5.2** The essence of SMART and FAST agreements

precision of both role appointments and mutual service level agreements. In contrast to SMART, a different philosophy as to how to define roles, called FAST, has evolved which was first described by Sull and Sull (2018). FAST stands for frequent coordination (F), ambitious formulation of assignments (A), specifying the detail of what is expected (S), and transparent sharing with each other (T). With the latter acronym, attention shifts away from mere content to the need for mutual coordination, although the content of role agreements continues to play a central role.

Above, we depict both approaches to role definition (Fig. 5.2).

Additional clarifications regarding the components of the acronym FAST show that, compared to the elements of SMART, they all focus on psychological issues likely to arise in collaborative processes, so that adult-developmental issues remain beyond consideration.

*The frequency of the dialogue (in FAST)* has the function of adjusting changing priorities, as well as allowing for the discussion of areas of tension that arise during role execution. The focus on tensions is further emphasized by Robertson (2016) who points to the value of addressing tensions in both operational and governance meetings. According to him, team dialogue should primarily focus on defining areas of tension and point to potential solutions.

*Ambitiously formulating* working agreements is meant to stimulate creativity in looking at the bigger picture, how an approach to work in a role evolves, as well as how to focus on the essential relationships it entails. In short, it is thought to lead to stretching the thinking of employees involved.

Being *specific* has two purposes. The first purpose is to translate agreements into concrete milestones and indicators of success or failure. This is in line with the SMART socket. The second purpose concerns clarifying toward each other what the chosen indicators mean for each participant, and in what way they are relevant or not.

*Transparency* refers to the need for all employees involved to share agreements. When agreements are shared in team dialogue, differences in the interpretation of the accords come to the surface quickly and become a topic of discussion. Focusing on transparency, one can avoid that too high expectations, as well as the role, feedback, and performance discrepancies arise, all of which are known to lead to stress, dissatisfaction, and mutual irritation.

The essence of FAST dialogues is that they invite participants to think more fluently. It is not the speed in the substantive dialogue that is central, but the speed with which one creates depth in the subject under discussion. FAST conversations make it possible to take into account employees' meaning-making involved while exploring the breadth of the necessary working arrangements. In this way, using FAST, one avoids that joint working arrangements get reduced to shared documents instead of enabling shared understandings.

The differences between SMART and FAST dialogues are now becoming more apparent. While the former type of team dialogue mainly focused on abstractions such as "objectives," FAST dialogues are taking a step in the direction of defining working arrangements around people and their psychological and motivational limits. Role interpretation begins to be seen in the light of people's developmental

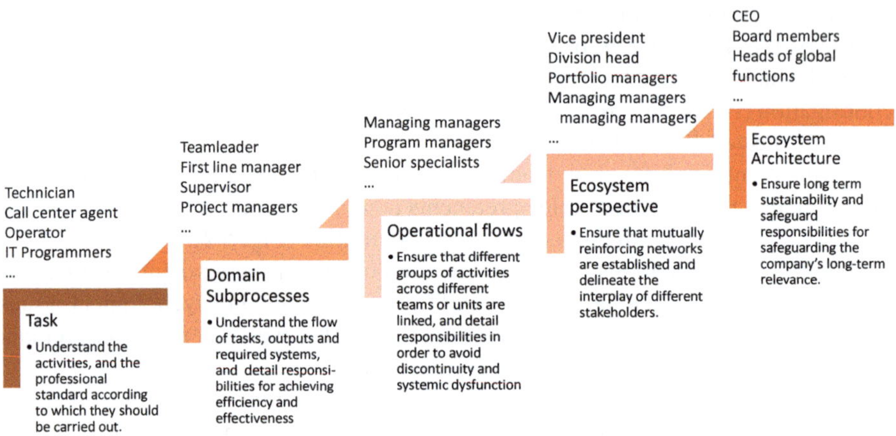


**Fig. 5.3** Different foci in role descriptions

resources which determine what kinds of decision-making and what tasks an individual in a specific role can handle at a specific time.

### 5.1.6 Activities Versus Contribution

The SMART framework is often used to draw up role descriptions, which include responsibilities, tasks associated with a role, related activities to pursue in a role, and role titles. Figure 5.3 presents a summary. Reading the picture from left to right, the complexity of role assignments increases.

#### 5.1.6.1 Size of Role

*Size of role* is a term coined by McMorland (2005) simultaneously with Laske (2005), both of them building on Jaques (1989), who understood roles cognitive-developmentally, not just behaviorially. Jaques was the first researcher to suggest and elaborate that decision-making in a role is an outflow of the individual's present level of cognitive development. His basic tenet was that employees commit to their work through the type of decisions they make. Their contribution to an organization is defined by the quality and timeliness of their decision-making.

In following Jaques, Laske (2005) showed that work delivery is a function on not only the level of cognitive but also social-emotional development of role holders, thereby contributing to the theory of decision-making. Van Clieaf (2016) detailed the differences in contribution at different levels of work complexity in terms of performance indicators.

Importantly, Jacques saw a correlation between the length of the time horizon associated with a task and the complexity of obstacles that arise during task pursuit. In a repetitive activity, such obstacles are kept under control. For example, the decision-making of operational staff (in customer services, on machines, in essential services to customers), repetitively done short term, is well served by simple, common-sense reasoning. These employees are expected to continuously check their work during role execution, as to whether the quality of their work meets prescribed standards and procedures in the short run.

What work at higher levels of complexity requires is dramatically different. It is higher levels not only of the fluidity of thinking and complexity handling but also of holistic thinking: seeing a whole composed of parts. We expect team leaders and supervisors to understand systems, and thus to intervene when quality criteria and procedures are no longer in line with what customers are thought to expect. Such people's decision-making follows causal reasoning; they can put individual events and situations in context. Managers who manage lower-level managers also need to be able to think systemically, thus be able to imagine a hierarchy of interdependent functions. Their decision-making often follows specific models, that is, hypotheses as to what might be optimal outcomes.

In contrast to Jaques' work, developmental thinking about decision-making in a role is mostly absent from organizational theory even today, nor has that theory absorbed the distinction between social-emotional meaning-making and cognitive sense-making. Instead, role behavior and decision-making are still pervasively evaluated from a narrow behavioristic perspective to the detriment of organizational functioning. When discussing employee contributions pragmatically—in contrast to understanding them developmentally—the main focus ought to be on the difference a role holder is expected to make within the larger organizational whole, his or her value added.

#### 5.1.6.2 The Size of the Person

"Size of the person" is a term coined by Laske and McMorland in the same year (2005), by the first on adult-developmental and by the second on behavioral grounds, under the influence of Jaques' work. Laske (2005) shows that the behavioral

| Type of Accountability & Type of performance indicators | Main perspective & mindset |
|---|---|
| Reshaping relative competitive position<br>Growth, profit and return from new business models | Policy<br>Deep transformational thinking |
| Creating breakthrough and reshaping profitability<br>Development of new viable producs/services/markets & customer portfolio management & growth and return on existing/new capital investments | Design<br>Transformational thinking |
| Rethinking operational flows and value streams<br>Current business value for current stakeholders: yearly revenue, expense and/or profit | Integration<br>Systemic thinking |
| Service Differentiation and optimization<br>Efficiency & Effectiveness Measures of Current Processes & Procedures | Alignment<br>Complicated logical analytical thinking |
| Quality & Service delivery<br>Quantity, Quality & Service Excellence Measures | Fulfillment<br>Expert Mindset |

**Fig. 5.4** A behavioral hypothesis of the complexity of role versus main perspectives and mindsets at different levels of work complexity. (Color codes by Kashmir Birk 2016)

attributes of a person are mere symptoms of developmental level. The term indicates the mental size of a person acting in a role, measured in terms of developmental scores (such as level of thought fluidity). On each level of development, the structure of human decision-making is different. As a consequence, there is no general answer as to what decision-making is before investigating individuals in specific roles. However, one can formulate *hypotheses* as to what strengths and weaknesses particular behavioral traits together with developmental levels may entail.

Figure 5.4 summarizes a behavioral hypothesis without disclosing its implied developmental grounding.

The main notion, established by Jaques, is that for work to be *requisite*, "size of role" and "size of person" have to match. Based on the interwovenness of developmental and behavioral factors in decision-making, one might hypothesize, for example, that when a person finds a task insufficiently challenging, his or her size of person might be larger than that of his or her size of role; as a consequence, he or she may become unmotivated. In the opposite case, where a person feels overstretched (size of role transcending size of person), the person might risk burnout. In making matching decisions within traditional human resources, the developmental-behavioral correspondence is pervasively left out of the account. Rather, following outdated competency models, a relationship is seen between a person's experience, skills, and competencies, on the one hand, and the activities forming part of his assignment, on the other. As a result, fundamental developmental/behavioral mismatch is never detected and never corrected.

### 5.1.7 The Storyline Approach to Role Commitment as a Cornerstone of Employee Dialogue

The basic idea behind story mapping is to describe every company role not only by way of the added value it creates in a collaborative context but also in terms of the differences individual employees *should* make in their work delivery relative to broader organizational concerns. Focusing on this aspect of work delivery from the perspective of what roles "should" or "could" deliver opens up a new kind of dialogue with employees about their contribution to organizational work. It allows helping employees to become conscious of the specific relevance of their roles, their individual value-add.

Some critical questions addressed to individuals relative to added value creation and contribution are listed below:

- What difference does your role make to internal and external customers?
- Through which decisions have you made a difference to customers?
- What difference does your role make to increasing innovation?
- What difference does your role make to the management of resources?
- What resource decisions would allow you to make a difference for customers and promote innovation?

- What difference do you make in your role regarding issues of planning and coordination?
- What planning and coordination decisions have allowed you to make the difference to customers and innovation we think you have made?

These questions are derived from the work of Beer (1985). In his *Viable Systems Model*, Beer uses an organismic model to describe the layered character of human work organizations. As he sees it, in the blueprint of each living system, one can distinguish five subsystems.

The first subsystem concerns the function of the system in its environment. In an organization, this might be said to correspond to the difference a company creates for customers. A second characteristic is the set of mechanisms in place for carrying out vital internal operations. The organizational parallel might be the planning, adjustment, and coordination of primary activities. A third system exists for providing the means to adjust required operations to each other. We might liken this third aspect to an organization's responsibility for managing resources. A fourth aspect of natural systems is that they regenerate themselves as open systems. Translated into ethics, one might think of an organization's responsibility for innovation. As the fifth characteristic of a natural system, one might mention the fact that the system ensures the coherence of the four previous ones aspects mentioned. The organizational parallel to this could be seen in the norms, values, and identity of an organization.

**Table 5.1** Example of a story line

| |
|---|
| [Customers] I build lasting relationships with customers. To this end, I seek dialogue with them, collect and evaluate feedback and suggestions, anticipate their needs, and ensure that all (sub) processes are cleverly linked and organized. I anticipate evolving customer expectations and formulate solutions to create value. I am particularly interested in the product-service-combinations we can offer. The fact that we can now enjoy a considerable increase in performance is due to the relationships I establish between shared customer-specific questions/problems, reusable solutions, and the development of long-term customer relationships. |
| [Innovation] I recognize when systems and processes need to change (or need to be redesigned) because they no longer meet customer needs and wishes. I obtain cooperation for this from different angles. I also recognize emerging and new technological innovations that may be relevant to the development of solutions for specific groups of customers with shared challenges and problems. This means, among other things, that market developments are recognized, assessed, and translated into solutions. I conceptualize and implement inclusive approaches by strategy and the search for opportunities to improve our effectiveness. |
| [Resources] I see how the realization of planning, budgeting, and forecasting evolves, and adjust my approach accordingly. I am also looking for how to keep the product and service complexity manageable. I focus my attention on the continuous improvement of our strategy in such a way that we can achieve more with fewer resources. |
| [Planning] In addition to my work towards customers, I also organize and plan my development process. This enables me to keep my knowledge up-to-date and to support colleagues in their development. I also pay attention to the efficient planning of my agenda and that of the teams in which I work. We also regularly look back at how the plan is realized and learn from experience. I keep an eye on the critical agreements in terms of milestones and deliverables and adjust where necessary to meet the agreements made with customers. |

In the real world, in terms of roles, Beer's five accountability dimensions are rarely aligned. For instance, a company may strive to realize accountability toward customers without having sufficient resources to do so.

Each of the five subsystems of the Viable Systems model comprises a set of processual building blocks. For example, the building blocks of a call center operator involve the processing of complaints, the launching of commercial actions, the booking of appointments, the conversion of calls into billable work. In the organizational context, processual building blocks are usually broader than mere activities, being also targets of meaning- and sense-making in employees' work. For this reason, these blocks—which are really processes—lend themselves to addressing the difference employees are asked to make for the sake of value-add. The story mapping methodology provides a way to clarify that difference. (The critical role clarification questions above correspond to the first four systems in the Viable Systems Model.)

Storylines can be built in teams where they become shared. An example of this is seen in Table 5.1. The storyline in question stems from a fast-growing, medium-sized software company shared among employees. It dealt with contributions to continuous improvement tasks and resulted from an in-depth dialogue in a focus group of employees who thought that company employees should evolve from a focus on individual professional excellence in meeting customer expectations to differentiating and optimizing their activities.

The storyline came into being as follows. The focus group selected the most critical subprocesses it thought everyone should engage with, such as recognizing emerging and new technological innovations; understanding the market, customer needs, and wishes; performing a root-cause analysis of problematic customer experiences; anticipating future customer needs; evaluating and prioritizing market opportunities; transferring and consolidating knowledge; and realizing the planning, budgeting, and forecasting required to satisfy customers.

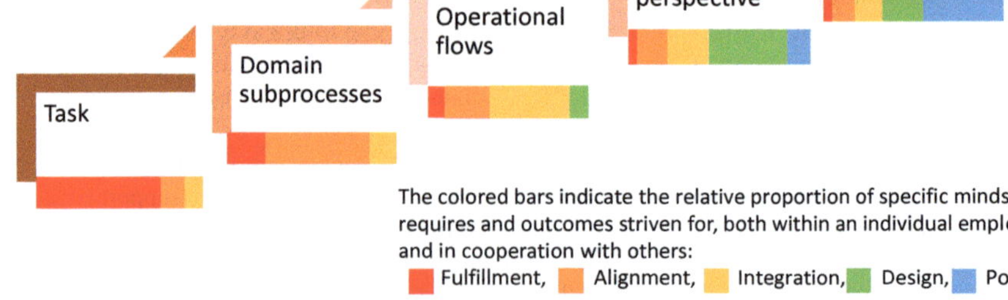


**Fig. 5.5** Developmental differences in different We-Spaces and activity-domains

The storyline below, a set of self-reports, summarizes the essence of a shared role:

The discussion of this storyline in a team has the following benefits for introducing *dialogue* in a group of employees:

- It invites employees to reflect on the perspectives they take in their current work and on how the perspectives on their work color their decision-making and the interpretation of their activities.
- It allows employees to discuss among themselves the effectiveness of their decisions and to challenge each other regarding the breadth of their perspective-taking.
- It encourages employees to formulate their development points (not all employees feel equally strong about every dimension of their work) and to seek mutual support for their development.

Story mapping is a compelling method to link the creation of value-add to employee contribution. Developing different storylines for different roles also makes it possible to map them to each other and thus get an idea of contribution differences in teams, as well as getting a closer look at the upwardly and downwardly divided dynamics of teams.

In our experience with story mapping, the diversity of adult-developmental levels, both in the social-emotional and cognitive domain, is considerable, both across different role domains and We-Spaces. Figure 5.5 summarizes what we found.

Figure 5.5 illustrates a framework for understanding the dynamic dialogue structure defining three different We-Spaces, as well as the impact their differences have on how roles are organizationally conceived, discussed, and put in practice.

At the top, we plot the different We-Spaces discussed earlier (Chap. 2). Below that, one sees the different foci in activities in distinction from those in classic role descriptions. As the reader will notice, the emphasis of work in different We-Spaces and the roles they subsume is dramatically different:

- In the continuous improvement We-Space, employees are mainly active in roles focusing on tasks and subprocesses.
- In the value streams We-Space, employees focus on and are responsible for subprocesses, and operational flows.
- In the We-Space of business model transformation, employees carry out responsibilities for the ecosystem and organizational architecture.

Underneath the We-Spaces and their consecutive foci, the color bars indicate the relative proportions of mindsets and aligned perspectives dominating a particular level of work complexity (We-Space). Although there is no one-on-one relationship between work in a specific domain of responsibility and the mindset and perspectives associated with it (as suggested in Fig. 5.4), we can speak of a certain tendency of "how we think here" to be shaped by what is the major focus of specific roles in a particular domain. By "tendency," we mean a mindset or dominant perspective from which the added value within a field of activities is thought to become realized.

For instance, in terms of Fig. 5.5, taking on role responsibilities for subprocesses is more comfortable from an alignment than from a fulfillment mindset. The creation of new ecosystemic collaborative relationships is most successful on account of a transformational mindset. It is these differences between We-Space mindsets and their associated perspectives that underlie the dynamics of cooperation and explain the need continually coordinating role agreements (see Chap. 4). For example, as seen in Fig. 5.5 in the continuous improvement We-Space, there exists an inherent tension between the fulfillment and the alignment mindset. This tension is essentially a cognitive one, having to do with the fluidity of thinking and capability of complexity handling which is either absent or present in a team. One could speak of a team's "workplace epistemology," or typical way of thinking, as we showed in the previous chapter. (Such a workplace epistemology has long been missing for managers at various levels of work complexity.)

We have seen that when moving from a passive role-taking to constructivist role-making, team dialogue about roles moves into the foreground. This accounts for the greater degree of realism of the latter approach. But "dialogue" is an abstraction. To understand its full impact in real time, below, we present **four different dialogue practices** in detail. As previously, we consider dialogue quality in a team as rooted in team members' sense and meaning-making maturity as it shows up in their internal dialogue, as outlined throughout the book.

One way to go beyond the role-taking approach is to add a role-making component to it, as we do below. We begin with two dialogue practices in the field of continuous improvement, namely, examples of (1) dialogue on the operating framework and (2) a prioritization dialogue. Following this, we discuss (3) a performance conversation that overlaps the continuous improvement and value streams We-Space.

**Table 5.2** An example of "red lights," "roundabout agreements," and "team agreements" in the background of a home nursing company

| Red lights | Roundabout agreements | Team agreements |
|---|---|---|
| Red lights must be followed by everyone | Roundabout agreements are non-negotiable—but there is freedom in how one realizes them. | Teams make consensual agreements (in line with an adopted framework) and everyone respects them. |
| *Examples*<br>Labor regulations: not wearing sharp rings.<br>Protocols: when and how to apply hand hygiene.<br>Framework: Every care worker uses the EVS-protocol | *Examples*<br>An intake for each new patient.<br>The team organizes itself within itself.<br>A team is responsible for the contacts with general practitioners but decides for itself how to follow up contacts. | *Examples*<br>Allocation of patients to rounds.<br>Agreements on the use of medical devices on patients.<br>Establishing agreements on boundaries, involving other care actors in the context of socially responsible care. |

We wrap up (4) by relinquishing the role-taking dialogue within the value stream We-Space, discussing role integration.

## 5.2 Four Dialogue Practices by Which to Explore Work Commitments

### 5.2.1 The Dialogue on the Framework Within Which One Delivers Work

One of the ways to weaken the rigidity of the role-taking model in the area of quality service provision is to introduce framework agreements into role fulfillment. These are dialogues about the freedom that individual role holders have in fulfilling their role. Framework agreements make a distinction between mandated nonnegotiables and points of individual decision-making for the sake of achieving precise minimum specifications requiring team agreements.

Table 5.2 presents an example of framework agreements in a home nursing organization. A threefold distinction is made, that between "red lights" appointments, roundabouts, and team appointments, represented by table columns.

1. *Red lights* are the working methods everyone has to follow, such as hand hygiene, wound care, dementia care, and the administration of medication. These red lights are described in the employment regulations and protocols.
2. *Roundabouts* specify the minimum standards for home nursing work. For example, it is essential to give injections in a hygienic environment. However, this is not always possible, and the nurse must find solutions to avoid contamination. These minimum appointments act as decision points as to what to do in a specific situation. The idea is that there are many nursing tasks for which to put forward one correct approach is impossible since what a person does in practice is determined by the concrete situation. To enable nurses freedom of choice, the organization periodically organizes "theme days" for exchanging experiences, for example, on wound care, and for coming to learn about innovations within specific care provision areas. The roundabouts invite employees to start playing their role in a context-sensitive way, allowing them to think more specifically about their particular contribution to a specific patient relationship.
3. *Team agreements* concern mutual agreements within a local nursing team. For example, a team is free to determine how it organizes individual patient rounds, how it responds to each other, and how it involves other healthcare providers in patient care. These agreements are valid for all nurses of a team regarding tactical choices concerning how to develop care in a specific district or region. The time perspective implied establishes a connection to an evolving larger project regarding which teams decide how best to monitor patients in their specific context.

As we recently observed in a company, the transition from a focus on activities to be carried out to an agreement about making care decisions within a patient-specific context has significantly increased staff satisfaction. It also reduced the perception of work pressure and reduced staff turnover by two-thirds. However, this transition has been experienced as difficult and has, at times, created clashes between different team members' conception of nursing work.

To compensate for this, the company has formed a team of coaches that the groups can call upon if they are overwhelmed by a multitude of opinions or options. These coaches act as mediators; they primarily focus on the quality of communication, explaining the underlying reasons for employee standpoints and broadening participants' perspectives. Participants work with a set of *blue* and *green* cards. When clashes occur, they raise a blue card, which is an invitation to all concerned to distance themselves from the immediate situation to explore common ground. It is also a modest step toward encouraging participants in the consultation to step outside their own present socioemotional frame of reference by which they define themselves in relationship to themselves and others. With a green card, an employee invites a specific colleague to share his or her perspective on a particular issue. This is often a colleague who has remained in the background in the dialogue up to that point.

### 5.2.2 The Dialogue on Priorities for the Sake of Transcending the Short-Term Focus on Quality

Employees focused on daily delivering quality in continuous improvement initiatives do not find it easy to free up time. The everyday pressure exerted by customers often makes thinking about how to evolve one's practice, study new technologies, or pay attention to changing competitors' practices difficult. However, customer expectations change, exchanges in communities of practice become more frequent and increase complexity in role fulfillment. Therefore, employees need to commit themselves to the evolution of their role as a way of learning to deal with increased complexity.

Following a pure role-taking logic, Lean and Kanban methods have introduced the concept of *priority sign*—a way of mapping workflow, monitoring the execution status of subactivities (usually divided into "to do," "doing," and "done"), and structuring discussions about responsibilities. The drawback of this approach is that the needed dialogue about subactivities is not considered requisite.

We followed the issue of prioritization up further. In consultation with workers on the shop floor of one of our client company's workplace, we experimented with a template allowing for a more highly developmentally oriented dialogue on priorities between coworkers.

Team members begin by agreeing on the "big" themes they want to work on, in this case of our client, (a) meeting customer expectations, (b) safety, and (c) innovations in production technology. When a group member had a specific idea, he puts it on the board. Every week team members go over the new and the old post-its. The team leader leads a dialogue about new post-its, asking the team to assess how the ideas expressed on new posts contributes to taking a metaperspective on the work to be done, both in terms of better understanding the work as a whole and of stimulating questions about the potential impact and feasibility of a specific concern posted. In the developing team dialogue, different interpretations of both the bigger picture of the group's work and particular notions expressed in the post-it have a chance of being continuously discussed.

For example, the idea of updating some of the safety regulations may lead to a discussion about different views of preventive maintenance, while an idea of changing the route on which forklift trucks are allowed to operate may lead to a dialogue about increasing safety for employees. The different interpretations of higher-level concepts, such as *safety*, further influence the understanding of an initially formulated and posted idea. Ultimately, new conceptions of employee safety can affect the prioritization of updating safety regulations.

Through such a continuous dialogue about priorities, workers learn to think from a process perspective. This helps them in their thinking about possible next steps, obstacles, and tools for realizing a specific idea. An exchange of views on posted issues unfolds, and the parties involved stimulate each others' thinking. Absolutist thinking, in which only a single way forward is seen, is replaced by critical thinking allowing for multiple solutions.

After a group dialogue, the idea, whether or not it has been reformulated, is put back on the priority board. Employees are then able to put themselves forward as candidates for working out the idea further, rather than relying on the person having posted the idea to provide a solution. The team as whole gains in awareness of the complexity of work involved.

### 5.2.3 The Group-Focused Organization of Performance Feedback Aiming to Achieve Commitments Toward Broader Role Fulfillment

The practice of role feedback in groups was developed in contexts of self-organization and is based on a role-taking, rather than a role-making, approach. The method consists of employees first making a self-evaluation and then inviting three colleagues to challenge it. For self-evaluation, team members use a template emphasizing fields of expertise and areas of competence (listed in a competence matrix). Individual employees are asked to score themselves along a points scale and provide evidence for themselves that justifies the outcome. Colleagues then challenge the score by, among other things, providing counterexamples. At the end of the evaluation, three points regarding behavioral "development" are agreed on with the person evaluated.

We developed a variant of the role feedback procedure in the continuous improvement domain for the sake of increasing its dialogical component. Three adjustments were made, each of them discussed below.

First, to broaden their holistic thinking, we invite employees to a personal reflection on their contribution to two larger themes, customers and internal cooperation. To stimulate employees to think outside of their comfort zone, we emphasize unmet uses of opportunities and possible contributions to larger projects. Concretely, we invite employees to prepare their self-evaluation based on the five questions below, two about past and three about future work assignments. The questions themselves build on aspects we have integrated into a story mapping approach.

- What has been my most significant contribution to customer orders in the prior period, and what indicators can I use to support my claim?
- What has been my most significant contribution to colleagues (and the teams of which I am a member) in the prior period, and with what examples can I substantiate my claim?
- Which opportunities have I not taken advantage of in my client projects and/or internal cooperation, and how am I going to put them into practice in the coming period?
- How can I contribute to better uses of all resources at our disposal, including my own planning and coordination of initiatives?
- What concrete contribution would I like to make in current cross-divisional projects I am part of, and how does this intention strengthen my personal growth?

Second, to invite employees to critical reflection about their own thinking, we add to the choice of three colleagues as devil's advocates, an agency we call a "white raven." It is the task of the raven, impersonated by a critical facilitator, to question the thought process of all those involved in feedback to a specific self-evaluation. The facilitator is familiar with the use of complex thinking in the form of DTF (Dialectical Thought Form) thought forms that expand participants' thinking beyond merely contextual descriptions, by introducing reflections referring to process, relationship, and transformation.

The critical facilitator acts as a censor of statements made by participants working from a cognitive DTF perspective. He does not allow comments that do not unravel the (obvious or less prominent) implications of themes, dynamics, relationships, or fields of tension introduced as a topic. Instead, he or she urges that descriptions using these nouns be refined and differentiated further. For example, if someone says he or she wants to "organize consultations with customers better," the facilitator will explore with the person evaluating himself of herself what this might look like because of the larger issue of customer consultation in the organization. In addition, the facilitator may invite reflection about stratification, for example, within a customer consultation, and urge taking it into account in the preparation of a dialogue with a customer. Also, the critical facilitator might bring forward different interpretations of a specific customer consultation viewed from different contexts (e.g., the financial framework of project development, the contribution of a customer project to the company's innovation programs, and the pilot character of a new form of cooperation). In short, the role of the white raven is to open minds.

The third adjustment to employee self-evaluation has to do with the scope of commitments, thus with social-emotional issues. Employees are asked to formulate, not only agreements with themselves but also agreements regarding collaboration with others. To do so requires choosing at least two of the three colleagues with whom a contributor has been engaged in intensive cooperation. As a result, the feedback conversation, initially only about a single individual, becomes a conversation about an employee's relationship with colleagues. In this case, the critical facilitator needs to be knowledgeable about social-emotional issues that concern how an employee makes meaning of not only external but also an employee's internal "others" that are prominent, indeed predominant at the stage of other-dependence.

We found it anything but easy to get this process on track in the continuous improvement We-Space given the tendency in this space to discourage, if not suppress, employees' own thinking and internal dialogue. Employees initially have difficulty formulating their contribution to a work process with precision since it requires holistic thinking. They also have a hard time discussing boundaries of their role relative to the roles of others, as well as with spelling out how they want to make a difference. Clarifying mutual role expectations requires an awareness of the constant give-and-take between group members, thus an ability to take a metaperspective on being a group member.

### 5.2.4 The Role Integration Dialogue Held in Terms of the Scaled Agile Framework (SAFe)

In line with the Agile Manifesto, various approaches have been developed to improve the flexibility of executing software development projects. For this purpose, the Scaled Agile Framework (SAFe) formulates several principles of role integration; it explains whole processes, defines core roles for agile project execution, and suggests a roadmap for achieving optimal results.

The SAFe framework stems from reflections on the layering of software development projects which—with considerable errors of omission—have been generalized to organizational projects. The framework is based on strictly logical and contextual thinking and thus does not answer questions about processes and relationships between its components. As formulated, SAFe distinguishes four levels: (1) a team, (2) a program (to be developed), (3) a value stream, and (4) a portfolio.

The SAFe framework distinguishes three protagonists, a "product owner" (who is in close touch with a client), a team called "the crew" or *scrum team*, and *the Scrum Master* who is in close liaison with the product owner. Scrum team members are responsible to the product owner for their work progress and communicate with him via the Scrum Master. Their process is conceived in terms of short—2–4 weeks—periods called "sprints" at the end of each of which they deliver results (e.g., pieces of software). Together with the scrum master and product owner, they decide the priorities for the next process iteration.

An iteration starts with a planning discussion at the end of a sprint in which the team decides which user stories (e.g., functional questions asked by customers) or features (specific functionalities desired by customers) they can provide. Every day, the scrum team discusses its progress. At the end of an iteration, team members demonstrate the results obtained to the product owner, to make sure that they have delivered what the client required. They then reflect on where their previous work can be improved, to get ready for the next iteration that starts the work cycle again, starting with a new planning meeting.

The team member directly responsible to the product owner is the "Scrum Master." He or she ensures that the team works within agreed-upon processes and collaborates effectively. In SAFe, several groups work simultaneously on the same software. All teams must have the same sprint start date, end date, and duration. Planning is expected to guarantee synchronicity of the planning in different teams—an important starting point of what is referred to as "developing in cadence."

Although detailed descriptions for all roles in the SAFe framework exist, the interaction between roles and their influence on each other is not captured by them. Rather, existing role descriptions simply outline contributions and highly concrete activities, neglecting processes as well as relationships between task components, as is to be expected when a behavioristic role-taking approach is followed.

SAFe role descriptions, although conceived of as necessary ingredients of a change process, are static entities that assume that colleagues involved share corresponding responsibilities, for example in optimizing working methods, rethinking value streams, and redefining the business portfolio. However, the size of SAFe role fulfillment does not always correspond to the scope of the operational or management roles with which the role holder is thought to consult. This correspondence is essential for achieving transparent communication and preventing downward team dynamics.

Another limitation of SAFe role descriptions is that different levels of a change process may follow different time horizons. For example, the organization's broad choice of investment themes is part of a strategic process in which decisions are made relative to a long time horizon. By contrast, adjusting value streams is part of the operational process of improving efficiency and effectiveness, which have an immediate impact on the bottom line.

In addition, the SAFe framework insufficiently deals with inherent tensions between different levels of work complexity (team, program, value stream, and portfolio). For example, flexibility to change value streams is often limited, making new business models more difficult to formulate. The realization of certain value streams often requires of functional disciplines to greatly exceed their present expertise, while at the same time continuing to create value for customers within their current expertise. Furthermore, tensions may exist between possible business model transformations and boundaries reached in implementing new technologies (such as combining big data and artificial intelligence with blockchain technology and robotics).

SAFe works with a concept of an "Agile Release train," which defines a format of periodic coordination in which all those involved in an Agile project are brought together. Gatherings that result may comprise up to 150 employees who, in changing subgroups, discuss parts of their projects to plan the next steps. In such an Agile

**Table 5.3** A selection of questions for accountability stretch explorations

| Context | Process | Relationship | Transformation |
|---|---|---|---|
| How does this occurrence disturb the equilibrium of your work situation? | Are there undisclosed aspects of your work that hinder us from better understanding your contributions' future development? | How are the components of your work interrelated, and what team tasks need connecting for you to contribute more effectively? | What conflicts, dilemmas, or contradictions make your contribution to teamwork instable? |
| How in detail might you contribute to social tensions within the social system you are part of? | In what regard is our perspective on your contribution and that of others deficient? | What interrelationships between component tasks of your work need safeguarding for the system to function effectively? | How might social tensions in your team enhance its developmental potential, as shown by which indicators? |
| What are the undisclosed assumptions being made that account for the instability of the ideological system within which you deliver work? | What team dynamics implicitly or explicitly determine your contribution to teamwork? | Are work contributions in the team reciprocal or characterized by indirect mutual support? | What arrangement of individual contributions seems to have the highest potential for transforming our present work situation? |

Release train, it is assumed that all projects can be synchronized which in practice is not the case.

After all, individual project members, at all levels, work based on their own, idiosyncratic interpretation of their role. As a result, some projects run into delays, while participants in other subprojects find solutions to speed up development.

The Agile Release train offers an opportunity to discuss interpretations in roles, and the corresponding areas of tension between the different levels. To steer such discussions in the right direction, we developed periodic "accountability stretch dialogues" with role holders at all levels. These are governance meetings in which participants examine tensions arising at different SAFe levels. After all, it is tough to coordinate different workflows consistently and permanently. Technological evolution may create new opportunities for adjusting value streams which may lead to developing new features for applications at the team level. At the business model level, advancing insight may make the continuation of the development of particular features redundant, and so forth.

An accountability stretch meeting involves (1) sharing tensions were experienced by participants, (2) exploring the multidimensionality of such tensions (and perhaps reconceiving of an area of pressure), (3) clarifying how different parties interpret the ongoing process, and (4) taking a critical look at the governance structure that is presently in place.

To carry out this kind of critical facilitation and thereby weave a role-making component into the classical role-taking model, we used Laske's DTF framework

(2008) as a basis of supporting dialogues by which participants can stretch what they conceive of as their own role accountability. The framework generates questions that help participants achieve a more in-depth exchange of ideas about their respective accountabilities. Table 5.3 gives an example of such questions (for an introduction to the DTF framework, see Chap. 2).

The interweaving of these questions in team dialogue removes tensions and leads to making company-specific, continuous adjustments to the SAFe framework.

**Key Insights and Practice Reflections**

The central issue addressed in this chapter has been the influence of developmentally sourced diversity of employees' sense- and meaning-making on making work commitments in each of the We-Spaces we distinguish in this book. We conclude that the deficiency of role-taking approaches lies precisely in the fact that it does not take into account either differences in the cognitive complexity of work arrangements nor employee differences rooted in the present level of adult development. This deficiency bears the hallmark of behaviorist thinking that remains closed to empirical findings in adult development since 1975.

Specifically, we have shown in this chapter that the deficiencies of the role-taking approach to work delivery— which are rooted in purely contextual and logical thinking—not only lead to the misconstruing of the nature of organizational collaboration in general but equally account for the trivialization of the complexity of team collaboration in specific situations. The behavioristic tenor of the approach is also responsible for the shallowness of hypotheses brought forward to explain and promote effective collaboration in teams of the same, and between teams functioning at different, levels of work complexity (We-Spaces).

Over the course of this chapter, it has become clear that strengthening the clarity of role assignments requires a developmentally grounded dialogue about role commitments focused on implementing two mental shifts: *first*, finding a balance between SMART and FAST agreements and *second*, having team members explicate the broader organizational ramifications of delivering work in light of developmentally diverse role interpretations.

Making the first shift in practice entails waking up to the interaction between employees as developmentally grounded interpreters of roles. The second shift consists of taking note of, and learning to use, a dialogue framework through which one can assess and explain the functional relevance of specific activities as parts of the larger whole of an organization's work culture. We began to demonstrate that such a framework enables critical facilitators to stimulate reflective practice and to heighten the quality of team dialogue.

Both shifts are grounded in the distinction, first made in the Introduction, between employees' *external* (physical and social) and *internal* (mental or epistemological) workplace, as well as in the notion deriving therefrom that the internal work is actively constructed by role holders in real time and decides how work is delivered by an individual in the external workplace. Both shifts are anchored in the hypothesis, that the external workplace—in which roles are typically stipulated and defined—is unceasingly and unremittingly subject to role holders' meaning and sense-making that dramatically changes over their life span.

Without considering employees' internal workplace and its lifelong reconfiguration, roles remain mere abstractions, however theoretically conceived and pragmatically organized they may be or how logically they are reasoned about in designing palliatives for easing team tensions. In fact, team tensions have their roots in precisely the developmental diversity of team members which these palliatives not only disregard but have no influence on.

**Practice Reflections**

1. How do different views of the nature of role contribution influence role expectations in your organization?
2. In your organization, how are the different role responsibilities (for customers, innovation, resources, planning, and coordination) distinguished from each other in different We-Spaces and, on account of that, sufficiently aligned with each other?
3. To what extent do framework agreements strengthen employee role "ownership" in your organization?
4. How would you restructure forms of employee dialogue in your organization in order to improve how far they are able to connect their own role with the broader organizational context?
5. How would you reshape performance appraisals such that they strengthen the inner dialogue of employees as a basis of improving their collaboration?

# 6 Coherent Action: Linking Role and Work Contributions to Each Other Through Real-Time Dialogue

*One could say that team discussions are characterized by cognitive asymmetry: a downward momentum tends to push destabilization away until only familiar, clear, and unambiguous views remain, while the upward momentum raises, tests, and supplements ideas. An oscillation toward and away from important focal ideas of a discussion is moreover congruent with how coherent action arises: there is a continuous dance between upward and downward dynamics in teamwork.*

**Abstract**

In this chapter, we look more closely at the dialogical dimension of collaborative action. Specifically, we address the issue of how organizational coherence, even culture, is created through real-time dialogue. For this purpose, we distinguish four configurations of teamwork that give rise to collaborative action in successively more complex forms: coordination, cooperation, co-constructing, and co-modeling.

We point out that, pragmatically, discussions for the sake of achieving collaborative coherence are characterized by asymmetry. By this, we mean that in every team, a downward momentum tends to push destabilization away until only familiar and unambiguous—and thus largely meaninglessly abstract—views of projects and goals remain, while an upward momentum tends to further the development, testing, and supplementation of new ideas. An oscillation toward and away from important focal ideas of a discussion is seen as constituent of how coherent action arises: there is a continuous dance between upward and downward dynamics. Overall, we propose ways to facilitate and enhance those dialogue processes in each of the We-Spaces that create organizational coherence grounded in collaborative action.


J. De Visch, O. Laske, *Practices of Dynamic Collaboration*, Management for Professionals, https://doi.org/10.1007/978-3-030-42549-4_6

In this chapter, we look more closely at the dialogical dimension of collaborative action. Specifically, we address the issue of how organizational coherence is created through real-time dialogue. For this purpose, we distinguish four configurations of teamwork that give rise to collaborative action in successively more complex ways: *coordination*, *cooperation*, *co-constructing*, and *co-modeling*.

We hypothesize that the cognitive (sense-making) process underlying teamwork encompasses two contrasting dynamics which derive from the kind of reflections and questions participants raise in working together. In previous chapters, we referred to these dynamics as "downwardly" and "upwardly" oriented, respectively. In the present chapter, these terms that initially describe the dynamics of a whole team assume a slightly different meaning. Rather than describing two different kinds of dialogue, they describe the interweaving and interpenetration of two distinct tendencies in the same team conversation. We attempt to make the interleaving of these opposing tendencies explicit and show in what way they ultimately produce failed or positive outcomes.

Pragmatically speaking, we view the creation of organizational coherence through dialogue as a result of managing both developmental diversity (of team members) and behavioral contrariness and opposition of individuals in three different dialogue spaces. Each of the dialogue spaces is characterized by a different level of emotional and cognitive complexity (We-Spaces). Overall, we propose ways of facilitating and enhancing dialogue processes that create organizational coherence through collaborative action.

## 6.1 Two Models of Organized Cooperation

How employees collaborate in an organizationally coherent way is an unresolved issue. Approaches to better understanding this process draw their inspiration from two opposing models: one hierarchical and the other defined by self-organization.

The first model builds on two principles: hierarchy and functionality. Mutual coordination and coherent action result from the work of individual managers who guide a range of output-oriented activities within networked functional processes. To produce a car, for example, involves a flow of pieces from a warehouse that is assembled, undergoes quality checks, and then feeds into more elaborate processes with a predesigned logistic. To a large extent, managers determine what the concrete elaboration of substeps should look like; which production model is to be used; which interactions need to be coordinated, and in which way; and how to plan communications using routines and kinds of automation.

In this scenario, organizations are conceived of as systems that predictably perform their assigned functions. The reasoning is that the better the integration of activities is designed, the more consistency is created by employee action and the better the latter can be managed. The logic rests on the assumption that one can describe all required activities in advance and that proper procedures and agreements lead to interlinked initiatives with coherent outcomes.

When coordinating activities in this scenario, one looks at the sequencing of specific activities "objectively," rather than from the perspective of individual participants in the collaboration. How one shapes interactions follows from an analysis of what one wishes to achieve. The activities to be coordinated are seen as existing separately from the people involved, who are relied on to carry out these activities. If everything is well designed, then each subprocess has a clear objective. With the help of measurement and control systems, work processes are controlled and managed. In this "objective" way of looking at production processes, attention is paid to design choices that allow for proper coordination. These choices involve decisions concerning the grouping of activities into separate coherent entities and procedures, as well as information flows designed to allow for coordination within the organizational environment in its entirety.

In the self-directed model, the process described above looks very different. To begin with, mutual consultation is central. Coherent action is the result of a dialogue between the parties involved. It is the employees themselves who need to arrive at a shared understanding of how to collaborate which is in no way predesigned. Their exchange of ideas requires coordination of developmentally different perspectives as well as a series of specific rules deriving from the self-steering approach they choose.

The sociocracy approach consists of working in circles. Everyone should formulate proposals via the decision-making process, most often in the absence of objections (see Chap. 3). Also, there is a "double-linking" rule that specifies that the connection of a subcircle with a higher circle should occur through the participation of two members of the subcircle in consultation within the higher sphere, namely, the one which leads the subcircle and a representative of the employees in the subcircle. In coordination processes following this model, subjectivity is critical for arriving at collaborative action. In this "subjective" way of proceeding, building coherence starts with the perspectives of individual employees on their role, objectives, and technological possibilities. In short, we are dealing with distributed management where participants are conceived of as autonomous (and thus, at least implicitly, capable of autonomous decision-making—a dubious assumption). **Predesigned hierarchy has been replaced by quick, subjective decisions made in real time, and by dialogue structures whose quality varies between individuals and teams.**

One would expect that those researching self-directed approaches to work would focus on the question of what is the nature of the dialogue needed to make the distributed management succeed. But this is not the case. Instead, researchers have focused on environments in which rapid reaction is central, such as emergency services in hospitals, medical trauma teams, fire brigades, and police environments (Schakel et al. 2016), only to find that coordination of activities through prior design is not easy to accomplish. Since employees are apt to deviate on-the-spot from procedures put in place and agreed upon, especially in crises, organization designs drawn up beforehand work only moderately well.

This fact raises the question of the extent to which integration can be programmed. It also implies that the value of predesigned integration is difficult to assess without an inquiry into how a dialogue between first responders (for instance) takes place in real time. The vital research questions become centered on how working agreements are made and ideas about workflow are exchanged in real time. But research into the details of how employee dialogue concretely happens, and how it should be conducted for collaborative action to emerge, is still a terra incognita. In short, employees' meaning- and sense-making processes are the real issue.

## 6.2 Layers of Collaborative Action

As Ricci et al. (2003) suggest, the first need is to investigate the specific structure of dialogues instrumental in leading to concerted action. In Fig. 6.1, we distinguish four different dialogue structures: (1) coordination, (2) cooperation, (3) co-construction, and (4) co-modeling. We also refer to these structures as "dimensions" of the organizational dialogue process at large, with a focus on teams.

The differences between the four dialogue structures are the following:

1. Coordination concerns the routine aspects of collaboration. It aims to ensure that employee interactions are in harmony with the immediate and unreflected social and physical environment. Employee dialogue, therefore, centers on instructions and orders (scripts, rules, or procedures). Guidelines, thought of as in no need of interpretation, regulate how activities are to be carried out. There is little or no reflection. Therefore, the organizational environment is taken for granted. Employees act accordingly. They aim to function as cogs in a machine. Because assigned role or function descriptions are relatively fixed, employees are not expected to question them. In practice, of course, there are always irreconcilable beliefs and perspectives. Instruction failures or omissions lead to excessive workloads, wait times, lack of flexibility, and failure to meet quality requirements, all of these are taken as "cost to do business" and do not elicit much reflection.
2. Cooperation is more complex. It regards how participants in a joint venture carry out activities based on prior agreements. The desire for a certain degree of predictability and stability in joint action is central. Employees have a high degree of freedom and decide among themselves what they want to focus on as a matter of priority and how to align their actions with those of others, including how they might influence colleagues for the sake of working toward a shared perspective. In this dialogue space, objectives are relatively stable, and dialogue focuses on planning the deployment of resources. The cooperative dimension of work gets tested when interdependencies between collaborators shift, for example, because customer expectations change, new technologies cause the work to be reallocated, or power relations between teams evolve (as a result of which, for example, the perspective of another party begins to dominate the interplay of the partners).
3. The co-construction dimension of collaboration is still more complex. It comes into play when a deeper understanding of interdependencies and interactions is

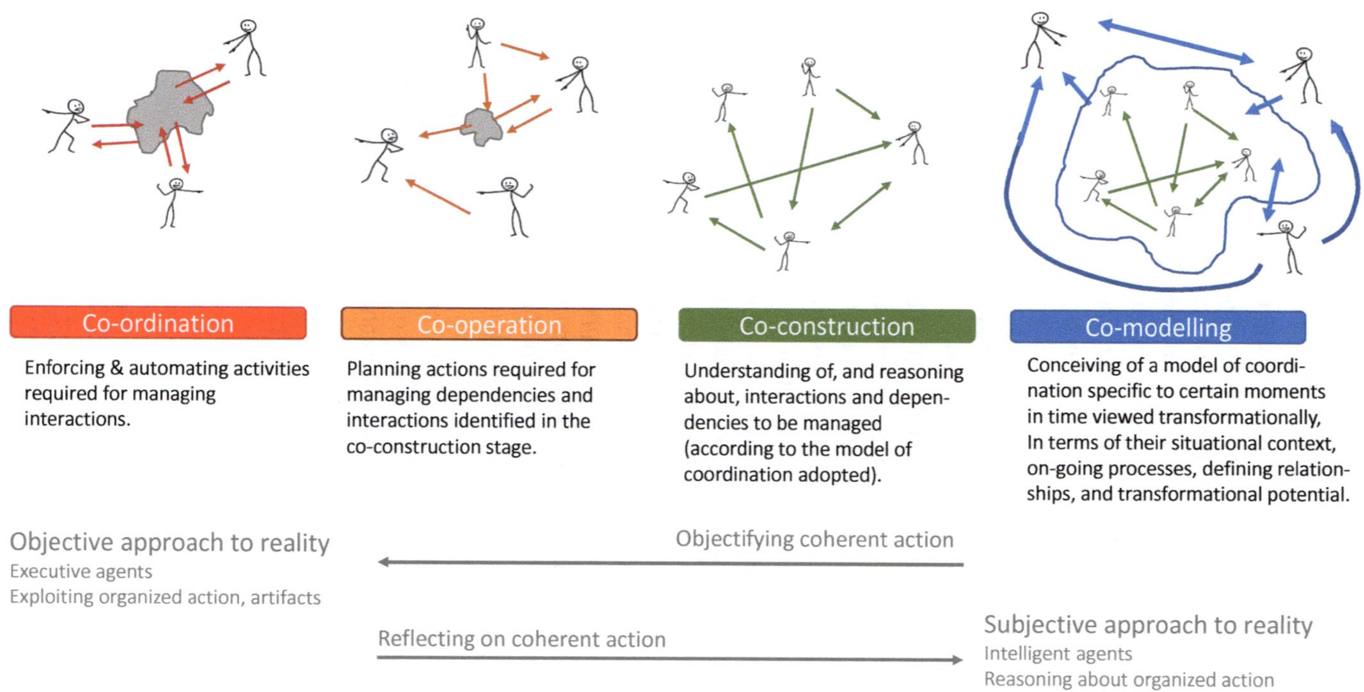


**Fig. 6.1** Four different dialogue structures for generating coherent action

sought, and when their redesign may become topical. Participants in this work configuration see their activities as interdependent and exchange different interpretations of them. They are open to reinterpreting the grouping and sequencing of operations, their flow, and the objectives associated with them. Nothing is considered as fixed, neither scripts and ways using resources nor the grouping of activities and associated schedules. Team dialogue primarily focuses on reinterpreting interdependencies for the sake of achieving stable cooperation. Often, conversations go hand in hand with reformulating the objectives they refer to.

For example, a library that sees itself as an institution that keeps books in an orderly manner will manage other interdependencies than a library that sees itself as an institution that focuses on lending out books. In the first library, the conservation process between employees will be critical, while in the second setup, the approach to visitors and borrowers will be fundamental. In the first library, dealing with library visitors and borrowers is complicated (and perhaps best avoided); in the second, visitors and borrowers are the reason for the library's existence. Co-construction is challenged when the underlying model of collaborative action changes, for example, when one moves from an analog to a digital approach to customers, or when one breaks through other boundaries of former activity groups such as happens with outsourcing.

4. The co-modeling dimension of organized action is the most complex way of working together. It refers to how design choices regarding collaborations to be shared are communicated, thus interpreted. The dialogue focused on co-modeling entails many abstractions, such as the extent to which the organizational design put in practice allows for a flexible response to the environment, supports operating in specific markets and strategy implementation, or prevents forming internal silos. The use of such abstractions presupposes a view of the broader context, ongoing changes, critical relationships, and the potentials for transformation in which these abstractions are embedded. In turn, such abstractions form the framework within which the co-construction takes place.

Coherent action rarely takes place in only one of these four dimensions. While distinct, they should be seen as integral parts of an encompassing whole. However, distinguishing between them helps differentiate ways of achieving coherence

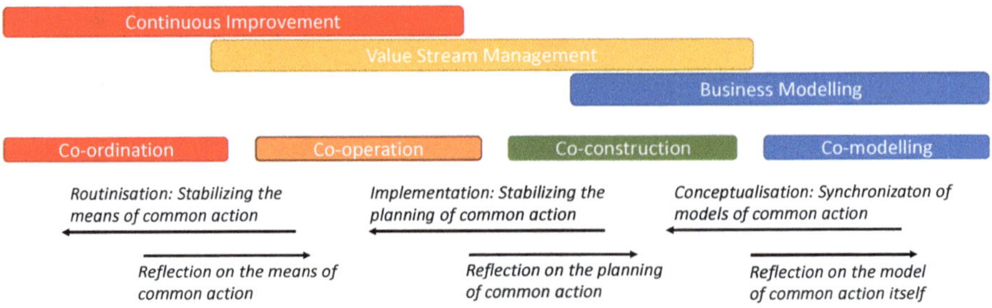


**Fig. 6.2** Four types of dialogue around organized activity characterizing different dialogue spaces

between different dialogue spaces and thus helps arrive at insight into causes of upward and downward team dynamics. What matters is the topic that dialogue parties focus on (whether consciously or not), and how, based on their dialogue, organizational coherence can, when in jeopardy, be adjusted or restored.

Figure 6.2 spells out the dialogue foci characterizing the three We-Spaces (on top), followed (underneath) by the four approaches to the dialogues we distinguish. As seen, each of the three spaces potentially comprises two of the four dimensions, with a potential tension a team may experience between them (e.g., a tension between coordination and cooperation).

In each of the dialogue spaces, we speak of an "upward" movement when there is a reflection on a theme that ensures coherent action, while at the same time, there is an attempt to engage with areas of tension entailed by organized collaboration.

In the continuous improvement We-Space, we anticipate (the need for) reflections on the use of resources and the planning of resource deployment, on the one hand, and on attempts to achieve greater predictability and routine within collaborative action, on the other. Reflections in the value stream dialogue space focus on interdependencies between streams and on improving the quality of planning them. Thoughts in the business model We-Space regard shaping organized action and steering participants toward improving the linkage between interdependent values streams.

## 6.3 Coherence-Creating Moments of Collaboration

How does team dialogue work in practice, and what creates the upward and downward dynamics in dialogue spaces we have spoken of? How is cognitive sense to be made of cooperation in real time? We suggest that answers to these issues involve understanding the questions team members ask themselves that regard the realism of their thinking about what only seemingly is "out there," but really is a matter of how they handle concepts.

It is the concepts people use and the way they use them that lets one know how complex they think. Talking about services is starkly different from speaking about business models. But considering concepts per se is not the issue. What needs attention is where the referents of the concepts in question lie, that is, the interplay between the collective action aimed for and the abstract ideas that guide it. When we talk about achieving coherence in collaborative effort we have a twofold focus: (1) the objective aspect of collaboration, of how to achieve differentiation and integration of activities and (2) the subjective aspect, of how it might be possible to transcend fragmentation (lack of connection) in the way employees make sense of—conceive, understand, infer from, link to—their collaborative work in real time. After all, achieving coherence in how people interact with each other to collaborate is a process of high complexity that has nothing preordained about it.

One can deconstruct dialogues in many different ways. Here, we follow the ideas laid down in Laske's *Dialectical Thought Form Framework* introduced in Chap. 2, a methodology that distinguishes four separate but interrelated dimensions of

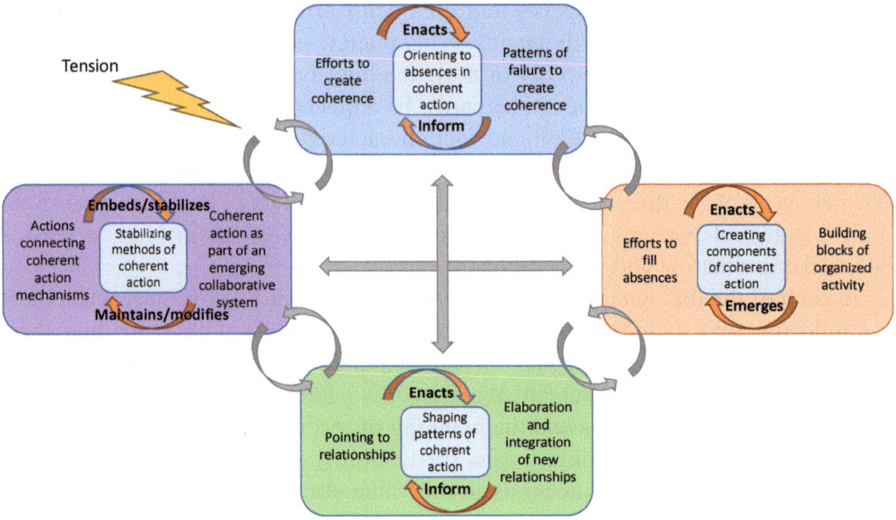


**Fig. 6.3** Moments in the reflective practice of organized collaboration

dialogical thinking: context (C), process (P), relationship (R), and transformation (T). Taken together, these four dimensions offer us at least 12, if not 28, different ways of using and evaluating any concept in light of its referent, the real world, answering the question of whether the world team members aim to understand is a static one (C), is in constant motion (P), is a set of relationships (R), or is in constant transformation from one state to another.

By entering into these four dimensions of complex thinking and their associated "thought forms," we can explore in detail how discussions, for example, about collaboration, unfold in different We-Spaces. Figure 6.3 points to the four aspects of collaborative action team members striving for coherence in their activities may need to dialogue about:

- Causes of difficulty in concerted action, associated with ongoing evolutions in cooperation (in blue)
- Procedures of adjustment (change) in a collaborative effort, related to the estimation of relevant context (in orange)
- Structural relationships between adjustment procedures (subprocesses) used in collaborative action (in green)
- Structural transformations of ways of working collaboratively (in violet)

## 6.4 The Continuous-Improvement We-Space: Routinization and Reflection on Planning

In the continuous improvement We-Space, attention goes to improving people's daily work and to achieve predictability and stability. Attention to instructions, procedures, cooperation agreements, and routines prevails. Even when the topic is agility, the dialogue remains purely logistic, resolving around the means for achieving agility.

Often, dialogue about coordination is not conducted explicitly, especially not if it involves manager. The latter's task is to decide who does what, and this conception translates into standardized instructions, procedures, and coordination meetings for planning to achieve greater efficiency. As a consequence, coordination is often an outcome of implicit knowledge as happens in routinized workplaces.

Accordingly, ideas about coordination often take the form of shared assumptions playing out in the background, and a small group of work designers often determines such assumptions. These designers assume that standardized, sequentially switched activities lead to predictable results. The production of the Ford T is an excellent example of this. Its manufacture follows a standardized path of purposefully linked activities. People who carry out predefined, clearly limited, activities themselves become objects, or else links within a system as envisioned by Taylorism.

Figure 6.4, which adapts Fig. 6.3 for the continuous improvement We-Space, can be considered as a template for discussions on collaboration in the continuous improvement We-Space.

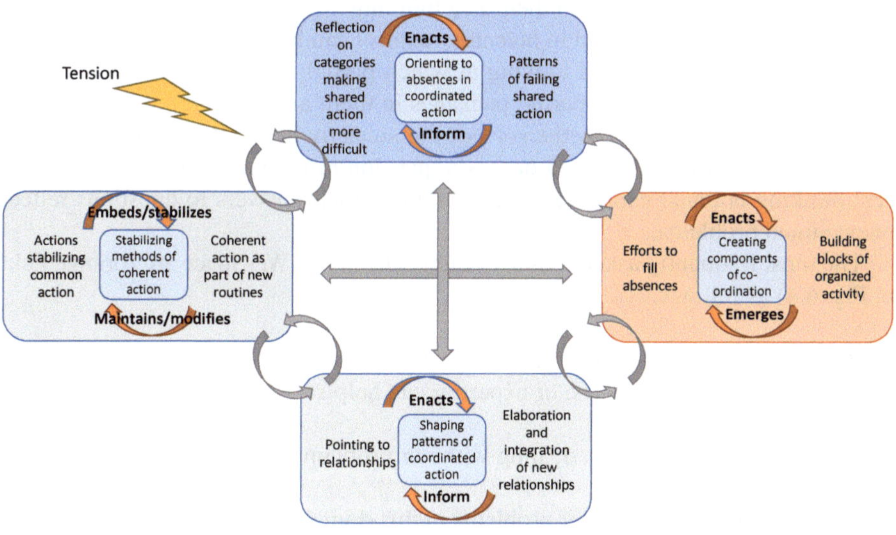


**Fig. 6.4** Moments of the reflective practice of organized collaboration in the continuous improvement We-Space

### 6.4.1 Orienting to What Does Not Work in Coordinating

Participants in this We-Space indirectly question collaboration and coordination after experiencing difficulties in carrying out activities according to prescriptions. They discuss persistent problems such as workload, waiting lists, quality problems, and lack of flexibility.

The most frequent (process) questions raised in this We-Space are (blue field in Fig. 6.4) as follows:

- How can we make sure we can guarantee quality?
- Have we seen this problem before?
- How did the problem come about, and how can we prevent it?

The questions provoke a reflection on where difficulties in joint action originate.

### 6.4.2 Getting a Grip on the Dynamics of Coordination and Cooperation

The sense employees make of problems in their work together is in line with their predominant instrumental thinking and other-dependent meaning-making as partners in team dialogue. Predominantly, team members approach problems in a strictly logical-analytical manner, meaning that they do not think holistically or systemically and have no inkling of emerging change and intrinsic relationships constitutive of their work. Rather, they treat their own activities as objects outside of themselves as if separated from their own thinking.

For example, the workload in inventory control can be examined by subdividing the stock records further and looking at which partial activities have increased in volume, then distinguishing partial packages in them and allocating some of them to a different employee. Whether or not the subactivities still need to be carried out—given that time has moved on—is a question rarely raised. Because employees' thinking is linear cause-and-effect thinking, their answers to questions reflect unexamined problems.

The most frequently asked (context) questions in this We-Space are (orange field in Fig. 6.4) as follows:

- What is the situation, and what are "the facts" and their variables?
- Which tools, competencies, or expertise can help solve this issue?
- What do experts say?
- What needs adjustment in dealing with our problems?

Strikingly, the discussion of problems in this domain straightforwardly revolves around finding solutions, while the problem itself is never conceptually reflected upon. One is trying to solve problems at the same level at which they arise, which right away creates narrow boundaries within which to search for ways of improving coordination. Logical sense-making itself creates fields of tension regarding how one might improve planning, by opening up a dialogue on details of what a problem involves, or how to plan cooperative work comprehensively. It is employees' logical thinking itself that turns obstacles into unquestionable, static entities stifling the planning dialogue. The use of the gray color in Fig. 6.4 reflects the absence of these ways of relationship and transformational thinking in the continuous improvement We-Space.

This situation gives rise to the question: how could the planning dialogue be opened up to more complex ways of thinking? Such reasoning would delve into what is otherwise taken for granted. It would enable employees to explore (a) how experiences in the workplace relate to the greater whole (= context perspective). In addition, employees could (b) analyze experiences from several different timelines (= process perspective) and (c) scrutinize essential relationships initially overlooked (relationship perspective), as is in more detail shown below:

- Exploring context (objectives, customer expectations, technology developments, etc.)
  - How do the standards and procedures help us achieve our goals (and where not), and which aspects of our actions are not covered by rules and procedures?
  - How do the standards and procedures help us respond to the customer (and where not), and where do our rules and procedures misconstrue client expectations?
- Exploring process:
  - How can we investigate our experiences from a temporal perspective, of a few days, few weeks, and months, and envision the evolution of work with customers from different time perspectives?
- Exploring relationships:
  - What remains invisible to us apart from intended workload, striven-for quality, and reoccurring flexibility problems?

Within this dialogue space, answers to mind-opening questions tend to remain, for the most part, purely analytical, and thus disregard the larger organizational whole, intrinsic relationships, and transformations that are not yet manifest. Were these answers more complicated (as a result of more complex questions asked), they could enable conversations on how to conceive of deployment of resources in the first place. This would help avoid narrowing of agendas, which occurs when essential concepts worked with daily are "cast in stone" and thus never questioned.

### 6.4.3 Exploring Structural Relationships

One always risks losing insight when conducting conversations in a reductionist manner, especially if they disregard structural relationships. Employees pay attention to detail, accuracy, and realization of instructions and consider required skills and competencies. But that may not suffice. When encountering difficulties, parties typically look for apparent answers; they may find them in using technology more efficiently, reformulating instructions, or improving competencies for putting guidelines into practice more fully. But they are often clueless when more careful planning, efficient use of resources, or different ways of deploying them require of them transcending local solutions?

Essential dialogue questions in this We-Space are (at the bottom of Fig. 6.4) are as follows:

- What instructions need to be updated?
- How can we ensure stakeholders follow instructions?
- How can we redistribute the work to shift responsibilities?
- What are the pros and cons of newly proposed ideas?

When formulating questions such as the above, there is little room for exploring essential relationships more profoundly. The way questions are formulated forecloses making fundamental changes, except perhaps for the last question above. By viewing employee and team activities as "given" (leaving them unexamined) and seeing them as parts of a mechanically conceived whole, one bypasses asking questions about how employees respond to assigned work, and whether or not the work assigned is healthy. Already in 1979, Karasek found that work can have pathological effects on participants when job demands are out of balance with individual job control. According to his research, high task requirements ought to be associated with high control possibilities, thus flexibility.

### 6.4.4 The Dialogue on Anchoring (Newly) Coordinated Action

Wherever a role-taking, rather than a role-making, model defines a We-Space, participants are expected to follow the working methods officially embraced, whether they are old or new. This holds true, especially for the continuous improvement workspace. In this We-Space, all kinds of measurement and monitoring systems have been set up to guarantee predictability. Often, the predictability mindset is further indoctrinated by the unquestioned notion that automation of activities enhances predictability. In short, a metadialogue about invigorating efforts to strengthen planning and efficiency of work is absent. Pure reliance on new technology as a means of solving problems is counterproductive since new technology requires new thinking.

In this context, it makes sense to open up the dialogue by reflecting on the limitations of new procedures just because such a discussion is not typically conceived of as fruitful in purely analytical frameworks. Procedures are simply not "seen" as interdependent in this dialogue space. As a rule, employees at this level of work complexity are not thinking beyond static entities and thus remain unaware of the emerging change and reciprocal relationships. Without a concept of the total flow of activities of which they are a part, they are damned to end up with suboptimal solutions. To counter this lack of thinking makes it important to introduce a systemic perspective when using purely analytical tools, such as perspectives on input-throughput-output relationships that constitute the broader context of the activities employees carry out.

### 6.4.5 Upward and Downward Dynamics in Continuous Improvement

In practice, the four grounding moments of dialogue—context, process, relationship, and transformation—are closely intertwined in the real world, but not always in people's thinking about the world. As a consequence, a downward dynamic often arises in teams' dialogue about coordination. These dynamics hinder new planning since planning remains deficient if relationships between procedures are disregarded. Only if this can be changed through thought leadership in teams can employees increase available resources or make better use of them. The continuous improvement domain as a whole is crying out for more complex ways of thinking to be used by employees, something that would ultimately serve their own personal development, not just what is Tayloristically referred to as their motivation.

## 6.5 The Value Stream We-Space: Roadmaps and Reflections on Interdependencies

In the value stream We-Space, dialogue about organizing the interplay between employees is more explicit. Participants reflect on dependencies between activities and deliberate on how to achieve a coherent give-and-take between them. One of the essential experiences in this We-Space is that environmental factors put the smooth internal interplay between roles at risk and that, therefore, the coherence of what roles output relative to the environment is never a foregone conclusion. Of course, the risk of lack of coherence of activities takes different forms in building cars and establishing a digital platform. As a result, end-to-processes in various work environments take on a commensurately different shape.

Organizational domains and associated task environments result from processes of legitimation through which a consensus emerges on how to align activity clusters making up a consistent whole, both in themselves and relative to the organizational environment at large. Importance, therefore, attaches to developing a shared mission, vision, and strategical objectives, to arrive at a shared understanding of the work system established. Only when these pieces are in place can one expect organized cooperation to emerge within the system.

In the value stream We-Space, dialogue on cooperation focuses on actions taken to safeguard interdependencies between activity clusters. Guaranteeing coherence becomes central. To achieve it, employees from different disciplines and departments are brought together, people who need to do a specific job jointly based on shared objectives. The conviction in doing so is that only in close collaboration with each other can work be done with systemic efficiency.

The principle of agreeing on common objectives is realized in dramatically different ways, even in the same industry sector, such as financial services. Different ways of conceiving of such services lead to different designs of the required end-to-end services. For example, employees of a financial institution focusing on private customers and aiming at high satisfaction in its services organize themselves differently from employees of a financial institution that focuses on small- and medium-sized enterprises to support entrepreneurship. Cooperation within the first institution takes place via microsegmentation; to limit the occurrence of disruptions from various subtarget groups, professional advisors are made maximally autonomous within their domain. In the second institution, cooperation takes place via processes through which different specialized disciplines (e.g., investments, financing, tax optimization) are combined in ways suiting a particular client.

In this dialogue space, tensions between cooperation and coconstruction are a central concern. Cooperation is based on agreeing on action plans dealing with interdependencies between both work processes and work output, while coconstruction requires understanding the nature of existing interdependencies and is thus a more complex thought process.

The underlying conviction in the field of cooperation is that the transparency of mutual agreements is required for achieving coherent planning and cooperation. Two different scripts are followed: one focusing on customer service level agreements (SLAs) and the other on internal operation level agreements (OLAs).

SLAs are agreements between service providers and customers. These agreements define not only the nature or scope of service but also the set of indicators that

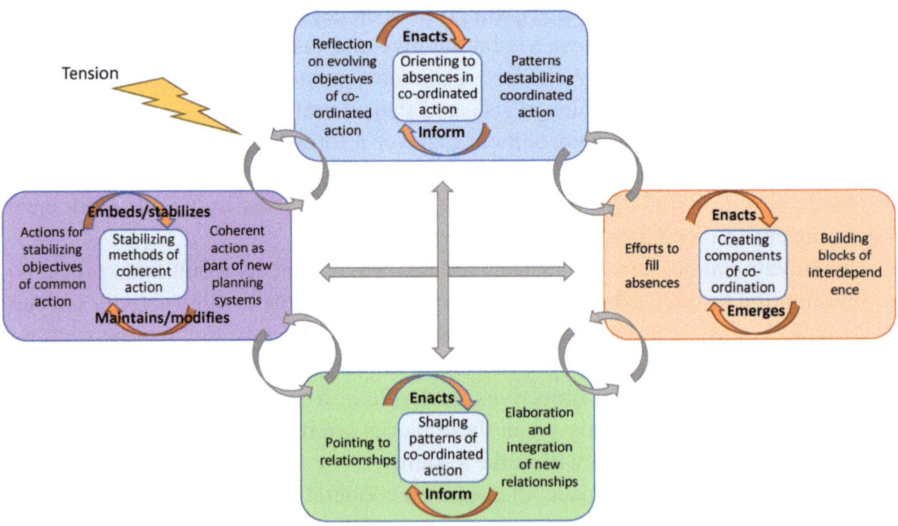


**Fig. 6.5** Moments in the reflective practice of organized collaboration in the value stream We-Space

a service must meet. These are often indicators of delivery time, quality, availability of service, and acceptable error rates. The breadth of their own view of the service process determines what they do and do not include in these agreements. If service providers only start from quality indicators, they will enter into a much narrower agreement than service providers that take into account the subprocesses on the customer side. In the latter case, the service provider also takes into account how a customer will proceed with the service provided. By contrast, OLAs define essential relationships between, for example, different functional departments such as IT and other departments, that influence the execution of a service level agreement.

The difference between an SLA and an OLA is that an SLA contains commitments to customers, for example, what an IT organization promises at a service level, while an OLA relates to the interplay between internal departments to realize the SLAs, for example, what different functional IT teams agree upon together. Very often, an OLA reflects the existing functioning of an organization, and it is not easy to question OLAs. The current control and audit processes are considered to be facts in such agreements, independent of the thinking of the stakeholders involved.

In the co-construction process, the parties involved develop a metaperspective on the interdependencies between the different stakeholders involved, and the awareness grows that the model of the interdependencies is related to the view that the parties involved a likely to take.

Figure 6.5, which depicts fields of tension in the value stream We-Space, guides our discussion of the nature of the dialogue around organized cooperation in the present space. The different colors of the fields refer to the four moments of dialogue, respectively, process (blue), context (orange), relationships (green), and transformation (violet).

### 6.5.1 The Orientation Around What Does Not Work in Cooperation

The dialogue around what is not working in this We-Space is most often triggered by failing to achieve objectives or to meet appropriate indicator levels. The conversation on cooperation then focuses on removing disruptions for the sake of attaining goals by minimizing the uncertainty created by environmental factors. Generally, this dialogue explores how deviations from planning evolve, and whether and how to adjust planning agreements. Often, temporary groups rather than individual task packages or departmental layouts are used to organize work. Following the principle of not excluding people from whom one is dependent, participants in consultation on these topics typically are interdependent stakeholders who give operational shape to the work system.

### 6.5.2 Questions About How to Get a Grip on Evolving Cooperation

To evolve cooperation, participants fall back on principles and models by which they give meaning to interdependencies between activity clusters within the external environment in which these interdependencies play out. The most critical dialogue questions are (blue field in Fig. 6.5) as follows:

- How to revise present intentions or ambition levels (actual or planned)?
- What cause-effect relationships account for the problems posed by the work system?
- What does revising the present work system entail?
- What are the options for revising the present work system?
- How are revisions going to be implemented?

The above questions invite participants to look at the situation in a sophisticated logical way. Participants assess issues from a cause-effect perspective of the work system's components. Unintentionally, they abstract from the greater whole within which problems occur. Often, dialogue participants work with existing problem analysis frameworks that can be straightforwardly applied. Many of them use root-cause analysis templates (Six-Sigma, Fishbone, Pareto). What these templates do not deliver is a process of thinking-through relationships between parts and the whole within the problem space, as well as detailing what creates stability in the work system.

To complexify the dialogue for discussing the issues named above, we suggest to ask the following additional questions:

- Which larger entities (we are presently ignoring) lead to deviating from our objectives?
- How can we get a better grasp of relationships between parts and the whole of the work system?
- Are the deviations that have occurred typically in the context in which we defined SLAs, or do they refer to other factors not sufficiently taken into account by us?
- What kind of a system is established through the SLAs and OLAs we defined, and what do our definitions overlook?
- Are the problems the work system poses for us layered, and if so, how?

Dialogue on these issues if often sabotaged by following automated templates and dashboards that lack any holistic perspective whatsoever. Their fatal error is that they make their users believe that one can control a work system based exclusively on working with its parts, without a grasp of the system as a whole and its underpinning intrinsic part–whole relationships. For instance, expecting to achieve predictability in reciprocal service provisions simply by monitoring indicators derived from objectives is illusory since dashboards do not provide sufficient context to do so successfully.

### 6.5.3 Deepening Structural Relationships and Interdependencies

However, one does encounter automated systems that do invite users to consider interrelationships central to cooperation. An example of this is MuleSoft, a digital platform technology that enables its users to oversee and manage customer journeys in their entirety, from a customer's request to the conclusion of contracts, order processing, invoicing, and aftercare—activities that usually take place in different departments. Using Mulesoft help users think about customer contact points in their totality, even if associated information flows through different channels. Doing so helps establish monitoring mechanisms facilitating optimal customer service, especially since they uncover faults in the flow of information or low data quality that point to the necessity of examining work system interdependencies.

Specifically, MuloSoft invites users' thinking about mutual interactions within a value chain. Through such thinking, the boundaries between the responsibilities of departments can be redrawn. For instance, invoicing can shift from Accounting to Customer Care for the sake of achieving faster customer service. Also, MuloSoft facilitates following up specifically related indicators in such a way that work is distributed among those who have a direct impact on relevant indicators.

In this dialogue space, attention focuses on deepening one's thinking about relationships. The following questions arise:

- What is the nature of connections between the template components (e.g., different functional disciplines involved)?
- What information flows do the components share, and what critical delays or failures are found in the information flows? (An answer to this question provides information about the adequacy of the boundary between components of a work system)
- What are the effects of nonlinear relationships between system components (e.g., batch order processing, manufacturing, packaging, and shipping)?
- How can existing interrelationships of importance be conceptualized differently?

These questions are grounded in complex logical thinking in which one looks at organized wholes in terms of the interrelationships of their parts, such as stocks, flows of information, responsibilities, and resources. Attention focuses on the speed, reliability, and flexibility of collaboration at points of variation of key variables such as unexpected increases or decreases of work, additional investments, or changes in the regulatory environment. Based on such thinking, initiatives can be taken that improve planning and create more stability in a cooperative work system.

The limitations of such an exploration of connections from a strictly logistic-analytical perspective are that those analyzing connections remain fixated upon their perception of present reality and thus are insufficiently aware of possible new practices. This situation often results from using MuleSoft which structurally hinders from rethinking existing value streams. One falls victim to the perfection of a static model rather than engaging in constructive dialogue about alternative ways of proceeding, reenforcing the status quo.

The alternative to blindly following models is a co-constructive dialogue. Such a discussion aims for a better understanding of interdependencies that participants in the conversation have direct experience of. How productive such an exchange can be hinges on the extent to which participants exhibit fluid and holistic, as well as objective, thinking. After all, such a dialogue strives to be a critical reflection in which taking formulated criticism personally is beside the point. Dialogue questions that support thinking more objectively and integrally are, for example,

- What is the mutual influence of different teams or departments on each other? What patterns can we distinguish in their cooperation?
- What impact do these patterns have on each other? Where do they reinforce or weaken each other?
- Are there dimensions not encompassed by the relationships in question that have a powerful impact on such patterns?

In co-constructive dialogue, thinking about cooperation from a transformational perspective, for example, as to the fragility of connections between subsystems, is typically missing. Such a view is, however, required for implementing interdependencies that have been reconceptualized. When applying MuleSoft to rethinking a customer care department, for example, the issues encountered have to do with imbalances that arise when redefining interdependencies that affect the department's work in practice. In such a situation, being able to think in terms of thought forms that focus on the transformation of customer care practices is priceless.

### 6.5.4 The Dialogue About Anchoring Co-construction

In conversations about how to anchor cooperations culturally, the notion of a "roadmap" is central to work in the value stream We-Space. A roadmap is a strategic plan in which one specifies objectives of the desired change, details the different steps to be taken, and defines requires milestones and deliverables. For this purpose, a flexible planning method is needed that enables creating a set of initiatives conceived from different time perspectives. What most roadmaps share is a vision around the objective and a hypothesis about how to realize it. Such a roadmap is prescriptive, not merely descriptive. However, it is often forgotten that a business roadmap derives from a set of hypotheses, levels of ambition, and the mental models used by those who defined them.

Also, a tool that worked well when describing a situation (with MuleSoft) does not necessarily work for those engaged in shaping new realities because those realities are nonlinear. Creating new realities cannot be approached in a deterministic fashion such as a roadmap implies, which neglects to consider that relations between subsystems of a work system are constantly changing. For example, if you develop a multichannel strategy for approaching customers, then the way consumers' relationships with technology changes over time will have to be captured by the digital dimension of the strategy.

These reasons speak for developing not one single roadmap, but sharply different roadmaps, each of which starts from a different perspective on the tensions to be managed during a business transformation. Not all roadmaps are created alike. There are roadmaps that safeguard the potential of including digital components, roadmaps that link fields of pressure to desired business model shifts, and roadmaps that highlight collaborative relationships strongly dissimilar to each other.

Dialogue questions that produce insights into sustainable transformations start from evaluative comparisons of different roadmaps, as exemplified by the questions below:

- Which of the roadmaps has a more significant potential to achieve the desired transformations, and which integration procedure characterizes it?
- Which aspects of the roadmaps we are considering help us evolve our identity, while at the same time allowing us to preserve aspects of our previous identity?

Answering these questions presupposes business model choices. These are choices around how a company or business unit intends to create value, for example, by combining complementary activities or assets, setting up alternative structures and governance mechanisms, or locking in customers or stakeholders. Business models are abstractions for use by stakeholders who need to make choices around interdependencies constitutive of value creation. Business model options are best created through a dialogue about how to co-construct critical drivers of value creation.

### 6.5.5 Upward and Downward Dynamics in the Value Stream Space

As in every dialogue space, systemic thinking in the value stream We-Space benefits from following the four moments of complex dialogue (Context, Process, Relationship, and Transformation, CPRT) we have demonstrated throughout the book as interwoven dimensions of complex thought. If team members cannot harness such thinking—in this case, if there is no in-depth discussion on how to reconceptualize value stream interdependencies—the team's dynamics may turn out to be downwardly directed, and the team's agenda may be sabotaged.

One potential outcome of this is that existing interdependencies, rather than being questioned, are simply replicated. As a result, too many employees are invited to projects and workgroups. This is a clear indication that those who desire change lack a notion or image of what is crucial for the transition to a new value stream configuration to succeed. The coherence of action then gets pinned to the lowest common denominator in the existing operational process, instead of reconfiguring the work system more proactively.

As a counterpart to the above, we can imagine a way of engaging with change by which a team becomes able to balance thinking-through interdependencies and roadmap-based planning such that it achieves coherent action, and thereby realizes an upwardly directly kind of collaboration. The latter way of working together leads to a better co-construction of evolving value streams, as well as the interplay between parties required for realizing it. Such a team is characterized by a vibrant dialogue on value creation (work system reconfiguration) and exerts a positive impact on attempts to reconfigure an organization's value streams.

## 6.6 The Business Model We-Space: Money-Making and Reflection on the Coherence of Developmental Direction

The term "business model" became popular during the dot-com revolution. Compared to more traditional companies, at that time, online companies competed with very different revenue and cost structures. By now, the term business model has come to refer to the choices a company makes around its income and costs in general. The model is, as it were, a formula for creating profit. Within a given industry, different business models may be used at the same time, even within a single company.

Business models are a cornerstone of executives' strategic thinking since major decisions can be anchored in it. They comprise a storyline around how a company or business unit creates value and can keep doing so in the future.

In the literature, the term "business model" has many different meanings. Researchers study business models without giving them an explicit definition. For some, it is a conceptual model or configuration tool (Osterwalder and Pigneur 2010); for others, it is an architecture or structural template (Amit and Zott 2001), and still, others see it as a set of patterns of doing business (Brousseau and Pénard 2007).

Different approaches to the notion of a "business model" have in common the assumption that it is the translation of a company's strategy into a proprietary logic, sometimes called a blueprint, based on which to make money. The design of such a model includes choices about the type of customers to be served, channels through which to approach customers, the variety of products and services to provide, and the technologies needed to ensure value creation.

Essentially, business models synthesize choices around boundaries, delineating critical subcomponents of a work system as well as the interrelationships of subsystems as a function of market changes. When defining model boundaries, designers determine where a business model has an open or closed edge. Business model "edges" cover groups of people who may or may not be part of the internal organization of a work system. (For example, civil society organizations are part of the business model of some organizations but not others.) By thinking-through closed borders, for instance, designers attempt to make an organization resistant to disturbances or undesirable influences from the ecological and market environment.

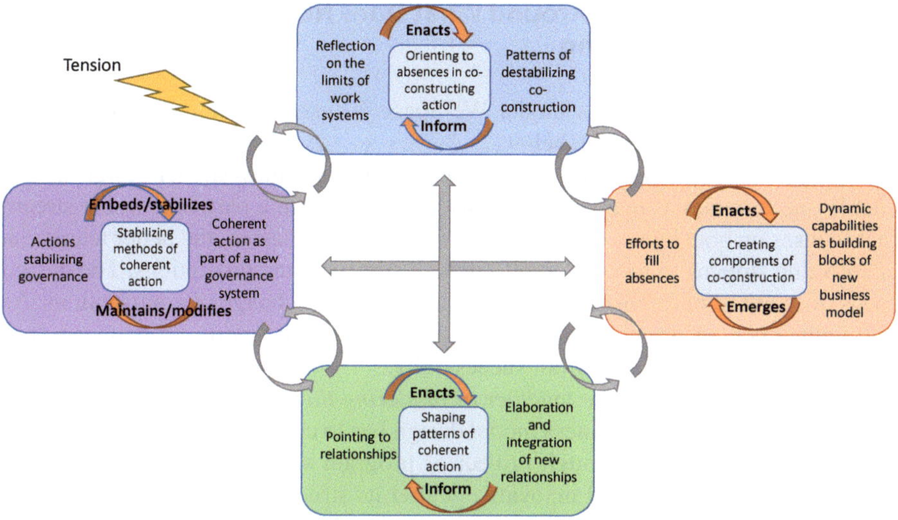


**Fig. 6.6** Moments in the reflective practice of organized collaboration in the business model We-Space

The most critical challenge for companies is business model innovation. In business model innovation, the focus is mainly on how a company's value proposition evolves and how the collaborative setups of a company need to change, including changes in decision-making, setting objectives, motivating employees, information flow, and consultation structures.

The main area of tension in the dialogue on business models revolves around co-construction versus co-modeling. The difference between these needs explaining. In co-construction, the conversation focuses on making design choices supporting coherent action. Design choices have to do with requirements of achieving customer segmentation, value propositions, deployment of resources, revenue, and cost streams.

In co-modeling, the focus is on reflection and learning together, for the sake of creating coherence in a developmental direction. Researchers such as Felin and Powel (2016) speak of *dynamic capabilities*. Dynamic capabilities have to do with how one develops, expands, enriches, and combines "average" capabilities thought to permit a company to identify and exploit opportunities, synchronize business processes, and influence a company's organizational environment. They are most often understood behaviorally, for example, in terms of "leadership skills" enabling a company to redraw value capturing mechanisms. By contrast, in this book, we advocate viewing *dynamic capabilities as processes of complex thinking toward the goal of creating work system coherence in a developmental direction.*

Figure 6.6 forms the backbone of our discussion of the dialogical thought processes focused on achieving organized cooperation within the business model We-Space.

### 6.6.1 The Orientation Around What Does Not Work in Co-constructing

The dialogue in the business model We-Space focuses on three different design choices discussed in sequence below.

Firstly, *bringing together or splitting activities*. A business model design should enable one to retain as many activities as possible within a particular value stream that focuses on how inputs beget outputs. The better the design, the better teams can adapt value streams to respond to all kinds of surprises and disruptions. The design focus does not refer to positions but transactions: the exchange of contributions. As the fault lines in keeping activities together become more pronounced, co-construction is harder to carry out successfully.

Secondly, *bringing people together or hindering them from developing relationships with each other*. A business model design has to comprise the actors needed to do a specific job, either through project or program work. It must break through silos of the work system and innovatively alter its structure. A design is successful if it helps reduce or omit unnecessary organizational complexity, such as collaborations. An efficient work system should comprise enough variety in competencies and affiliations, as well as task and contribution differentiations, to carry out the work required. Sociotechnically speaking, it should focus on internal control capacity, so that there is sufficient space for making decisions in a reasonably autonomous way, not only about working methods but also the division of tasks, adjustments, and goal clarification. Co-construction and its associated internal control capacity come under pressure when decision-makers who do not play an executive role inside the value stream begin to influence decision-making, whether they be hierarchical managers, design teams, or planners.

Thirdly, *establishing the meaning of a work system*. A work system derives its relevance from its external environment: the appreciation of services or products by all kinds of stakeholders outside of it. These comprise not only customers but also regulatory governments, civil society organizations, and competing organizations. The basic idea underlying the work system is that group members of value streams are responsible for managing the system's relationships and boundaries with its environment, also referred to as "external control capacity." When the participants of the work system become isolated from its outside stakeholders, co-construction becomes difficult. Due to their isolation, they are unable to take into account the bigger picture, ongoing changes in the environment, and essential interdependencies.

The three design choices just discussed, namely, those about (1) bringing together or splitting activities, (2) connecting people or hindering them from establishing relationships with each other, and (3) establishing the meaning of the work system for stakeholders, determine what the boundaries of a work system are and, at the same time, also the limits of a work system. These limits concern the meaning given to specific work processes, namely, the issue of what kind of business an organization is "in."

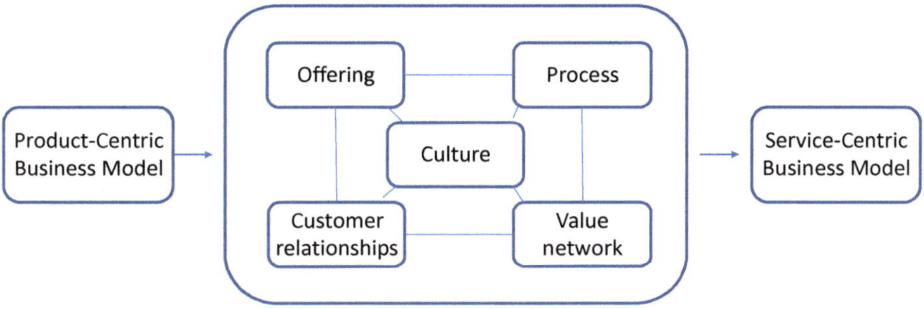


**Fig. 6.7** Shift to service-driven business model innovation. (Inspired by Kowalkowski and Kindström 2014)

For example, if a school considers its core process as the transfer to learners of subject-specific specializations, it makes sense that teachers organize themselves into departments for accumulating subject-specific knowledge, developing teaching packages, and so on. If a school chooses process-driven learning, then before they know it, teachers, educators, and even students will focus together on one particular issue. In other words, boundaries of collaboration are not fully defined by formal organizational structures—they are also a function of underlying convictions. The underlying beliefs also create boundaries for change. Initially, those involved who work more in silos will find it much more difficult to implement new curricula imposed by governments, which require intense collaboration between teachers.

Thinking about the limits of a work processes needs to start from mind-opening questions such as the following:

- What is the maximal level of conflict the work system can bear, whether on account of task content or task process?
- What intellectual frameworks need to evolve to view our work processes realistically?
- How do conceptual frameworks of stakeholders change based on which stakeholders they connect?
- What conceptual frameworks do stakeholders use to assess, maintain, or alter work process efficiency?

To answer questions like these succinctly, it is often required to create a new metalanguage that facilitates understanding new ways of doing business. Examples for significant metalanguage shifts in the market are the shifts from a "product-centric" to a "customer-centric" work system, from an "analog" to a "digital platform" environment, or from "value chains" to "value networks."

### 6.6.2 Co-modeling as an Integration Process

Usually, the dialogue on business modeling starts from a relatively static conceptual framework. Figure 6.7 visualizes a framework that is used to start a conversation around the creation of a service-driven business model.

Each of the building blocks in Fig. 6.7 contains a more detailed list of subprocesses. For example, the section “value network” invites users to reflect on the whole of the networks in which a company is embedded, thus facilitating new thinking about the structures that connect actors and create new value constellations. The “customer relationships” section encourages users to reflect on their proximity to customers, and how they can use the various points of contact with customers differently. “Culture” refers to the mindset needed to bring about change and the role that managers can play in promoting it.

In a business model dialogue, both *culture* and *structure* are usually seen as notions crucial to achieving coherent action. “Culture” refers to both the ability to deal with issues intellectually and the ability to handle emotions. The ability to deal with problems relates to how one handles content, the design, and implementation of a change process, as well as putting in place co-construction. These are constructive contributions aimed at achieving substantive tasks. The ability to handle emotions, however, refers to how to experience feelings without being lived by them. It is about creating a holding space in which emotions can be understood, filtered, and handled. In the business model environment, “structure” is often synonymous with governance, the whole of organizational design choices, committees, and charters. These define how one role should function in an interplay with others.

The disadvantage of adopting abstract frameworks for conducting a dialogue about business models is that abstractions and associated checklists used are easily mistaken for components of the real world. The hypothetical nature of abstractions is easily forgotten. Specifically, abstract images tend to ignore relationships between parts (here, the five building blocks involved) as well as the larger wholes involved (in Fig. 6.7, the current product-based model, and the desired service-centric model). Therefore it makes sense to ask the following additional questions when working with Fig. 6.7:

- How do the individual building blocks depicted relate to the broader context, and to what extent are they context-dependent (unreal when isolated)?
- Do the building blocks chosen assure the new organization’s stability?
- How stratified are the building blocks, and what is the influence of their stratification in a specific context?
- What different perspectives can one take on the coherence resulting from using such building blocks?
- What is a relatively small investment trigger able to set in motion a broader process of business transformation, and what nonlinear feedback is likely to occur?

It is vital for the success of a business model that its transformation integrates a variety of different perspectives. By questioning, introducing contrasting ideas taken from the outside of the business, and by creating doubts about current organizational habits and procedures, one can broaden participants' views to avoid coming up with an "integrated model" prematurely.

The main challenge partners in a dialogue about a new business model encounter is to create coherence in a developmental direction. To reach this goal, they need to explore matters from as many possible frames of reference as possible, explore a mix of options, and develop multiperspective views of the business in question. Such exploration also offers the opportunity to legitimize new perspectives on actions to be taken that derive from implicit knowledge inside of an organization. If a lot of the people involved in the dialogue have been trying to find their way around in an unruly environment to achieve transformations, it can be taken for granted that they have found constructive ways to proceed that do not correspond at all with ideas and professional views adapted from the outside of the organization—ways that are intuitive and informal and do not carry an official label.

### 6.6.3 Integrating Structural Relationships

When constructing new business models, one needs to build insight into how to coordinate streams of organizational action with their purposes outside of the organization. A reflective effort is needed to make the ways of thinking used to do so explicit, including the structurally vital relationships that tie activities together. Special efforts are required to capture nonlinear and multidimensional aspects of collaborative work, as well as essential correlations between unlike processes. Rather than using abstract nouns attached to barely breathing verbs, narratives provide ways to preserve experiential richness; they ensure that relationships are not lifted out of context and that emotion can be harnessed as generators of insight. Narratives also safeguard aspects of the ambiguity of a process or situation; they encourage multiple interpretations of complex subject matter that otherwise could not be conceived of.

In the present context, particular attention must be paid to describing:

- patterns of interaction between different but related parties
- structural aspects of relationships, for example, between workgroups
- intrinsic and invisible relationships that underlie observable connections

### 6.6.4 The Dialogue Around Anchoring New Co-modeling

Each newly formulated business model has a displacement effect in that it silences other models. It excludes perspectives that did not get a hearing when it was formulated. Wherever its formulations sound "rational," it makes it easy not to investigate certain matters further. For this reason, it is essential when postulating new models to examine how much of the previous status quo has crept into them under different labels, how much they silence the articulation of different perspectives, underline positional power, and control or exclude certain groups of people—in-house or in the domain of customers—whose presence remains essential.

The primary fault of business models is that they neglect to consider that human insight into the real world is tremendously limited. This most clearly shows in the fact that most models are anchored in a vision of the real world as stationary rather than in motion. Reduction of process complexity leads to a neglect of fields of tension between different perspectives, overlapping processes, and structures, to minimizing attention to emerging trends, and lack of attention to fragile, always shifting equilibria. Notable absences in business model innovation regard attention to the potential inherent in conflicts and ambivalences that might propel a company's evolution in a positive direction. Such evolution could consist of higher levels of integration and/or inclusion, of effectiveness and efficiency. Types of value creation that are commensurate with a business's social, ecological, and societal dimensions get short shrift. Designs that are built on nothing but human-made data are not models of how the real world works.

Business models gain in critical realism when participants pay attention to the creation of coherence between systems, by asking questions such as:

- How do different subsystems of the business models (existing and new) influence each other, what challenges do they create in their interaction, and how can the interdependencies be attuned to each other?
- What are the relevant criteria of coordination of business models components, and which functional relationships between them are central?

Business model innovation does not start from scratch. Participants need to identify those elements that remain constant from one model to another. Often, what needs to be held constant is the identity of existing partnerships. This fact leads to questions such as:

- Where is the new business model untrue to what employees identify with?
- How does the new business model help employees take steps in self-development without making them lose their acquired identity?
- Have we considered that employees and managers are on a developmental journey that sets limits to what they are capable of doing or even envisioning?
- Have we introduced supports for self-development that makes employees and managers want to engage with our journey into the future?
- Have we safeguarded uniquely human capabilities or sacrificed them to reduction by mindless digitization?
- How will the new business model influence employees and managers in answering the question: "what are we hiring the organization for to strengthen our self-development?"

### 6.6.5 The Upward and Downward Dynamics in the Business Modeling Space

The complexity of dialogue required to put in place new business models becomes more transparent and thus manageable from listening to a team dialogue in terms of the four dimensions of complex thinking previously referred to as CPRT—*context*, *process*, *relationship*, and *transformational system*. These dimensions are always inseparable from each other (rather than little buckets), which is the crux in determining the degree of fluidity a team's thinking can attain. Whether such fluidity exists or not determines the dynamics of the team's cognitive development as well as efficiency; it makes the quality of a team's collaborative energies predictable.

A downward, low-fluidity, dynamics in business model discussions is endemic wherever best practice examples—which by definition represent the status quo—are chosen as frameworks for defining the future. A best-practice focus leads to co-construction, that is, the intervention in interdependencies seen as success dimensions, but not to co-modeling. In co-construction, one focuses on the realization of systemic connections as if they were given, and thus overlooks specificity of context, emerging changes, and structural relationships. As a result, a single model, rather than a portfolio of models that can be explored in some depth, is focused on. As a result, a mindset of experimentation has only feeble chances to emerge. No shared evolutionary lines along which the business can evolve are envisioned. Instead, the emphasis is put on the governance system as a control mechanism for monitoring coherence in the chosen developmental direction, whose realism may be in doubt.

Business model discussions that focus on a single model, even if not pinned on best practices, are usually too narrow-minded to yield authentic transformations. Required for an upwardly directed, high-fluidity dialogue on future business is not a single model but rather a portfolio of possible models that each create a set of levers that facilitate change. The dialogue focused on co-modeling engages with many abstractions and even ventures into the development of a new language. Those abstractions take broader contexts, ongoing but open-ended changes, critical relationships, and transformative potentials into account.

For instance, in developing a governance model, the dialogue should be focused around the common directionality, transformational agenda, and possible transition paths aligned with the company's natural transformation process. Essential for formulating promising business model transformations is the explicit use of sensitive intervention points (SIPs). When defining SIPs, one looks for tipping points allowing a complex system to evolve based on changing the underlying system dynamics and the rules of the system itself.

An example of such a way of proceeding is stipulating the goal to evolve toward a climate-neutral business model. To realize such a model, participants need to redesign relationships with producers of raw materials and machines and build collaborative relationships with research institutes and authorities. They also need to rethink their cooperation with logistics partners and distribution channels completely. When this can be done, one needs to have a governance dialogue in which the definitive business model is not fixed but is considered as being in progress within a range of alternative models. After all, the new business model needs to be complicit with how the real world works, not with past illusions of linear progress.

**Key Insights and Practice Reflections**

In this chapter, we outlined organizational activities that gain coherence through handling the dialectics between four different modes of collaboration in teams: coordination, cooperation, co-construction, and co-modeling. We showed that in each of three We-Spaces we distinguish, discussions of organizational coherence need to address tensions between two of these four modes of dialogue (one more demanding than the other) simultaneously and that this dialectics can be handled by a team in a "downwardly" or "upwardly" directed manner.

In more general terms, rather than classifying teams per se as either "downwardly" or "upwardly" directed—which retains its usefulness—one could say that team discussions are characterized by *cognitive asymmetry*: in every team, a downward momentum tends to push destabilization away until only familiar and unambiguous views remain (largely abstractions), while the upward momentum is one based on developing, testing, and supplementing new ideas. An oscillation toward and away from important focal ideas of a discussion is congruent with how coherent action arises: there is a continuous dance between upward and downward dynamics. Where upward dynamics prevail, participants are not just confused, but use this confusion to handle complexity more efficiently, being confused at a higher level.

Throughout this chapter, it became clear that enlarging and refreshing a team's mental space by continuing to play with ideas is essential in all three We-Spaces. Keeping discussions open is facilitated by using mind-opening questions originating in teachable "thought forms" that, with practice, revamp contributors' mode of communication on account of closer listening to others and oneself. Such a way of working is, however, (initially) hard to realize without a critical facilitator who keeps a team on its toes regarding the quality of its dialogue. A dialogue has high quality if it consists of a continuous process of doubting, searching, clarifying, questioning, and envisioning those team members, especially in the continuous improvement domain, have never encountered and would say they "have no time" for.

Indirectly, we demonstrated the stark limitations of a purely logical-analytical approach to real-world matters that are based on nothing but linear causal thinking, without any second thought about emerging change, intrinsic relationships, and unceasing transformation. There is always a call to simplify gained insights, not to "reinvent the wheel every time," even though the real world constantly moves on. This accounts for how insights gained are translated into bite-sized education and training programs that nourish holistic thinking. Due to a pervasive lack of thought fluidity, organizational cultures move into downward dynamics and almost automatically back themselves into instability.

**Practice Reflections**

1. What different areas of tension in the dialogue about structuring collaborative relationships do you recognize in your company?
2. Choose a specific collaboration project in your company. Which of the different subdialogues (coordination, cooperation, co-constructing, and co-modeling) do you recognize, and to what extent do you find an upward or downward dynamics in the making of agreements?
3. What possibilities do you see to enrich the planning dialogue within the continuous improvement We-Space in your company?
4. How can you deepen the reflection on interdependencies within the value stream We-Space?
5. How can you tilt the dialogue in the business model space to achieve integration and coordination of relevant context, ongoing changes, and critical relationships?
6. How broad is your notion of business model transformation: have you taken the adult-developmental potential of contributors including the CEO into account?

# The Development Dialogue: How to Strengthen Employees' Capability to Take on Real-World Complexity

# 7

*A development dialogue entails becoming aware of the quality of one's internal dialogue (depth of reflection) and results of its interweaving with the emotional and cognitive processes of others. A crucial piece of the awareness-raising process is what we refer to as "double listening."*


**Abstract**

In this chapter, we develop and demonstrate the notion of "double listening" as a foundation of team collaboration and effective communication in general. We base this notion on empirical studies in adult cognitive development as being geared to transcending formal logic, which has its root in cognitive assessments using Laske's DTF (Dialectical Thought Form) framework. We formulate hypotheses about how contributors can develop double listening in and among themselves: (1) by becoming aware of their own thinking in real time and (2) by experiencing thinking together with others. In addition, we unfold the novel notion of "critical facilitation" as a form of cognitive coaching, showing that and how it amplifies and strengthens executive coaching in its conventional form.


In this chapter, we develop and demonstrate the notion of "double listening" as a foundation of team collaboration and effective communication in general. We base this notion on empirical studies in cognitive development *beyond formal logic*. Work with executives using Dialectical Thought Form (DTF) since 2000 showed in detail how organizational contributors reason about three dimensions of their internal workplace referred to as the *Three Houses*: their tasks and roles, their environment, and their own professional agenda (Task House, Organizational House, and Self-House; Laske 2008). On the basis of empirical findings from these cognitive




J. De Visch, O. Laske, *Practices of Dynamic Collaboration*, Management for Professionals, https://doi.org/10.1007/978-3-030-42549-4_7

assessments, we formulate a hypothesis about how double listening can be developed by contributors: (1) by becoming aware of one's own thinking in real time and (2) experiencing thinking together with others (see Fig. 7.2).

On this methodological basis, in addition we develop in this chapter the novel notion of *cognitive coaching* as a discipline of critical facilitation of individuals and teams that amplifies behavioral executive coaching. Starting with a concrete example, we show how a cognitive coach acting as a "critical facilitator" can assist managers like Robert in the task of "de-constructing" (reflecting upon) their own thinking, thereby paying attention to the individual thought forms one is using in real time. As our studies have shown, such deconstruction yields with large benefits for revolutionizing an entire team's thinking. We attend to the motivational side of cognitive transformation by pointing to three specific attitudes that have been shown empirically to boost double listening. In brief, we are proposing a way to strengthen organizational transitions from hierarchical functioning to self-organizing work systems by emphasizing their cognitive-developmental preconditions.

Making sense of the world is like breathing; it stops only with death. However, the majority of employees and managers are entirely unaware of this fact. Based on our experience as critical facilitators helping employees unbury their internal dialogue, we propose practical ways for employees to recover an awareness of the unceasing sense-making they are engaged in, for the betterment of their work together and the organizations they hired for boosting their self-development. Specifically, we discuss what it takes for contributors to grow in their capability of taking on real-world complexities that, in purely logic-analytical thinking, get lost or do not even surface.

Overall, we propose that enhancing the *critical realism* of employees' thinking entails two consecutive steps: (1) becoming aware of one's own thinking as occurring unceasingly and (2) beginning to experience oneself as a "thinker" by closely listening to, and thereby thinking in concert with, others. We demonstrate that these

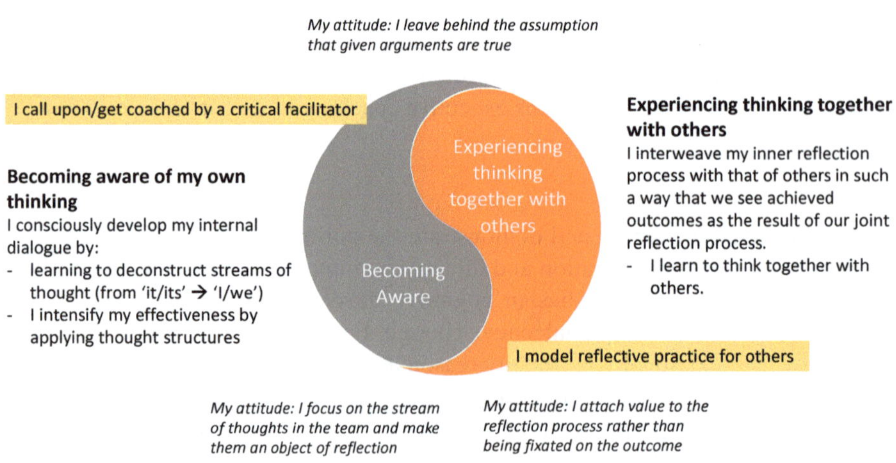


**Fig. 7.2** Experiences leading to developing one's internal dialogue

two steps toward cognitive fluidity are tied together by what we name *double listening* and examine how to school such listening in all three We-Spaces we distinguish.

The most urgent reason for learning to "re-think" how one conceives of the identity of one's role at work, and how one makes agreements and acts in that role, is presently the potential obliteration of one's career by technology. Since all ways of purely logical-analytical thinking are potentially replaceable by software, evidently to keep one's job entails invigorating one's capability to handle real-world complexity, particularly in the domain of dialogue with others (team dialogue) where existent apps completely "fall down."

## 7.1 The Case of Robert B.: Steps Toward the Development of Internal Dialogue

For the first time in his career, Robert B. had to confront project failure. A year ago, after completing an MBA program at the age of 35, he was asked to lead a sizeable lean implementation program. As a high potential, he was well regarded throughout the organization. The focus of the program entrusted to him was the improvement of the value chain linking sales and production. He had put all his energy into understanding the baseline situation, involved all the key players in making a thorough analysis, developed alternative scenarios, and built up a good business case for operational change required. He used the full best practice toolbox that he had learned in his MBA program.

Robert's initial enthusiasm declined over time due to not achieving acceptable results in several subprojects, budget overruns, and decreasing stakeholder involvement. His credibility as a successful manager came under pressure. Doubts arose in senior management. How was it possible that someone with such a strong portfolio of competencies could fail so badly? Based on the remaining trust, the management team offered Robert an executive coaching program.

The first step in executive coaching was a developmental assessment. Classical assessments focus mainly on behavioral strengths and personality. A developmental evaluation examines a contributor's present level of social-emotional meaning-making and the ability to engage with thought forms underlying complex thinking. A developmental review examines how a person conceptualizes and views coherence, formulates hypotheses, and builds theories, such as about what drives a lean approach, and how this approach can or cannot support overarching strategy (e.g., toward cost reduction), which is the most suitable roadmap for driving projects forward and so on. Such an assessment does not focus on thought content but instead on the thought forms based on which a contributor articulates insights and perspectives. The central question is *epistemological*: how a person understands his or her environment and himself or herself in cognitively complex ways, and how on account of his or her understanding, he or she orients himself or herself in the social world.

By way of recording and evaluating a semistructured 1-h interview, Robert's coach demonstrated to him, based on empirical data, how he went about making decisions, formulated objectives, dealt with ambiguity, planned and organized, and conceived of and built internal and external relationships. The coach also pointed to differences in how Robert approaches tasks and roles (Task House), conceives of his work environment (Organizational House), and formulates his own professional agenda (Self-House).

Having evaluated the outcome of the developmental interview in terms of thought forms used by Robert in these three different domains of his internal workplace, the coach did not share results with his coachee right away but began by helping Robert to become aware of "how Robert presently thinks." The coach did so because the coach concluded from his experience with other coachees that immediate detailed feedback was not the most useful starting point for initiating a transformational process in clients of the coach, whatever their instrumental level of adult development at the time of the interview.

Concrete thinkers (who are overfocused on thought contents, their own and those received from the outside) have a hard time reflecting on their real world as well as inner experiences, in large part because they fuse them and thereby cannot discern that what they call "the real world" is actually constructed by them in real time. Consequently, they are too attached to their own truths (about the real world and themselves) to gain new insights, except for controlling the little world around them. Once the coach had outlined the essence of cognitive coaching for Robert, he was able to create some initial awareness around how Robert approached the real world, namely as something "out there" as if it had not been his own construction all along.

The coach made it clear to Robert that he, Robert, was actually coconstructing that world out there "in here," by way of his own internal dialogue of which he had found by means of the interview that its quality was not exactly outstanding when it came to transcending purely contextual thinking even in Robert's Self-House where transformational thinking tends to be most fluid. She showed her client, how he consistently neglected using process and relationship thought forms especially in his approach to tasks (Task House), but also in the way he viewed the organizational environment (Organizational House), and therefore ended up where he did, despite all of his documented competences. (The reason is simple: "competences" are something one "has," whereas capabilities point to what one "is," and while one can decide not to use competencies one has, one can never decide not to use who one is.)

To summarize her observations, the coach drew the following picture (Fig. 7.1).

The message of the coach was simple: Roberts' success as a change manager depended not merely on what he was thinking but even more on the inner place from which he operated both as a meaning-maker and a sense-maker (thinker). The purely contextual outlook Robert was acting from led him to think in strictly logical-analytical terms, with the result that he primarily focused on detailed functional descriptions of variables he trusted to represent his "real world." The coach conveyed to Robert that mental growth would take place only if he could step back from his "tower" and open some new windows that would permit him to see aspects of

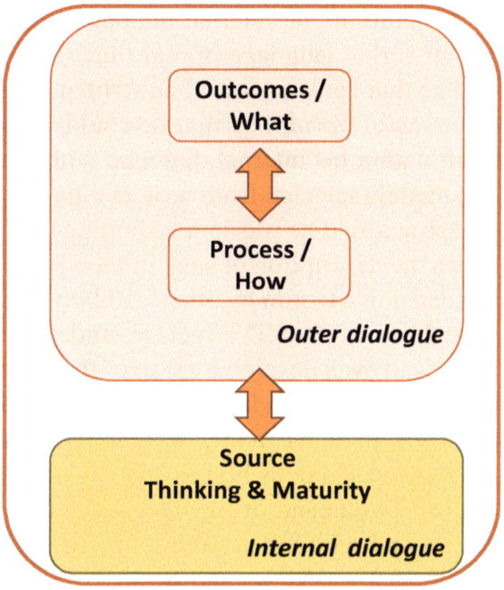


**Fig. 7.1** Internal and external dialogue as a function of developmental maturity

reality now escaping him. Robert could then "walk around" his mental tower and go from window to window, passing from context to process relationships, and even transformation to enlarge his purview of what was "going on." This new flexibility of thinking would, however, emerge only if he paid more attention to "what he just said," i.e., the internal dialogue that led him to speak to the coach and reflect on what he had been saying (i.e., how he had just "constructed" a piece of his reality).

Robert had trouble understanding what the internal dialogue was all about. Every day, he thought about problems he was facing, most of them vaguely defined and inviting him to use a range of enlightening models and frameworks of somebody else's making. Robert thought that using such models would lead to confronting problems in an effective way, such as asking: "How does all this cohere?" or "What can we do to change this situation?" or "What assumptions have we made?".

The coach, schooled in DTF, made it clear to Robert that from a four-dimensional CPRT perspective, such declarative questions would not suffice for opening up an internal dialogue in himself. The referent of Robert's questions was located "out there," in an assumed real world not of his construction, instead of being anchored in Robert's momentary mental processes in real time that kept track of "HOW exactly he was thinking right now." The reality he was looking for was thus much closer to him than he had an inkling of: what was required of Robert was a deeper level of questioning flowing from reflecting on his own mental processing. The "deeper questioning" required had to do with using thought forms by which each individual is unceasingly creating his or her "real world," one different from that of another person since each person had their way of configuring what was "real" for him or her. **In short, what Robert needed to grasp was that there is no "real world" without his constructing it in real time and keeping track of the thought forms he was using to do so.**

In addition, the internal dialogue required of Robert was closely allied with his use of verbal language in real time (as a speaker). As a speaker, Robert needed to realize that spoken as well as written language does not simply describe, but actually create, *World*, i.e., that he could not speak of a "real world" without speaking from within his internal dialogue with himself. Therefore, he could not effectively use models selected from writers outside of him without reflecting on their conceptual structure if he was indeed hoping to understand "what was going on"—however much the description of such models promised to solve his problems. To use models handed down to him by others, Robert would have to develop a critical sense of their thought form (CPRT) structure, understand their conceptual and practical implications, and even develop a grasp of the conceptual implications of the *practices* these models led him to adopt, which is what captains of industry, CFOs, and CEOs, had been able to do when they were successful in creating future value (De Visch 2014).

The coach did his best to explain to Robert that deeper questioning has to do with the intertwinement of the internal and the external dialogue, the first with himself, the second with others. While the internal dialogue is a process of de- and reconstructing world views and perspectives received from others, the external dialogue to improve by Robert was one that interweaves his own movements-in-thought with others' mental processing as was constantly happening in team dialogue.

Robert, a man of action, soon felt entangled in a paradoxical exercise. He wondered, "How can I start thinking about what I cannot yet think about?"

Individuals like Robert are not in the minority. Our present educational system is fact- and model-oriented and thus produces many of them, some with respected high-level degrees. The trouble is that contemporary education has lost the breadth of "liberal education" in which individuals were schooled in taking different perspectives, partly by engaging with humanistic studies that showed them how individuals in history had faired in their time.

However, there is no need to return to the past. The modern developmental sciences have made big forays into "how the mind works" in empirical, cognitive-developmental terms. Although most of them remain bound to formal logic (Commons 1984; Fischer 1980; King and Kitchener 1994), there are some, like the DTF framework utilized in this book, that break new ground in loosening the grip of logic as a control system on the unfolding of individuals' cognitive resources. DTF is closely aligned with social-emotional studies which put heavy emphasis on the development of self-awareness as a "stage" that transcends mere self-authoring (Laske 2005).

When considering self-awareness pragmatically, it seems to comprise two components. As Fig. 7.2 suggests, complex thinking based on one's dialogue with oneself in real time (component #1) is potentiated by experiencing "thinking together" with others (component #2). The link between the two components entails that what is referred to as "thinking" never happens in isolated human heads but is rather a "dialogical" (rather than "monological") process. By using the Yin/Yang metaphor, Fig. 7.2 also suggests that thinking can only be comprehensive and thorough when it is happening in dialogue with others, and thus grounded in every interlocutor's own internal dialogue. In other words, the highest quality of team dialogue stems from both unburying the thought forms carried by one's thinking in response, as a response to the internal dialogue of other speakers to whom one is closely listening. This entails that the boundaries between becoming aware of one's own thinking and experiencing (one's) "thinking" together with others are very punctual and therefore very fuzzy. In short, these boundaries are "dialogical," and thus transformed continuously in real time.

Pragmatically, it is tough to go through the first process (of becoming aware of one's own mental process) on one's own, rather than being supported by a critical facilitator. Once one has a grip on deconstructing one's own thinking held as an object, one can make a conscious attempt to make one's own reflective practice transparent not only to oneself but also to others, and thus modeling it for them in real time.

As shown further below, developing self-reflection, and thereby transparency of one's internal dialogue, is effortless to the extent that one is able to embrace three novel attitudes. The first attitude is (1) to abandon the assumption that given arguments are true. A second attitude is (2) to open to focusing on one's movements in thought and making them an object of reflection. The third attitude is (3) to rebalance the fixation on outcomes with an emphasis on the reflection process itself.

## 7.2 Developing *Double Listening* Through an Awareness of Cognitive Structure

Figure 7.2 has broad implications. It suggests that becoming aware of one's thinking directly leads to being able to experience oneself as thinking together with others. But this is an oversimplification, made to point the reader's attention to the reciprocity of the two components of the figure. Double listening is not based on any linear relationship between figure's yin- and yang-part, but rather on their intertwinement, here conveyed only implicitly by the assumed unceasing flowing into each other of "becoming aware" (yin) and "experiencing" thinking in concerts with others (yang). As a result, the "experiencing" referred to is not located "in" anybody separately but floats above everybody's mind in the team as a whole. **"Mind" is a team mind, never that of an isolated individual**.

More appropriately, then, *double listening* is listening to oneself as a moment of the process of listening to others and using others' thinking as a critical backdrop to scrutinizing one's thinking. When this interaction succeeds, an intertwinement of two or more movements-in-thoughts results, each of which "clarifies" and "sharpens" the other. Deeply listening to "what I just said" becomes a tool for experiencing "how others think," while listening to others becomes a tool for clarifying one's own movements-in-thought. When all members of the team have this "dialogical" experience, we can say that they are indeed "thinking together."

The following discussion between Robert and his coach, of a situation in Robert's work context involving the alignment of two subprojects, will make these notions more evident in a pragmatic way.

*Coach: "Why was it important to you in not letting the conflict between two of your project managers escalate?"*

*Robert: "I wanted all team members to follow the same roadmap, but they showed themselves unable to do so. As a result, a discrepancy between the two project leaders as to timing their projects was threatening to arise. If I hadn't been able to avoid conflict between them and their work, the two sub-projects would have evolved independently of each other rather than in alignment."*

*Coach: "Help me understand what you refer to as 'the alignment in time of two subprojects'."*

*Robert: "Well, it has become a priority for us to simplify handling complaints and inquiries from external customers. To achieve this goal, it is essential to possess a work agreement that makes clear who is responsible for what unique data input, and who is responsible for editing and for using available data and thus also the relationship between the three tasks involved. The two projects we are speaking of are meant to prepare such a work agreement. The work associated with the first project is to identify the questions customers ask and the information for answering their questions. The second work project maps out what information we keep about customers in different systems, and how employees use this information. The first project is to make an inventory of the information necessary for answering queries, while the second produces a list of ways of how to handle data captured from clients. You need to know both projects to understand the work agreement between two subgroups of the team, something we refer to as a 'master file.' If we were to complete one sub-project after the other, the project as a whole would be delayed."*

There are many ways for a coach to listen to Robert's utterances, above, for the sake of intervening in his mental process. Classically, we make a distinction between the "content" of what is said and heard, and the structure of the mental process ("the thinking behind it") by which the content is conceptually constructed. In the short interview fragment stated above, Robert focuses mainly on the roadmap, the interdependence of the two projects, and the need for their alignment in time. He focuses on the content of what needs to be done, without reflecting on his own way of constructing that content, presenting the content important to him in a strictly linear and analytical way, and moreover fixated on outcome.

To a person knowing DTF thought forms, it is evident that Robert could have formulated the content he conveyed (C) in many different ways had he been capable of reflecting on the processes (P) and relationships (R) involved in what he conveyed. To such a listener what Robert said would have documented Robert's present "cognitive profile" that would explain why he failed as he did and would have suggested the kind of cognitive coaching he was in need of.

What we have referred to as "double listening" requires not only listening to oneself in terms of the content to be conveyed but also having an awareness of the form in which it is conveyed, or as we say in this book, the "thought structure" of one's utterances. We make this distinction being aware of the fact that what is presented is always just one among many possible interpretations of a real-world issue and that a different person, making sense of the situation in question differently, would present a different interpretation. In both cases, the listener learns as much about the speaker's understanding of the real world as about what is spoken about since both aspects are inextricably intertwined.

As a thinker versed in DTF thought forms, a cognitive coach is searching for the conceptually richest description Robert can give of the issue he is speaking about. He or she does so because he or she knows that rendering real-world complexity matters for the quality of the work that is delivered. By searching for conceptually rich stories, a cognitive coach tries to find out, not primarily "what," but "how," Robert is thinking, paying particular attention to the concepts Robert uses, as well as Robert's awareness of how the concepts used are linked to implied or associated concepts.

In the above example, the coach chooses to reflect on the idea of "interdependence," but he could also reflect on the notion of "roadmap" or "downscaling the escalation." The first level the coach listens on in what is said is defined by the concepts that Robert himself uses in interpreting events, observations, and experiences, while in the next step, he or she would consider the implications of the concepts used by Robert and form an idea of how Robert's utterances would shift in meaning were they to use concepts different from those he has chosen, or if the implications of the concepts Robert used were to be made transparent.

Listening to a person's (or client's) thought structure is done in cognitive coaching to understand on what level of complexity a speaker is presently making sense of the real world, as well as of how aware he or she is of the used concepts' implications or links to other concepts. The coach would ask herself: is what is presented by a speaker part of a whole, central to understanding changes implied by the issues talked about; does the speaker's emphasis lie on relationships and the common ground different concepts share; or does the speaker realize the transformations the issues discussed could undergo over time?

In the above example, Robert uses relationship thinking in a very simple way, by focusing on the need for the simultaneity of two subprocesses making up a whole. He refers to a common ground that of constructing what he calls a "master file" that links the two projects not only externally but intrinsically (since they are meant to form a larger whole). Had Robert pursued a different intention, he would have constructed the issue differently, perhaps in a strictly process-oriented or contextual way. He could even have conceived of the issue as a transformational one in the sense that should both subprocesses end up fully aligned, and they could have transformed the company's way of servicing clients and capturing their data.

To explain the CPRT aspects of utterances a little further, let us consider the following.

Answering the coach's question to Robert from a strictly contextual point of view could look like this: "The two project leaders both claim to possess the information essential for improving a company response to customer inquiries. However, in my view, they lack a shared vision on the value-add of this project. Above all, they want to ensure that each of their employees can continue to do the work they are used to doing. But when working from a common vision, more clarity about what the interdependencies between the two subprocesses involved is required."

In this answer to the coach, Robert refers to context elements (namely, each project leader claims to possess task-essential information) and to the need for managing interdependencies (i.e., a strong shared vision). He "contextualizes" both parties' mental processes in order to be able to come to the conclusion that their (implicit) vision of the project is not shared between them.

From a process thought form point of view, Robert's description of how the two project leaders handle client inquiries would focus on changes occurring in real time and on how one process might be embedded in, or lead to, the other. Thus Robert could have said, "The two project leaders seem to construct their work process differently since they appear to follow a different path in creating a valid Master file. To the extent that they fail to adhere to the timing of the project agreed upon, not only will its next phase be delayed, but other projects will be equally delayed. This misalignment would have risky consequences for the entire enterprise."

Robert could also have chosen to formulate his thinking in terms of relationships. Referring to a different kind of delay having to do with price increases, Robert might have said, "We cannot dissociate the reciprocal responsibilities for data processing from future price increases and renegotiations of contracts with customers. To renegotiate contracts, we will have to do highly individualized analyses for customer groups. Such analyses would then not only determine how we would design the flow of information right now; it would also determine the future content of the service, i.e., who will have to do what."

A transformational answer by Robert to the request of the cognitive coach could look like this: "The lack of correct and unambiguous information about customers currently creates ambiguities, and thus dissatisfaction among customers as well as frictions between departments in our organization. Paradoxically, the departments cannot achieve their performance indicators because we often review decisions, and precious time to create a Master file is lost. Coordinating the two subprojects offers their leaders an opportunity to discover how best to complement each other's work, and thus to improve the overall customer experience. The two project leaders would be able to come to transparent agreements on their respective responsibilities so that their teams are able to improve their work, as well as reshape how they communicate with each other. This would instill greater stability into the two project teams' outcomes, which, in turn, could shift customer responses to company offerings."

Only a highly developed transformational thinker could have given such an answer. It is a way of thinking imbued with sensitivity to the fragility of systems due to existing imbalances, and the potential developmental gains (in meaning- and sense-making) arising from tackling them. Transformational thought structures inspire highly inclusive perspectives (such as the total customer experience) based on which coordination decisions should be made, but present contributors at Robert's responsibility level have developed the tools for such thinking.

### 7.2.1 Summary of the Notion of "Double Listening"

The notion of *double listening (DL)* challenges conventional ways of listening as well as of responding to communications in that it requires schooled attention not only to the content of a conversation but also the four-dimensional conceptual structure (CPRT) of the *sense* the communication conveys. If I say "my house is on fire," I am establishing either a fact or a hypothesis, and these are the contents of my utterance. However, I am implicitly referring to a process that I perceive is taking place, as well as the relationship of that process to the object it is about to change (i.e., the house), and even to myself (as the owner) who is trying to safeguard the house as property. Without attention to these relationships, the core point of the message is missed, namely that without interfering in the ongoing process, my house may be doomed. Finally, the utterance "my house is on fire" is a call to action; it implicitly refers to an outcome that amounts to a total transformation of what the speaker calls "my house," which is a heap of ashes.

From this example, it becomes clear that DL goes to the core of how language is used in organizational environments, not only in teams. By broadening conventional listening to include four interrelated dimensions (CPRT), DL requires a form of listening that comprises both the conceptual content conveyed by an utterance and the thought structure based on which this content is generated and articulated. One moves from "monological" to "dialogical" thinking by assuming that, by speaking as well as listening, individuals experience a concept in multiple ways, namely, as a context, as part of a process of change (unburying of absences), a node in a network of relationships, or a transformational whole. Listening to the structure of speakers' thoughts in real time is listening to the way a person gives shape to what for him or her is "real" in the world at the moment of speaking. It is thus a truth statement about the state of the world, e.g., "my house is on fire."

There is no way for people to speak about the world without simultaneously speaking about themselves, and what sounds "factual" is equally a personal expression of a speaker's world view at the time of speaking. Whether a person creates his or her beliefs about the real world himself or herself by way of inference or observation, or absorbs them through interactions with others is irrelevant. Therefore, listening to a speaker and paying attention to the structure of his or her thought is equivalent to listening to an expression of a person's consciousness expressed in the here and now, and that consciousness can be changed by opening the person's mind by using thought forms the person has not considered using.

What does DL amount to in pragmatic terms? It entails that you listen to the concepts and their meanings of which storylines are composed, at the same time discerning shades of (alternative) interpretations of the real world implied by them. This leads you to discover the many meanings, and thus also alternative meanings, of what is being said by a speaker, meanings of which he or she is not possibly fully aware while speaking. You are thereby switching from a *monological* way of listening for which what is said is "fact" to a *dialogical* mode of listening in which the facts (contents) dealt with amount to no more than a set of interpretations of the real world, none of which is absolute and each of which begs for further inquiry.

The overriding strategy of a cognitive coach (or critical facilitator) is based on the assumption that arguments and storylines are composed of elements, some of which are less rich conceptually than others and therefore deserve less attention than those that need to be explored in depth. Thus, the term "interdependence," for instance, takes on different meanings depending on the context into which it is placed by the speaker, functioning as (a) part of a larger whole, (b) an ingredient of emerging change, (c) an element of a set of interdependencies, (d) an element causing instability, or (e) critiquing premature coordination. As far as the person on the receiving side of a communication, here the coach, is concerned, DL initially entails asking for an explanation, or perhaps clarification, for the sake of sharpening a concept's meaning. This initial step is the first step to searching for the specific interpretations the speaker "has in mind" that is not disclosed by what he or she says but either taken for granted, unclear to the speaker, or willfully withheld by him or her.

### 7.2.2 Learning to Deconstruct My Thinking

Strategically, learning DL comprises two steps: (1) accepting the richness and thus ambiguity of concepts and (2) assuring oneself of the peculiar interpretation attached to particular concepts by a specific interlocutor. Both steps together form the foundation of "deconstructing" what a communication conveys by way of four classes of thought forms. These classes are ways of interpreting concepts and spelling out their relationships with other, implied, concepts.

To appreciate the notion of "thought forms" fully, think of your mind as a fishing net and of the world as an ocean of complexity that far transcends the reach of

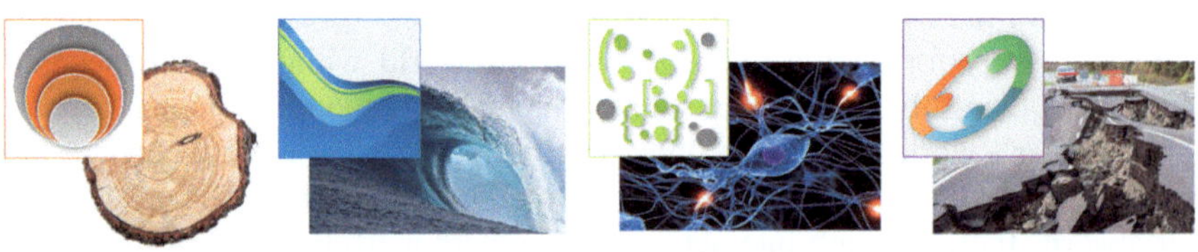


**Fig. 7.3** Four moments of dialectical thought (C, P, R, T)

human thought. What you can catch from the ocean depends on the form and structure of your net. Human thinking is embedded in thought forms by a process very similar to that by which the fisherman's expectation of the shape of the fish he or she is after becomes embedded in the design of the net he or she casts out to sea (De Visch 2014).

In this perspective on DL, we can distinguish four types of fishing nets our thinking activates when we speak either to ourselves or others. These are four translogical perspectives from which to view the real world holistically and systemically. Figure 7.3 visualizes the classes of thought forms we have in mind to which we can refer as "moments of dialectical thought" (Laske 2008).

In logical terms, we can consider these moments or perspectives as four *classes* of thought forms (TFs) and view each TF as a tool for identifying *absences in thought (thoughts implied but not expressed)*. Regarding the use of TFs in real time, we can distinguish three paths, also referred to as the PEL Sequence: p, e, and l. The first use of a TF is that of "pointing to" a subject matter or interpretation of it (p), while a second entails "elaborating" the meaning referred to by a concept (e); a third use, finally, is of "linking" of thought forms themselves, either those in the same class or different classes (l) (Fig. 7.4).

Using the PEL Sequence, above, is best pursued from a "higher" vantage point, distinguishing two types of "movements-in-thought," or ways of proceeding in the deconstruction of what is put out by an interlocutor: (1) *breadth-first search* and (2) *depth-first search*. In the first search, the person responding to an interlocutor chooses to place either the focal concept chosen into the vicinity of related concepts or else zeroes in on the focal concept itself to explicate its more extended meanings.

This procedure is visualized in Fig. 7.5.

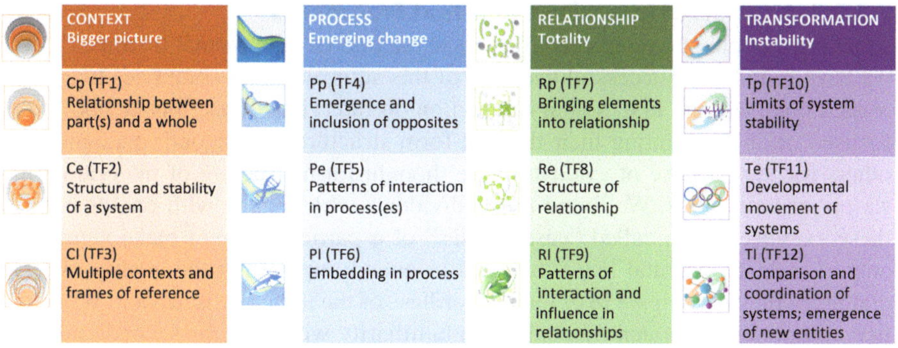


**Fig. 7.4** Four moments of dialectic and their associated TFs

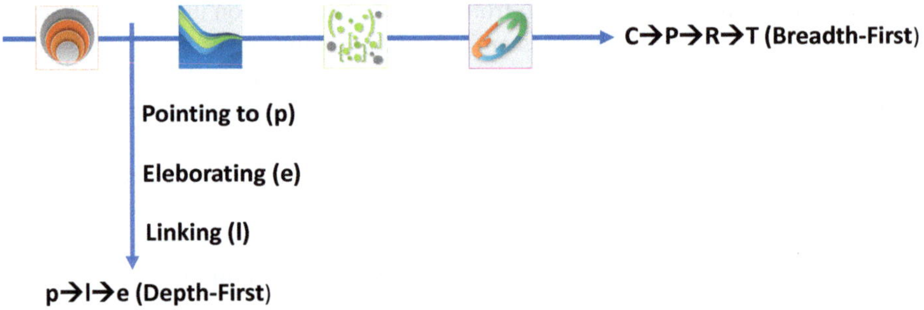


**Fig. 7.5** Two movements-in-thought: "breadth-first" and "depth-first"

### 7.2.3 Deepening the Practice of Complex Thinking

The framework for complex thinking outlined above assumes that all contributors to an organization are endowed with a potential for complex thinking that can be developed to its (expanding) limits. The framework distinguishes four perspectives in which to look at the real world and speak about it in search of the truth. Within each of these perspectives, there are many paths to proceed, above all, what we just referred to as "breadth-" vs. "depth-"first search. It is for these kinds of search that we use thought forms (TFs). Particularly when used in dialogue, all TFs function as "mind openers," enabling dialogue partners to delve into what is presently absent from our thinking.

When we think about the pedagogical and coaching side of the endeavor of learning complex thinking, the first important distinction we need to make is between "what humans think" and "how reality works." As we all know, these two aspects are separated by a wide gap, and it is this gap that we attempt to close by engaging in complex thinking.

There are several pathways along which to learn to use thought forms with increasing effectiveness: (1) the analysis of recorded interviews, (2) the study of storylines or arguments, and (3) the analysis of personal efficiency.

#### 7.2.3.1 Analysis of Interviews and Text Fragments

Teaching complex thinking over 20 years at the Interdevelopmental Institute (IDM), we have found that successful teaching of this subject matter comprises two interrelated components: first, solitary reflection on interview transcripts or book texts focused on understanding their thought-form structure and second, dialogue with others for the purpose of evaluating the thought-form structure of interview transcripts or book texts. We found that individuals who engage with one or both of these exercises in so-called "case studies" of a particular client make significant cognitive-developmental leaps that lead to quickly upgrading the quality of team dialogues they participate in or lead, regardless of the topic of discussion. While the first component, text analysis, builds up familiarity with TFs, the second, dialogue with others, helps practicing the TFs that have been acquired. It appears that it is the balance of understanding TFs by assigning them to text fragments (1) and subsequently using them in real time in dialogue with others (2) that makes for mastery of complex thinking in the sense of the DTF framework.

When we adapt this rather "academic" way of learning complex thinking to organizational practice, component (1), text analysis, has to do statements of a speaker (e.g., team member) about how the real world works. When scrutinizing such statements one can easily infer the thought forms used by the speaker. An example of a text fragment is the following:

> One of the tools we used in reviewing our business model was the "four actions framework." This was a powerful method of questioning our value proposition and exploring new customer segments while also deepening our insight into customer relationships. The following four crucial questions enabled us to challenge the industry's logic and established business model:
>
> - Which of the factors that the industry takes for granted should be eliminated?
> - Which factors should be reduced well below the industry standard?
> - Which factors should be raised well above the industry standard?
> - Which factors should be established that the industry has never taken note of?
>
> Answering these questions within a team gave rise to a discussion about simultaneously increasing value while reducing cost. A summary statement of this discussion goes as follows:

We are following two intrinsically related goals. The first goal is to lower costs by reducing or eliminating less valuable features or services. The second goal is to enhance or create high-value features or services that do not significantly increase the cost base. In thinking about the relationship of these goals, we came upon creating an entirely new industry by way of value stream differentiation and refinement, as opposed to continuing to compete in existing industries by simply modifying existing business models: rather than trying to outdo competitors in terms of traditional performance metrics, we decided that the company should start to explore a path of increasing value for customers by creating new benefits and services, while simultaneously reducing costs by eliminating less valuable features or services. With this approach, we hope to be able to increase innovation, at the same time rejecting the traditionally accepted trade-off between differentiation and lower cost.

In the above excerpt, the speaker summarizing the team discussion focuses on the relationship between value creation and cost (1), simultaneously bringing forward two oppositional ways of transforming business models (2). Under aspect (1), he is thinking in terms of outwardly different issues (such as cost and value) as sharing a common ground, in the sense that they are intrinsically related not only for the company but also for clients (which implies that there are limits to separating value and cost). Under aspect (2), he puts in opposition two modes of doing business, the traditional, "contextual," way of modifying existing business models and the more innovative, "transformational," way of increasing value and reducing cost, thereby establishing what he calls "a new industry." While aspect (1) is expressed in terms of relationship thought forms (column 3, *elaborating*, in Fig. 7.4), aspect (2) is articulated in terms of *pointing to process*, the first TF in the Process column of Fig. 7.4.

Complex thinking is decidedly learnable if the learning process comprises both text analysis in terms of TFs and team discussions in which the concepts focused on by analysis and their associated TFs became the focus of team dialogue. The texts involved can be financial newspapers, internal reports, strategic documents, or professional articles. The more they articulate the thinking of thought leaders, authors, or reference persons, the higher their value. Without a deeper study of TFs (as outlined above), our approach does not guarantee the development of rich thinking. Nevertheless, it does increase the likelihood that in team discussions about texts a multitude of thought forms (represented by TFs) will emerge in the team which, when analyzed by team members, will eventually foster a higher quality of team dialogue than would otherwise be possible.

#### 7.2.3.2 The Study of One's Storylines or Arguments

Since it is hard to combine on one's speaking in real time with searching for the thought forms one is using, the better way to discover thought forms is *to listen for them* when attending to another speaker. This second pathway to complex thinking entails inquiring into a stream of utterances in real time in which a speaker brings into play the four moments of dialectic and their associated thought forms, to shape his or her arguments. This kind of *cognitive listening* entails not only taking the conventional role of "listener," but changing from a conventional listening stance to that of an "interviewer" focused on an interlocutor. This upgrading of conventional listening implies expanding one's own mental space for carefully scrutinizing what is being said by a speaker outside of oneself in real time, for scanning which thought forms the speaker is actually using with what strength of articulation.

In this positioning as "interviewer," one can easily learn to scrutinize "what is said in real time" in two different ways: (1) at the level of (socio-)emotional meaning-making and (2) at the level of making conceptual sense-making. The first way of "social-emotional listening" scrutinizes how a speaker presently "makes meaning" of his social experiences, while the second way regards the conceptual, "sense-making" quality of the interlocutor's thinking in real time. This kind of analysis of an interlocutor's speech flow in terms of "stages" or CPRT sequences ultimately leads to deepening one's listening to oneself, that is, one's internal dialogue based on which one communicates with others.

Clearly, this kind of DL functions as an obstacle to taking fast and superficial positions toward a subject matter, even if only one of the options outlined above is used. Along both pathways of scrutiny, social-emotional and cognitive, DL enables one to detach from the flow of a conversation to make it an object of reflection. In so doing, one upgrades one's creativity by moving to a higher level of awareness "of what is going on" in the literal sense of "who is saying what, based on what thought forms, or from what stage of meaning-making."

We can imagine that Robert when reflecting on the options for the subject matter before him, and realizing that there is more than a single way to think about the matter, chose precisely the thought-forms that would succinctly express his intentions. Robert considered composing the governance committee for his program as follows:

*The governance committee should include the owners of the current sub-processes of the different business units as well as the key decision-makers able to assess the longer-term impact of formulated proposals.*

The above fragment reflects a rather contextual (descriptive) approach to governance. It focuses on the different categories of people that need to communicate with each other. By contrast, when Robert brought process thought forms into play (see Fig. 7.4), he formulated as follows:

*The governance structure should be aimed at overseeing and clarifying the field of tensions that arise during project implementation. In particular, project members should be able to assess the interweaving of inhibitory and enabling mechanisms that alternate, reinforce, and neutralize each other in such a field. In this way, our dealing with change will be tightly targeted. After all, it is not possible to foresee where we might get stuck, given the constants' shift of situations over time.*

This formulation reflects the awareness that nobody has absolute control of the future and that therefore what happens will have to be made apparent as it occurs. In the formulation above, Robert is focusing his notion of governance to be able to deal with ongoing changes.

#### 7.2.3.3 The Analysis of Personal Efficiency

A third track in deepening one's inner dialogue is to investigate one's personal efficiency. One can do so by reflecting upon how one uses one's psychological energy at work, as in M. Aderman's "Need/Press" Questionnaire (Hawkins 1970; Blattner 2001).

A person's use of energy in the sense of Aderman has to do with how a person balances inborn needs, ideals to be fulfilled by one's own professional agenda, and cultural and political pressures exerted on one's work by the work environment. Applied to Robert, the invitation is to observe his own needs as the context of his professional (especially role) functioning. Personal needs are situated within three broad (psychological) domains, of self-conduct, task approach, and interpersonal perspective (emotional intelligence). To give an example of interpersonal conflicts that can emerge from the compound of a person's needs, ideals, and experience of corporate culture, a strong need for affiliation aligned with an equally strong need for helping others can be at odds with pressure from the work culture to make principled decisions. Being made aware of such a conflict by a coach, or by answering a Need/Press Questionnaire (http://www.needpress.com/), can help a person open up an avenue toward behavioral change.

## 7.3 Experiencing Thinking Together: Multidimensional Listening

The deepening of one's internal dialogue ideally takes place in interaction with others. It means that one strengthens one's mental growth by stepping into a reflection process with others, practicing "multiple listening." Multiple listening comprises not only listening to another person than yourself but also DL to yourself. Multiple listening delivers a considerable benefit in delivering ever richer mindsets that can be modeled for a team in real time. Here too, we can distinguish three parallel tracks: (1) thinking together with others by questioning their reasoning, (2) constructing a synthesis from conceptual building blocks, and (3) understanding the gap between intention and action.

### 7.3.1 Thinking Together by Questioning Participants' Reasoning

Thinking along with others is an invitation to share reflections about a subject matter of common concern. It is often initiated by exhortations such as "let us reflect on how we are thinking here" or prompts like "can we take a moment to reflect on our thinking?". As organizational cultures go, this is an unusual intervention to make, because, in most conversations, thinking is taken for granted.

When following up on the first intervention, above, one is looking for a central concept around which other thoughts circle. In the second instance, one investigates how associated concepts and ideas relate to the fundamental concept chosen. In this pursuit, heretofore unmentioned or undiscussed questions will arise. These could become mind-opening questions, but only if, from noticing that a pure context perspective prevails (e.g., by thinking in discrete categories treated like independent "buckets"), a team member can raise the issue of how the context in question develops in real time. Reflections can then open up further to questioning the coherence or totality of elements of the context from which reflection started, or even to paying attention to how the focal concept of the conversation has the tendency to evolve in a particular direction by itself in a natural way.

De Visch's Rethinking Game (2019a) supports this process. The rethinking game invites participants to explore their collective thinking process playfully. Each participant receives a series of cards filled with mind-opening questions. The game entails that a "problem owner" puts forward a particular problem and invites each participant to choose a specific mind-opening question by which dialogue about the issue can be started. The person presenting the problem then chooses the question most strongly resonating with him or her, with the group looking for answers to the question. The group builds up its understanding of the problem further by choosing new mind-opening questions. There then ensues a creative search process, either breadth- or depth-first, in which different lines of argumentation unfold, alternatives are formulated, and reasoning about them is tested, which in the end leads to combining the best ideas that emerged. These ideas are then checked against the data from which one started, to assess their critical value.

The typical result of the game is that participants move from an analytical to an intuitive approach of addressing a real-world situation. Traveling the analytical path creates meaningful concepts and associated alternative variants, while walking the intuitive pathway helps clarify a problem's essence, and clarifies the latter through shared questioning made precise by thought forms leading to mind-opening questions.

### 7.3.2 Cliff Note Dialogues

A frequent task for teams is putting together different building blocks into a consistent whole. This task is similar to how what students call "cliff notes" are compiled. The term "cliff note" refers to summaries of complete books and series of lectures that facilitate cheating in academic tests. In an organizational context, cliff notes can be compiled for the sake of creating an intelligent simplification of a subject matter than interweaves different ways of thinking. The emphasis lies on finding what has a maximum of explanatory power regarding a problem, and how concepts focal for the problem overlap or strengthen and weaken each other. Such a compilation also shows where more explanation is needed, where there is too much repetition, what turns out to be controversial, and so on.

There are two subprocesses involved in investigating the process of sense-making. The first process is that of multiple listening. Multiple listening is a process of knowledge exchange and creation. The second process is a reproduction process in which one examines how to transfer insights reached to others. Reproduction is not a passive activity, but rather a slightly subversive activity because any synthesis of ideas by a person allows for further refinements of what was previously conveyed.

**Table 7.1** Robert's immunity-to-change map

| Commitment ("espoused theory") | Actions taken or not taken in violation of the commitment ("theory-in-use") | Implied and hidden competing commitments | Big assumptions made when taking action |
|---|---|---|---|
| Identify and follow-up opportunities for improving work delivery (even if they entail risking to lose others' support) | Strenuously avoiding surfacing adverse reactions in response to executing one's role: "I am trying to please everyone, especially direct reports." | To be well-liked throughout the company [indicating social-emotional other-dependence] | If I criticize my direct reports, they will avoid me and be reluctant to share ideas with me |

### 7.3.3 Understanding the Gap Between Intentions and Actions

A third track of deepening one's internal reflection and of weaving it into that of others is to examine the difference between what is said and what is done by a person. This topic, initially investigated by Argyris and Schon (1978), has been given a developmental slant in Kegan's *Immunity to Change* framework (Kegan and Lahey 2009). The central issue is that of making "espoused theory" (Kegan's "intention") congruous with "theory-in-use" (Kegan's "action"). While Argyris focuses on the organization as a whole, Kegan focuses on the individual contributor, spelling out the socioemotional factors that account for the clash of espoused theory and theory-in-use, referred by him as "hidden commitments."

Table 7.1 presents a hypothesis as to the mental template according to which Robert is acting. It can also be seen as a result of reflections Robert has been invited to make, as to how he has so far tackled real-world challenges. As shown by the map, Robert identifies what he has done "not or not otherwise" that has prevented him from fulfilling his role commitment, and spells out the, so far, hidden factors of merely espousing, rather than acting upon, his commitments.

Above spelling out the nature of his social-emotional meaning-making (showing him to be defining himself by expectations of others), the map also points to his way of making sense of the organizational environment and the individuals composing it. His hidden commitment being liked by others derives from a deficient way thinking about the nature of his role and of the consequences of being other-dependent. Specifically, Robert fails to explore the process ongoing between him and his reports, and therefore misjudges the structure of his relationship to them. By doing so, he fails to recognize the systemic consequences of his behavior, thus showing himself to be a not very complex thinker.

In the sense of Argyris, Robert's behavior only "espouses" taking responsibility for executing his role. His "theory-in-use" differs from his espousal, initially without his knowledge. When reflecting on his deeper emotional commitments and self-conduct, he is unable to distance himself from his "big assumptions" and incapable of cocreating a shared ambition with his teams (for instance). In terms of Argyris, he is not just acting upon socioemotional needs, but upon *theories* he is internally constructing (as a sense-maker). This way of proceeding amounts to misrepresenting to himself, his own self-concept and approach to tasks, and distorting the organizational reality he is part of.

It is important to realize that investigating the gap between intention and reality is not simply a matter of (social-emotional) meaning-making but of (cognitive) sense-making as well, and this is equally a matter of complexity of thinking. Keeping this in mind is crucial in helping executives as role-holders to broaden the diversity of their thinking and to build a broader understanding upon which to take action. Pragmatically, the aim in so doing is to help executives and team members generally, to increase the transparency of what they do and do not, not just what resonates with them in terms of meaning-making. The difficulty of this process lies in furthering ways of thinking that add value rather than commingling what people assume to be of value with their unconscious and never identified preferences. If role-holders fail to do so, they run the risk of encouraging ideas that are easy to "digest" but do not offer added value. Team members acting from a high level of cognitive development are likely to experience such ideas as commonplace or as irrelevant. In our experience, these difficulties in debugging one's sense-making can be reduced if team members develop three attitudes, further detailed below.

## 7.4 Three Basic Attitudes to Acquire

In our experience, developing an internal dialogue in oneself that is rooted in DL presupposes forming a set of interrelated attitudes:

- Attitude 1: Leaving behind the assumption that given arguments are true.
- Attitude 2: Focusing on movements-in-thought in real time, making them an object of reflection.
- Attitude 3: Valuing reflection processes by themselves, rather than remaining fixated on abstractions of "outcome."

As critical facilitators, we often initiate a developmental process by abstractly presenting these three attitudes, and then modeling what they look like in real time. In our experience, embracing these attitudes and gradually establishing them in oneself will strengthen contributors' internal dialogue, rather than the predilection of overfocusing on the external dialogue between parties as something "out there." Quite often, these *cognitive* attitudes clash with social-emotional meaning-making, which primarily focuses on personal relationships by putting the real world into brackets (so to speak). It requires a notion of "truth-seeking" and the acceptance of there being a "real world," not simply "out there," independent of speakers/actors, but as something that we unceasingly construct and refer to in speaking (without realizing it)—something that takes time to instill in individuals.

Below, each of the three attitudes is detailed further.

### 7.4.1 Attitude 1: Leaving Behind the Assumption that Given Arguments Are True

Several recalcitrant cognitive patterns complicate DL: (a) single-minded perspectives (e.g., logical reduction), (b) anecdotal knowledge, (c) untested practices, (d) organizational habits, and (e) undisputed values. Each of these patterns strengthens the idea that arguments per se are correct and true (rather than hypotheses), making it nearly impossible to embrace of ambiguity, even complexity.

We summarize these factors, mentioned above, in the three points below:

1. Single-minded perspectives and anecdotal knowledge each create a "window" on the real world that excludes complex thinking. They reinforce existing conventional and one-sided views. Typically, such perspectives are created due to a

lack of frameworks and models for looking at phenomena from different angles. Employees holding such perspectives rely on "best practices" and remain uninterested in (or unable of) looking beyond their discipline or profession. This attitude has the result that employees act as nothing more than "experts" (rather than thinkers) who with an ego-centrism look at complex issues from a single side, such as marketing or IT side. The perniciousness of this attitude is that it makes imagining new ways of dealing with issues impossible, especially when contrasting facets of a problem are disregarded. In such cases, not only do contrasting ideas remain out of sight, but the prevailing ideas remain blurred due to a lack of conceptual sharpness, making it difficult to bring one's own experience to the fore. For these reasons, no internal dialogue ever happens, and the knowledge dealt with remains sketchy, anecdotal, and abstract.

2. Whereas the previous obstacle to enabling internal dialogue consisted of not correcting opinions and beliefs by engaging with contrasting ideas, the second issue is a lack of critical realism because of failing to look into the mirror of practice, to learn whether actions taken actually lead to the results aimed for. This obstacle is not so much caused by the fact that one finds practice irrelevant but that one sees in practices only what one wants to see, thus stifling critique. In such circumstances, selective perception and biased interpretation win the day, something that easily occurs if, for example, the person devising an approach is not the one who carries it out, or if the approach is never implemented. A second way leading to selective perception and biased interpretation is one where the parties involved are too close to what they practice, and therefore lack the impetus to reflect on it. It then becomes easy to forego scrutinizing one's interpretation of what is happening and skip testing one's conclusions. In such cases, the link between what is said and done is broken, interpretations remain unscrutinized, and any conclusion is unhesitatingly accepted, even if doing so does not help make headway regarding a problem. There is then no link between intention and action, and what is claimed to be an outcome of one's practice does not truly derive from the practice referred to.
3. The third obstacle to internal dialogue results from eliminating ambiguity by fixating on values as "undisputed," and refusing to scrutinize them more closely, thus making it impossible to recalibrate one's views by adopting opposing ways of seeing actual outcomes (in contrast to mere opinions about what they are). Why create controversy if matters seem to be "clear," colleagues respond with consent and offer reassurance?

   This situation frequently occurs when assumptions on which consensus is based are never made explicit, so that they accrue to solid and untouchable organizational belief systems. When this occurs, developing an awareness of the balance between an organization's stability and fragility becomes very difficult, since the organizational transformation that occurred is taken for being merely a "change," changes being easier to conceptualize and understand. Fields of tension within a team then become simplified, and process responsibilities falsely appear as unambiguous. What is more, unscrutinized presuppositions hold sway and are defended uncritically, even though reports, policy papers, and other formal texts referred to distort the company's real status. One follows the rituals of discussion simply to "get something done."

The three patterns described above frequently result in what one might call "wilful one-sidedness," meaning that something is left to develop in arbitrary directions. Critical realism is then abandoned and truth-seeking comes to a halt. In the presence of anecdotal knowledge, one forgets that alternatives should be tested. The third pattern mentioned above seamlessly fits in with the first two: the less searching out the truth is seen as essential, the more undisputable dominant views and practices become. In such circumstances, letting go of one's unscrutinized truths and stepping into DL collectively can cause a thought revolution.

### 7.4.2 Attitude 2: Focusing on Movements-in-Thought in Real Time, Making Them an Object of Reflection

Teamwork is primarily about learning and evolving in maturity. Its major enabler is searching for a valid route to follow that is in line with team members more or less realistic notion of how reality works. Here, too, obstacles arise that make exercising DL difficult and change of team functioning hard to achieve. Two of these obstacles are hesitant to participation and outsourced innovation.

Amid rapid organizational change finding answers to complex issues is not easy for employees. With hierarchies largely gone, their own self-concept, based on fixed competences, is being put in doubt by themselves and others (Boyd and Laske 2018). When an innovation initiative is announced, it raises doubts among those involved as to whether to join in. To reduce this uncertainty, they appreciate being offered easily explainable approaches, preferably with guarantees that they will "work." The paradox is, the better a procedure can be explained, the less internal reflection it triggers and the less suitable it is to deal with complex realities. Getting an initiative started right away, and designing a tailor-made approach for it is frequently greeted with doubts because potential contributors engage only once confident that the problems to be solved can find a solution.

Another paradox plays a role once an initiative has started. Its implementation cannot be restricted to those involved because of the risk of following familiar routines that predictably lead to unsatisfactory outcomes. Leaving innovation to others does not work either because the parties involved need to think of themselves as part of the change required and aimed for. The only way to make this paradox generative of solutions is to invite team members to think together and to be open to multidimensional listening and critical reflection.

Listening to each other's movements-in-thought (not just "thoughts," which are their result) means that employees need to exercise critical reflection. In our experience, three intervention steps are useful in this regard: (1) slowing down, (2) making doubts explicit, and (3) reevaluating perspectives taken so far.

The first intervention step is to *slow down*. Once employees have explicitly communicated their truths, it is important to take the time to investigate these truths and continue listening to employees. Slowing down creates a holding space (Hirschhorn

1988), that is, a space in which to air uncertainties and thereby come to a deeper understanding by filtering ideas. Instead of following one's immediate reactions, it is more fruitful to find out from which common frame of reference opinions can be shared and how they can be clarified and refined. In this situation, the key lies in asking mind-opening questions for the sake of building a richer picture from thoughtfully exchanged arguments. Often, stories that initially seem to be helpfully concordant begin to show holes and cracks. An initial consensus on improving cooperation or implementing a new policy often peters out.

A second intervention step is to provide space for *sharing doubts*. It is important not to frame uncertainty as criticism but to label it positively as a process step serving further clarification. This works best if formulating questions is grounded in flexibility of thinking and abstains from trying to persuade. Often doubt springs from negative change experiences, and sharing doubts helps reinterpret history.

A third intervention step consists of *reevaluating previously adopted perspectives*. This kind of intervention is a search for more fruitful perspectives lying outside of what is known. The aim is to explore what is congruent with the involved parties' environment and commitment. If done well, this step leads to more than an inventory of wishes or consensus on goals. Instead, it results in investigating attempts to retreat into uninspiring ideas, e.g., about innovation. Performing such an intervention turns into learning as a team.

### 7.4.3 Attitude 3: Valuing Reflection Processes for Their Own Sake Rather than Fixating on Outcomes

A third attitude that helps develop internal reflection is one that values movements-in-thought over their outcome. This attitude detaches employees from step-by-step plans in which no more than broad outlines are laid down. It also prevents waiting for outcomes that never materialize since complex agendas, even when broken up into steps, never lead to predictable results. In complex plans, the time-horizon for completing work is of crucial relevance. Especially if the completion path is long, unexpected disturbances appear with the result that the more robust and uniform the plan, the more cogency it loses over time.

The remedy for this calamity is to spend more time on diagnosis ("reflex"), to understand a tough issue in greater depth initially, so that planning can become more precise. Of course, further analysis has its risks: it can become endless, and thus a paralyzing exercise. Resulting problem definitions retain random aspects. As impatience with the diagnostic phase increases calls for action multiply. In frustration, one seeks recourse in an action-oriented approach such as "best practices" trusted inside of the organization. In this situation of broken-off diagnosis, effectiveness most likely results from maintaining DL for the sake of building cooperation.

As the above review of three attitudes promoting DL shows, it is not "thinking" per se (certainly not logic-analytical thinking), but its timing and structure as well as critical realism relative to the real world that matters. In addition to being a source of sophisticated thinking tools, the four-dimensional (CPRT) structure of complex thinking provided by DTF also has motivational aspects that heighten circumspection, especially when the pathway to a solution is long.

**Key Insights and Practice Reflections**

Contributors' development dialogue entails becoming aware of the quality of one's internal dialogue (unceasingness of reflection) and of the requirement of interweaving it with the emotional and cognitive processes of others. A crucial piece of the awareness-raising process involved is what we have referred to as "double listening." As the reader may have noticed, we have given this concept a threefold meaning:

1. The ability to listen to oneself in both an emotional and cognitive way.
2. The ability to stand in other's shoes when listening to them as their "interviewer," adopting a "persona" detached from one's own subjectivity.
3. The ability to engage with others in a dialogue integrating the two preceding components in a critical (self-reflective) exchange with the "truths" brought forward in real time.

What we have called "multiple listening" is an interweaving of these three capabilities in real time dialogues.

We have shown throughout this chapter that improving these abilities is not simply horizontal "learning" but vertical "development" (over time) by which contributors advance toward higher social-emotional "stages" and higher phases of thought fluidity. Executing these capabilities presupposes at least three achievements: first, real-time experience of oneself as "thinking"; second, a detachment from one's own movements-in-thought; and third, embracing the thought flow of others from a stance of an emotionally detached "interviewer." On a metalevel, these achievements entail realizing that others are not merely one's clients but, in the long run, midwives of one's self-development. The detachment from one's ego-centric needs required in exercising these capabilities is not easy to achieve. Separating the emotional from the cognitive strands of dialogue, as well as separating speech content from thought structure underlying speech, is a challenge.

In addition, experiencing one's own, unceasingly occurring internal reflection process requires practice. It is instantaneous only in cognitively highly developed adults who have become "double listeners." Such a mental process is both the source and the result of thinking together with others. As a source, it opens the self to others as "co-thinkers"; as a result, it positions others in a place where they can be "heard" because what they say is intrinsically linked with one's internal dialogue, or else is discrepant from it in ways that invite further dialogue. Resonating with what others say based on the thought-form structure of what they convey, in contrast to fixating on the content they are conveying, is at the root of any high-quality dialogue. Such a dialogue is, moreover, characterized by a constant awareness of the gap between "how humans think," on the one hand, and "how the real world works," on the other. Closing this gap is the ultimate goal of any team-based enterprise.

In this chapter, we have reviewed organizational work as a set of pathways for becoming an adult both in one's meaning- and sense-making, and thereby amplifying an organization's "human resources" beyond the abilities of even the best HR department. We have shown indirectly that HR departments are far beyond in their recognition of what is known today about adult development, especially cognitive development. We have hypothesized that although adult development cannot be the direct and explicit focus of organizational work, it certainly needs to be the focus of organizing work in companies that strive to become self-organized. The reason for this is that the core of "human resources" consists of contributors' *dialogical* capabilities that so far no app, however smart, has shown to possess. We have thereby indirectly suggested that the hiring process in companies is twofold: (1) companies hire contributors to get needed work done, while (2) contributors hire companies to acquire opportunities for becoming adults. Companies who miss (2) are in for hard times.

Our focus in this chapter has been cognitive, not social-emotional development since the latter is sourced cognitively, and outside of cognitive resources can only be hand-waved by persuasion rather than solid tools such as DTF. We have shown the various ways in which employees can boost their cognitive development by using teams as a resource in which to acquire complex thinking through dialogue, most effectively whenever they see in others midwives of their own lifelong development (which becomes possible only at high levels of adult development).

We have suggested that an excellent methodology to follow for boosting contributors' cognitive development is Laske's DTF framework, which we have ourselves used in teaching complex thinking for a decade. As shown throughout the chapter, the four classes of thought forms contained in DTF address four aspects of the real world, which, when engaged with through dialogue, together make possible a holistic and systemic view of oneself as an integral part of the real world, as well as the real world itself.

When made use of in teams, the CPRT Sequence is a potent tool for closing the gap between "how humans think" and "how the real world works"—a gap that purely logical thinking can never close. We have shown that closing this gap is closely linked with boosting one's own sense-making, both in life and work. This is so because all thought forms, of whatever class, are not only tools for opening one's mind; they also generate an infinite number of compelling questions regarding the complicity of the real world to open to human initiatives. In logical thinking which constantly "objectifies" the real world instead of opening it up for action, this complicity vanishes into VUCA.

In addition to introducing and explaining DTF, we have given multiple practical examples of using its thought forms in a variety of circumstances (e.g., Robert). We have emphasized that employees do their best work together with a cognitive coach, at least initially. In a second step, they can develop their thinking further by working together in groups, scrutinizing texts of relevance to them for the sake of learning, and practicing thought forms in dialogue with each other in which they take the role of detached "interviewer." In our experience, doing so considerably enhances, over time, the quality of team dialogue. Since high-quality team dialogue directly contributes to dynamic forms of collaboration, efforts to learn DTF and its thought forms are an excellent investment, especially for organizations striving to become self-organizing. Daily stand-up meetings do not suffice.

**Practice Reflections**

1. What in your work–life hinders you from stopping to reflect on what you do or intend to do?
2. Do you use language only to describe things, rather than realizing that by speaking, you are creating new realities that the real world might be complicit in encompassing according to its own rhythmics?
3. What makes you overfocused on the social environment as being located "out there," not realizing that you are cocreating it (as you speak), as well as being under its influence (as you listen)?
4. Why might you be caught between an absolute and a relativistic notion of "truth" instead of consistently investigating truths by way of thought forms in real time dialogue with others?
5. How might you be able to open up your internal dialogue, and thereby augment the resonance of what others tell you as "co-thinkers"?

# 8 Viewing Human–Machine Interaction from a Developmental Perspective: Stepping Up to the Humane Organization

*In most general terms, the crucial limit of present machine capabilities ("intelligence") is their inability to produce or understand mental transformations. While their—in human terms "logical"—capabilities excel at capturing data contexts, external relationships between data and concepts, and lead to instantiating information processes, dramatic transformations as found in human development over the lifespan and capabilities such as complex human thinking are presently, and perhaps forever, beyond their reach.*


**Abstract**

In the last chapter, we scrutinize human–machine interactions from an adult-developmental perspective, for the sake of preparing pragmatic ground for fusing human and algorithmic intelligence while strengthening human freedom. We argue that the reduction of developmentally sourced human capabilities to what fits logic-derived machine notions of efficiency and effectiveness is particularly unwarranted in our time because of the urgent organizational need of integrating algorithmic intelligence into human work delivery. We return to the starting point of this book, of rehabilitating ways of thinking that transcend logic-analytical reductionism and behaviorism, for the sake of instituting a holistic and systemic kind of thinking of a transformational nature that is highly in tune with the apex, in human life, of both social-emotional and cognitive maturity.

In this spirit, we explore alternatives to *engineered determinism* as a basis of designing artificially intelligent systems that promise enhancing, rather than cutting down on, human flourishing. Our suggestions are based on arguments put forward throughout the book. We summarize these ideas by formulating six principles, all of them focused on the issue of creating opportunities for high-quality team dialogue and, by extension, vertical development of organizational resources beyond the Tayloristic paradigm of human resources.




J. De Visch, O. Laske, *Practices of Dynamic Collaboration*, Management for Professionals, https://doi.org/10.1007/978-3-030-42549-4_8

## 8.1 Introduction

Throughout this book, we have been rehabilitating human thinking as a capability that intrinsically references the real world, conceiving of it holistically, systemically, and "dialectically,"—in short, as something irreducible to logical-analytical thinking. We have conceived of human thinking about organizations as capable of addressing the real world as a place of conflicts potentially complicit with human agency, rather than as the VUCA (volatility, uncertainty, complexity, and ambiguity) world formal logical thinking declares it to be. To do so consistently, we have acknowledged that since Kant (1781), human thinking has become able to distinguish between "how humans think" (the world as it is "for us") and "how the real world works" (the world as it is "in and by itself"; Stewart 2016). This metatheoretical distinction is likely to amplify humanistic tendencies in organizational theory that bear on notions of human flourishing in conjunction with notions of fusing human and algorithmic efficiency.

In this chapter, we are taking a broad, empirical as well as philosophical, view of human capabilities that support dialogue-based collaboration in three different, successively more complex social spaces we call *We-Spaces*, those of (1) continuous improvement, (2) redirecting value streams, and (3) business model transformation. Within these three mental spaces of increasingly higher work complexity, we speak of two opposing kinds of freedom, referred to as "positive" and "negative," respectively, and see their dialectic as the driving force behind synthesizing two perspectives on human freedom. The first, positive, kind of freedom is that of contributors striving toward autonomy in working with others with an awareness of the totality of work involved. The second, negative, kind of freedom regards the constraints cultural and organizational environments impose on individuals' and teams' drive toward self-development.

We show in this chapter that of central relevance to understanding the dialectics between these two kinds of freedom are two opposing conceptions of human thinking: the first, *instrumentalist* and the second, *humanist*. We see ourselves as continuing the work of critical theorist Max Horkheimer (1947) who first realized that over the last 200 years (approximately) formal logical thinking has been drained of real-world insights by conceiving of logic predominantly as a control system, rather than a tool for holistic and systemic insight into how the real world works.

In this chapter, we exemplify this dichotomy between insight and control by drawing conclusions for human flourishing in organizations from the powerful sway of instrumentalist over humanistic thinking, which, for us, is linked with the two notions of freedom distinguished above. As we move through the three different We-Spaces distinguished in this book, we note a shift in the direction of positive freedom that is rooted in deeply collaborative learning processes. Our notion of algorithmic resources is that they fail to be "resources" if they cannot be shaped, so as to dialogically support such learning processes.

Throughout this book, we have stated our belief that the topics mentioned above cannot be fruitfully addressed except by more profound reflections on the nature of human cognitive development over the life span. We have noted the influence of conceptions of what is an "organization" on conceptions of human sense- and meaning-making. Our deliberations on the nature of human vs. algorithmic work lead us to the central question of this chapter: **how can human thinking be schooled to flourish, while at the same time, embracing artificial intelligence devices, and thus instrumentalist thinking in an objectified form?**

Our paradoxical stance in answering this question is that because human thinking is both "dialectical" and "dialogical," the seeming opposition between human and algorithmic thinking is not an absolute one; it dissolves when it becomes possible to (1) shape algorithmic devices by insight into adult cognitive and social-emotional development and (2) engage such devices as cognitive-developmental assessment and support tools that provoke their users to become "interviewers" of each other. We propose that as "interviewers" (rather than mere "listeners" or interlocutors), users of algorithmic devices can be engaged as "coaches" of their own cognitive and social-emotional development. We see this possibility despite our knowledge that depending on the We-Spaces we consider, human thinking itself is to various degrees subject to "instrumentalize" itself by way of thought-inherent habits, memorization, and automation.

In pursuit of answering the above question (in bold), we come to the following conclusions:

1. As *dialectical*, human thinking surpasses logical-analytical thinking in-depth and holism without losing a shred of the power of such thinking (Laske 2019a, b, c, d, e, f, g, h, i, j, k, 2018a, b, c, d, e, f, g, h, i, j, k, 2015a; De Visch and Laske 2018).
2. As *dialogical*, human thinking is open to receiving a boost from "dialogically savvy" apps to the extent that software is designed to strengthen individuals' internal dialogue and multiple listening.

As a consequence of our approach, we are evaluating digital platforms and templates that go under the neutral name of "business software" in terms of how they measure up to the challenge of augmenting the quality of dialogue in human work teams. We think that as far as they do not do so, they reinforce the calamities of purely instrumentalist thinking (Horkheimer 1947; Bhaskar et al. 2016).

In detail, this chapter's sections address the topics listed below:

- The instrumentalist-humanistic dichotomy
- Thinking shapes, and is shaped by, tools
- Considering the instrumentalist—humanist dichotomy from a developmental point of view
- Limits of present machine capabilities
- *Engineered determinism*: A suboptimal symbiosis of human and "machine" intelligence
- Contours of a humane organization

## 8.2 The Dichotomy Between Instrumentalism and Humanism

Talk about profit and shareholders aside, the real focus of management theories has always, if indirectly, been the nature of work, the topic of how to wisely engage human resources together with, and sometimes as, machines. Formulating management theories has, however, frequently been characterized by a profound dichotomy between two kinds of work delivery: by humans as virtual machines and by machines as "the real thing."

Over time, the notion of "machine" has turned out to be an extendable metaphor encompassing different types of routinization, mechanization, and automation. Since the arrival of computer algorithms in the mid-1950s, the notion of machines delivering "work" has come to include algorithmic intelligence in human thinking. We have now arrived at a turning point where what we envision as "humane" organizations hinges on finding an equilibrium between the deeply entrenched dichotomy between machine-based and human ways of delivering work. Paradoxically, a deepened inquiry into human capability from an adult-developmental perspective since 1975 has further problematized significant advances in artificial intelligence which are seen by some as destroying "human" ways of delivering work.

Substantial influence on how the human capability to deliver work has been conceived by organizational leaders derives from the over 100 year-old traditions of Taylorism. In its updated forms, as found in protocols of "agile" and "lean" ways of working, Taylorism is thriving but has not shed its blindness to the human capability of transformation which is demonstrated by empirical research on adult development over the life span. Research in adult development has shown that the optimal way to remain oneself far transcends the notion of mere change, being rather focused on unceasingly transforming oneself. In our view, it is this capability that also provides the greatest potential for realizing the integration of artificial intelligence elements into human work.

Tayloristic thinking conceives of everything in an organization as a raw material—activities, tasks, processes, value chains, and related data. The core of this mechanistic vision, first critiqued by the members of the Frankfurt School as instrumentalist thinking (Horkheimer 1947), is the idea that everything can be manipulated for the sake of achieving organizational objectives. The danger attached to such a vision is that humans themselves are seen as instruments that can be engineered, optimized, and programmed as if human minds themselves were nothing but a kind of technology. In Taylorism, we are seeing the triumph of instrumentalist thinking of a purely analytical type that even endangers human uses of artificial intelligence.

### 8.2.1 Outsourcing Thinking

Thanks to ever-present smartphones and other digital services, most of us are connected to an extensive, all-encompassing computer network that captures what we think, need, and do. The companies that control these networks are focused on achieving ever stronger control over how we think and what kinds of meaning we make of others and ourselves through their apps, sites, and services. At the same time, networked objects and applications are creeping into our homes and workplaces, promising to make our lives even more surveyed under the lure of increasing "comfort" and "convenience." Many activities we used to experience as difficult and time-consuming have become easier, requiring less effort and thinking, which reduces our capabilities of self-authoring. The risk we are taking in accepting convenience is that we lose our initiative and the sense of fulfillment, as well as belonging associated with shared intentional action.

When we transfer our initiatives to computers and their software, we start to lose control over our wishes and decisions. We "outsource," as it were, our responsibility for personal, self-defining evaluations of important slices of the real world by following programmers and the companies that employ them. Many people resort to algorithms to find out what films they might watch, what meal they might cook, what news they should follow, and which person they should date. Why would you think if you can click? By thus outsourcing personal decisions, we expose ourselves to manipulation. Given that the design and operation of algorithms remain largely hidden, it is a tough task to determine whether the choices proposed to us reflect our own preferences or those of companies, interest groups, governments, or other third parties. We want to believe that technology increases control over what we want to do. Still, using it without critical reflection renders us subject to technology almost as much as we already are in terms of adult development over the life span.

Jaron Lanier (2018) goes further and argues that today's digital technology prevents us from focusing on problems and challenges that are "real" for us. He calls social media "behavioral manipulation empires" that make us into "assholes." He believes that since social media continually monitor us, they have the power of having us fixate on negative feelings, such as fear and irritation, that can amplify like a snowball. Lanier's primary concern is the business model of social media, not the media themselves, since that business model makes it imperative to improve social media perniciously by keeping people's attention. Social media platforms refer to this effect as "engagement and conviction," while Lanier prefers to speak of addiction and manipulation. In his view, social algorithms lead to a feedback loop of negative emotions because they tend to reinforce experiences that lead to engagements within the limited confines of smartphones, in a way void of reflection.

### 8.2.2 Self-Made Difficulties

In our view, the unmitigated focus on efficiency and predictability, an outflow of instrumentalist logical and analytical thinking as encapsulated by Taylorism, is precisely the reason why present-day organizations are finding it so hard to conceive of, and "find," an equilibrium of algorithmic and human capabilities. The decisive difference between these two dimensions of work delivery is one of scope as well as depth. In contemporary rationalism, the meaning of the term "human" is easily reduced by formal logical thinking to routinized behavior, while in humanistic, including adult-developmental, parlance, the scope of the word "human" is much, much broader. Concretely, it includes adult development over the life span, a topic that organizations have tip-toed around successfully for at least 40 years and are still resisting to acknowledge today, as we think to their disadvantage.

Importantly, the difference in scope and conceptual depth of the term "humanist" relative to "instrumentalist" is closely associated with different conceptions of real-world complexity: for logical rationalism and behaviorism, the world is entirely circumscribed by empirical findings in the form of human-made "data" (facts), while for developmental humanism including *critical realism* (Bhaskar et al. 2016), the world is exceedingly complex, mostly unknowable, and in unceasing transformation—as are human beings and their identities themselves. In the real world seen by holistic perspectives, "VUCA" is (and has always been) the norm, not the exception. The VUCA world is, therefore, best diagnosed as a product of logical thinking finding itself barred from a world of constant transformation.

## 8.3 Thinking Shapes, and Is Shaped by, Tools

We are well aware that formulating a strict (undialectical) dichotomy between "instrumentalist" and "humanist" relative to thinking not only presumes that we have complete knowledge of what human thinking is but also minimizes attention to the fact that human thinking has always been shaped by tools and devices needed to deliver work. Take the evolution of fishing with spears to the use of nets, to the use of sophisticated radar equipment of fishing vessels. Using a lance to fish requires a series of skills, and these skills preshape our notion of the world and our functioning in it. Gradually, fishers have lost the ability to use spears for fishing. Due to modern fishing technology, more fish are caught with fewer people, creating opportunities for the fishing community to diversify, learn other skills, and explore different ways of organizing itself. As Winston Churchill said, "We shape our tools, and after that, our tools shape us." In short, there is always a feedback loop between human thinking and the tools chosen to support it.

From the vantage point of this book, it is critical to understand this coevolutionary process ongoing between human thinking and its tools. As is daily demonstrated to us, automated systems and robots, for example, perform specific tasks faster and cheaper, freeing up space for people to take on other, richer jobs. As well, automated tools seem to open the door to massive destruction of repetitive task performances on the one hand and create a range of algorithmically enriched jobs in which human skills are central on the other (Davenport and Kibey 2016).

Davenport et al. start from the observation that automation mainly concerns subordinate tasks, and seldom entire jobs. Every job can be seen as a sequence of tasks. Even though the ratio between automated and nonautomated tasks differs between jobs, there are relatively few jobs that have been fully automated. In the insurance industry, the repetitive aspects of underwriting insurance policies and claims handling, for instance, have been taken over by digital systems, and underwriters are evolving toward owning key client accounts regarding which they deal with the client in both the underwriting and claims handling dimension. The remaining non-automated tasks require conceiving of a bigger picture (e.g., the type of customer relationships desired for different target groups) or system integration (e.g., consulting or comparing various sources), as well as holding an interpersonal perspective on a situation (e.g., reassuring a customer).

The job augmentation argument regarding automation stems from a relatively simplistic way of reasoning, typical of thinking within the continuous improvement We-Space. In that space, a relatively simple cause–effect logic between the means and result is assumed. In this line of thought, automation brings about productivity, quality, cost-efficiency, and richer jobs. How the reality created through automation influences beliefs, values, and self-image of the people involved is not considered. For example, many managers advocating or establishing automated processing do not take into account how the professional identity of the employees involved is potentially turned upside down.

For instance, until recently, an underwriter in an insurance company had a completely different professional identity compared to a claims handler. It must be shocking for both to learn that supported by tools enhancing decision-making; they are now playing a role that seriously undermines their self-image as domain experts. Nor does this kind of flat argumentation in favor of automation take into account whether employees, working in the larger decision space, are actually prepared to function in it productively, let alone how they could be supported in growing their responsibility for partial processes, or whether they are equipped to monitor the weaknesses and strengths of the algorithms they are working with. Even less are artificial intelligence enthusiasts aware of the impact of "job augmentation" on employee interaction and collaboration they vaguely think of as "supported" by software.

From a cognitive-developmental perspective, we would predict that employees in the continuous improvement We-Space are able to question tools provided to them only to a very limited extent. This is the case since, for them, these tools *define* "reality" rather than open a strictly circumscribed window on small pieces of the real world, with the result that tools and reality get merged into their users' subjectivity—a blinding reduction as to how reality works.

Digital tools create their own, often savagely reduced, reality due to their inventors and users' lack of cognitive development beyond logical thinking. As a result, these tools shine a light on subject matter in such a way that most of it remains in the dark. This situation can move very close to the situation of a drunk looking for his keys in the light of a lamp nearby, rather than where he or she might have lost them. Importantly, this blind subjectivism creates the risk that thinking about human–machine interaction remains fixated on abstract outcomes as well as the "machine" dimension of work, with blinding advertising hype in close pursuit. In short, it is a situation of the blind leading the blind.

Although automated tools take many forms, they all share an inbuilt tendency to suppress human reflection. This is so since the cognitive structure of these tools is a single-minded extension of formal logic with which to take on how the real world works (not to speak of complex human thinking as demonstrated in this book) is pure fantasy. By subverting complex thinking, most apps extend the controlling function of formal logic to their users unbeknownst of the latter. Rightfully, therefore, Frischmann and Selinger (2018) see the impact of digital business software on work as a form of *engineered determinism*. Engineered determinism arises when digital systems based on strictly logical thinking, and thus structurally stifling users' internal dialogue, begin to determine how people think, behave, and relate to each other, offering control systems primarily pointed at users of digital tools, not at the real world, thereby reinforcing their subjectivism.

Digitalization is often advertised as "lean" and "agile." An example of a somewhat *critical* approach to working with algorithms can be found in matching applications on the Internet, where, for example, an algorithm selects candidates for open vacancies. The matching takes place based on algorithms that encode information deriving from curricula and job postings. They search for connections between two encoded sets of data. The unfortunate result of this procedure is that candidates who do not fit patterns arbitrarily stipulated as valid are no longer presented to recruiters at all. Candidates whose career history deviates from such patterns no longer have a chance to be considered. Even worse, recruitment professionals have so far not learned to inquire into the weaknesses of such algorithms and thus do not realize the narrow boundaries of the underlying data set they rely on. In this way, no data is included that would promote a candidate's ultimate well-being in a future job, enhance opportunities for the candidate to self-develop in the post offered, or provide information about a potential match with colleagues or supervisors associated with the job. In short, the algorithm simply reinforces impoverished recruitment procedures.

Frischman and Selinger also investigate the effect of so-called "mind-extending" technologies believed to support problem-handling. They suggest that the following three questions are never asked in engineered determinism, which is dominant in the continuous improvement domain:

1. *Who* is doing the thinking when humans use mind-extending technologies?
2. In mind-extending situations, *what types of thinking* do humans and apps do each of them, and how transparent to human minds being extended are the different forms of thought involved?
3. *How* does technologically extended thinking positively or negatively influence the natural development of human capabilities in the sense of adult development as occurring spontaneously?

Answers to these questions differ in different We-Spaces, as one would expect. In the continuous improvement space, the machine aspect of new technology is often glorified by way of a storyline in which digitization is praised as "fantastic," "preparing the future," and "cutting edge." This thoughtless ideology is part of a broader storyline in which employees who operate from an "instrumental" or "other-dependent" maturity perspective are likely to embrace uncritically, since they define themselves by others' expectations and therefore see technology as guiding, if not directing, human action. The perspective they adopt in no way addresses the issue of how humans can coevolve together with machines and thus represent the lowest level of thinking about technology. In our experience, an undeveloped perspective on the human–machine relationship leads to the suboptimal use of resources, disruptions in the value chain, and waste of human capital. The notion of a humane organization is meaningless at this level of work.

As we will show below, at higher levels of adult development, the human–machine relationship is seen from a much broader as well as deeper perspective.

The first question—**who** is thinking when humans use mind-extending technologies?—needs to be answered both from a social-emotional and cognitive vantage point since the human identity it points to, the self that does the thinking, is a thoroughly holistic issue. Given that thinking uses emotion as a pointer to what is relevant to an individual, thus as a source of insight as well as the valuation, the "who" that is thinking is developmentally determined by maturity level. Empirical findings tell us that while emotion is a "fast" system, "thinking" is a slow one, both in the sense that it "comes second" in real time and, more importantly, that it undergoes a long development over the life span. From this vantage point, cognitive development is not truly faster but slower than emotional meaning-making. In fact, "maturity" entails an equilibrium of both emotional and cognitive sources of thinking as well as of feeling which is a highly complex transformational achievement often possible only in late adulthood but not in one's work life. As a result, the "who" of thinking in the continuous improvement space (in which most adults work) is qualitatively starkly different from the "who" in the value stream or business modeling domains.

To give an example, the same platform meant to make meetings more efficient will be used very differently in the three We-Spaces we distinguish. The reason for this lies in the different positions toward the real world that template users take. Since most individuals working in the continuous improvement space make meaning of the real world at the instrumental and other-dependent levels, their natural response to templates is one of unreflective use, whether for the sake of controlling others (less adept at using technology) or as a way of reinforcing their group membership by which they define themselves as "I." The ill-considered use of Slack, for example, leads to the creation of unconnected files in which a group of users quickly loses its way.

The situation looks different in the second We-Space in which value stream redirection is topical. In this We-Space, we are dealing with teams composed of individuals that are more or less advanced in the progression from other-dependence (where "I" really means "We") to self-authoring (where "I" means "I"). This mix of two contrasting ways of positioning oneself in and toward the real world shifts the "Who" of thinking into a zone of ceaseless conflict. Individuals resolve social tension either to the side of other-dependence (following Kegan 1982, notated as "3/4") or to the side of self-authoring (notated as "4/3"), where the first integer identifies individuals' stage. When other-dependent team members wake up to the realization that their internal voices are those of others, not their own, they make a turn toward self-authoring, so that conflicts between "me" and "other" remain but are increasingly resolved in terms of self-authoring (notated as "4"). This means, for example, that decisions are made more on the basis of shared principles deriving from authentic value systems and less on the basis of consensus between other-dependent points of view stuck in an undifferentiated "We."

Where meeting platforms such as Slack are used in this We-Space, pieces of information are, in addition, seen in a more holistic frame of reference. The file structures of Slack reflect essential building blocks, dimensions, and interaction processes associated with this We-Space. They are set up in such a way that topics can be related to each other in a structured manner. As a result, fields of tension are more easily identified and become negotiable. Orchestrating discussions about central points of tension is also more easily accomplished. By making transparent how concepts used in a team influence its members' specific accountabilities, individuals are able to improve their contribution to the team.

The *Who* of thinking becomes even more free from other dependence, thus intrusion of dictates from templates claiming to promote thought and efficiency, when we move to the domain of business model transformation. In the business model We-Space, where the focus lies on strategically connecting concepts of central importance in different dimensions of the business model, a platform needs to support real-time conversations centered around strategic concepts that a discussion can move from one domain to another. The Nureva Span workplace software, for instance, allows for visualized movements-in-thought that enhance such discussions in real time. As a result, individuals active in this dialogue space, while conflicted between a self-authoring ("4/5") and self-aware way of meaning-making ("5/4"), have gained enough depth and independence of thinking that mere logical-analytical constraints built into templates have less of an impact. Individuals on this level of work complexity lead conversations of a much higher quality than we witness in the continuous improvement and value stream domains. They do so on account of radically different "world views" (implied by their stage of adult development), compared to their lower-level colleagues.

As shown above, the "Who" of thinking shifts according to levels of adult development.

## 8.4 Considering the Instrumentalist: Humanist Dichotomy from a Developmental Point of View

We have shown in previous chapters that collaborative intelligence—seen as a broad human capability instead of just some type of competence—is not without its own pathologies. These pathologies are intrinsic, not extrinsic, to human work since the latter easily becomes (1) routinized or even (2) mechanized *on account of human thinking itself*. This negative potential, if not counter-acted easily leads individuals to disengage with their own movements-in-thought. The individual then becomes estranged from himself or herself, by readily engaging with available forms of mechanization and automation, especially since present-day apps on their own do nothing to support the unfolding of human potential by boosting internal dialogue.

By contrast, we found empirically that in the continuous improvement We-Space, which comprises the majority of individuals delivering work, team activity is characterized by the pervasive use of templates that tendentially short-circuit complex thinking and thereby exacerbate the lack of maturity that is characteristic of a team at this level of work complexity.

Several authors (Gabriels 2016; Davenport 2018; Frischmann and Selinger 2018) point to the need for considering the downsides of the blind belief in human-made data and evidence-based analysis. In present organizational cultures, the premise is that what counts is what can be measured with reliable empirical methods. All too often, one forgets that mindsets, mental models, political beliefs, or worldviews determine the choice of these methods, the initial questions these methods foster, and what in light of them appears as apt to measure. One easily forgets that value-free empirical methods are fiction. This also applies to the range of technological applications. In short, it is essential to create mental spaces in which the conventional ideas and theories associated with engineered determinism can be challenged.

The notions here coming into play regarding the issue that the English term "development" has two entirely different meanings. The first, "agentic" one, is expressed by saying "we are developing this team," while the second, "ontic" (natural) one, is stated by saying "this team is adult-developmentally underdeveloped (for the We-Space it is in)." The first statement makes the illusory assumption that individuals are in control of their own adult development and can be "helped" by human resources and coaching to mature in their work, while the second, empirically correct one, states that individuals are subject to, rather than in control of, their own development—"agentic" interventions in the form of training programs and coaching notwithstanding. As a result, the quality of "collaborative intelligence" is a function of both ontic and agentic strands of "development." Behavioral interventions, supported by apps in particular, may have little of an impact on individuals' ability to collaborate.

What further contributes to the fragility of the (ontic-)developmental source of collaborative intelligence regards cognitive development in particular. The quality of thinking that guarantees collaborative intelligence is simply not available at the level of formal logical thinking but is a matter of complex (dialectical) thinking which itself is inseparable from social-emotional maturity. Since ontic development is known to progress in "stages," "human resources" (and thus delivery of human work) are *developmentally stratified* and differ by maturity level from individual to individual. Whether such resources become corporate assets or not, they comprise capabilities whose potential to be "schooled" is limited to what is, at any point in time, *developmentally possible* for individuals, and nothing more.

A further entailment of the adult-developmental sourcing of human resources is that while it is not organizations' mandate, to facilitate employees' development to maturity, organizations do themselves an awful lot of good if they actually set up the corporate asset called "human resources" in such a way that individual maturity becomes a focal point and accomplishment of corporate culture.

The reason for this is that the professional role individuals assume in an organization, whether the latter is hierarchically organized or not, is a reliable asset only to the extent that the individual in a specific role is mature. *Maturity* refers to acting from a unique and autonomous value system, something developmental theory refers to as assuming a "self-authoring stance" on the one hand and demonstrating the fluidity of thinking on the other. It is only when positioned in such a stance and viewing the real world accordingly, that an individual can develop both a holistic grasp of corporate culture and, at the same time, negotiate its requirements within oneself in terms of his or her personal value system.

It is only from a self-authoring position that one can act as if one were free. We can predict that an individual operating from a self-authoring stance is highly likely to show critical thinking in dealing with digital systems; moreover, he or she will be guided by an authentic (rather than other-dependent) value system relative to his or her role identity. In this developmental position, an individual can thoughtfully connect intentions and actions; developmentally sourced intentions become behavioral choices. The espoused theory is replaced by an awareness of theory-in-use (Argyris 1993).

These deliberations lead us to the question: whether a drastically and relentlessly engineered environment decreases the space for people to invoke their freedom. We arrive at the hypothesis that aiding people to move to self-authoring has become one of the most critical functions of directing organizational human resources (Kegan and Lahey 2009). On account of our research findings from developmental assessment, we have come to believe that taking the developmental roots of human resources seriously can dramatically reshape discussions about the dichotomy and possible equilibrium between "humanist" and "instrumentalist" contributions to work delivery. Such findings also lend a decisively different meaning to the term "humane," in contrast to "robotic," organizations than can be expected from a rationalistic and behavioristic mindset.

For one thing, since humans live in unceasing transformation as to understanding and experiencing the real world and themselves as a part of it, the term "humane" remains incomplete when not taking humans' development over their life span fully into account. Adult development centrally points to the unfolding of human *potential*, not to any status quo, and this *potential capability* needs to be focused on, assessed, and promoted in organizations. This can best be done by keeping in mind that adult development occurs "in stages" social-emotionally, and "in phases" cognitively, and that these two strands of adult development are not parallel but rather intricately interwoven in a way still largely unknown.

Secondly, a focus on humans' *potential capabilities*—rather than on current capabilities and present behavior alone—forces a reconception of the human–machine dichotomy deriving from Taylorism. As the success of Taylorism shows, humans are quite capable of turning themselves into machines, by merely being either forced to or consciously decide to adopt routinized thinking and behavior (which are closely linked). While in times when organizational hierarchies were unquestioned and reigned supreme, to turn oneself into an automaton was a fêted human achievement and amply rewarded—as soon as "agility" becomes a central organizational issue, the metamorphosis of humans into machines ceases to be a corporate asset. Rather, it becomes the greatest hindrance to self-organization one could invent.

From this vantage point, one should take seriously the likelihood that the use of template-based routines cuts down on the flexibility of thinking and behavior needed to achieve individual excellence and collaborative intelligence in teams. As we have shown, wherever routinized practice encroaches upon more complex We-Spaces such as those in which rethinking value streams and new business models are topical, organizations risk losing their competitive edge and diminishing their survival potential.

## 8.5 Limits of Present Machine Capabilities

We have seen that answers to the first question regarding machine–human interactions, above—*Who* is thinking when humans use mind-extending technologies?—is a matter of the level of adult development, both social-emotionally and cognitively speaking. When we move to the second question above: *what types of thinking* do humans and apps do each of them, and how transparent to human minds being extended are the different forms of thought involved?—we need to look at the current limits of the reasoning and dialogicality that digital systems are capable of. ("Dialogicality" is the ability of mind-extending apps to prompt reflection and thereby to open up users' internal dialogue.)

In most general terms, the crucial limit of present machine capabilities is their inability to produce or understand mental *transformations*. Computers—in human terms "logical"—capabilities excel at capturing data contexts, external relationships between data and concepts, and lead to instantiating information processes. Dramatic *transformations* as found in adult development over the lifespan and capabilities such as complex human thinking are presently, and perhaps forever, beyond their reach. This is so since logical reasoning does not allow any A to become non-A without the latter being thrown away as "false" (rather than integrated into A), which is the crux of complex identity transformation. Also, digital systems have not shown that they can promote the kind of equilibrium between emotional and cognitive capabilities that characterize human maturity, however late an achievement that equilibrium in humans may be.

While *transformations* embody changes, they are not identical to changes. Rather, they reside on a metalevel relative to changes since they entail a telos, although not always a known or even discernible one and often a telos that itself morphs into another one while setting the direction of events (Bhaskar et al. 2016).

Transformations are expressions of open systems whose identity is maintained principally by way of constantly changing themselves, as seen in human life. Transformations are not data but purpose, telos driven. They "trans-form" an entity by triggering intrinsically interlinked processes, redefining structural relationships, and embedding one context in another. Significantly one context may shrink and then morph into another context altogether. These characteristics derive from a logic other than, and more complex than, mathematical or formal logic, which is presently beyond the reach of linear, data-based algorithms, and is outlined in DTF, the Dialectical Thought Form Framework (Laske 2008).

For instance, it seems to be a human possibility to shift the relationship between social-emotional and cognitive maturation processes. The fact that at a specific point in one's life, one is more social-emotionally than cognitively developed does not foreclose the possibility that the relationship between these two developmental strands might at some point in life be reversed. Any open adaptive system is capable of such reversals except for digital systems. Triggered by life experiences, a person may indeed become "more cognitively developed" than he or she has previously been, thereby subordinating his or her level of social-emotional to cognitive development, for instance, due to hardship.

On the side of algorithms, such dramatic, life-changing transformations simply have not been found or produced. While present apps surpass humans in speed and accuracy of logical deduction and inferencing, as well as the thoroughness of data analysis, they are not (yet) "dialogically savvy" as humans are who dialogue with themselves when thinking, nor are they organisms that can adjust their abilities to external influences whose interpretation, based on "reflection," redefines their course. At this point, digital systems fail to anticipate, or even mimic, their users' movements-in-thought, although they may be able to predict (guess) them under trivial circumstances based on large arrays of data.

In light of these considerations, how could one forge a concept of "humane organization" that symbiotically comprises both human and machine capabilities?

Various deliberations on this topic are as follows:

1. In highly developed teams, introducing app-based intelligence at present risks downgrading existing levels of thought fluidity and thus of collaborative intelligence as well.
2. The symbiosis of algorithmic and human intelligence does not primarily concern the "form" of apps, but the options they offer for their holistic use in real time. (e.g., app-based developmental assessment that triggers heretofore unavailable app capacities such as cognitive and motivational prompts.)
3. Differentiating app functionality in terms of its users' adult-developmental level requires assessing the present social-emotional and cognitive profile of team members' functioning in specific We-Spaces.
4. Among the two structural assessments best suited to a developmental appraisal of teams, cognitive-developmental data sheds the brightest light on how intelligent apps need to be (re-)configured to increase team members' complexity of thinking.
5. Producing adult-developmental assessment findings and using them to improve app functioning short- and long-term should be part of an app's conception, rather than an after-thought.
6. Adult-developmental screening of app users equally benefits users of templates not in the form of apps, but existing in the form of management tools.

As our own recent app-building work has shown, using both social-emotional and cognitive data about app users, *elicited by the app itself*, is highly productive in the process of configuring an app's intelligence. Such work is critical of the assumption that the efficiency and productivity of app users are independent of stages and phases of adult development at which such users presently function.

## 8.6 Engineered Determinism: A Suboptimal Symbiosis of Human and Machine Intelligence

*Engineered determinism* as a design philosophy leads to a type of system design that optimizes convenience, maximizes efficiency, and minimizes transaction costs—as well as reflective deliberation. In our view, this type of design is put into practice at great cost, in that it may lead to obstructing and/or slowing down adults' unceasing (ontic) development. Behavioristic (agentic) notions of "developing people" take no account of the intrinsic development people are naturally subject to, and either disregard or distort individuals' adult-developmental resources. In addition, business software engineers are designing counter-productive apps due to neglecting 45 years of adult-developmental research.

By necessity, system design for human thriving is critical of engineered determinism, especially regarding the following three issues:

1. The importance of play
2. The need for semantic discontinuity
3. Imperatives of value-sensitive design

### 8.6.1 The Importance of Play

Ever since Friedrich Schiller's text on the *Aesthetic Education of Man* (1794), play has been seen as standing at the intersection of the workings of humans' sensual and moral nature, as well as having been considered a core ingredient of human freedom. In *Configuring the Networked Self*, Cohen (2012) renews this tradition by making a case "for a more comprehensive, structural understanding of the ways that the information environment can foster, or undermine, capabilities for human flourishing." She examines everyday practices of human beings situated within techno-social environments, the importance of "play" for human development and self-determination, and the role of legal and technical architectures in mediating everyday practices and play.

According to Cohen, "Social scientists who study play have concluded that its developmental functions extend into adulthood and remain centrally implicated in the process by which individuals orient themselves to the world. Particularly relevant to the domains with which this book is concerned are playing with objects and narratives, which locates the individual concerning material and intellectual culture and play with conceptions of empathy and morality, which enables individuals to form and pursue conceptions of the good. Play is both the keystone of individual moral and intellectual development and a mode of world-making, a pathway by which transformative innovation and synthetic understanding emerge. It is neither inherently frivolous nor essentially single-minded, but rather a process of open-ended encounter with self and world."

Kinds of play form a critical ingredient of our everyday lives as human beings situated within a technosocial environment. The freedom to play is essential to our development and exercise of capabilities; it stands against and requires freedom from engineered determinism.

### 8.6.2 The Need for Semantic Discontinuity

Cohen advances three principles that she proposes should inform the design of legal and technical architectures: (1) access to knowledge, (2) operational transparency, and (3) semantic discontinuity. Of these three principles, we would emphasize the third one because it relates to our call for supporting human development and the need for a countervailing design of work. In Cohen's words, "Semantic discontinuity refers to gaps and inconsistencies within systems of meaning, and to a resulting interstitial complexity that leaves room for the play of everyday practice. In an increasingly networked information society, maintaining those gaps requires interventions designed to counterbalance the forces that seek to close them."

Though admittedly, the notion of semantic discontinuity is somewhat opaque, this powerful concept is worth unpacking. Semantic discontinuity could be seen as a design principle for engineering technosocial systems affording its user different kinds of freedom. The central idea is that instead of striving for unremittingly "closed" systems characterized by nothing but efficiency, technosocial engineers should insert "gaps and inconsistencies into and between related systems. Despite pressure from an efficiency expert, risk manager, and other optimizers, we should sometimes sustain rather than close these gaps and inconsistencies."

Despite engineers' attempts to minimize imperfections, all man-build systems are imperfect by nature. "Perfection" is in the eye of the beholder. Often the flaws in our technosocial systems afford a room to play. Look, for example, at fitness tracking tools. The imperfections in the Fitbit data collection afforded students to play and thereby develop basic capabilities. Gaps in data collection leave open the possibilities of inconsistencies in the meaning of fitness data recorded and reported, and this sustains a higher degree of complexity in the intervening "space" between students, teachers, and third parties.

While much of the continuous improvement space is tightly closed off from human creativity, in the value stream We-Space, increasing opportunities for countering engineered determinism arise. One of them is to engineer levels of freedom into the way systems are designed. Safeguarding degrees of freedom is synonymous with creating transparency around the function of different stakeholders in the development of human–machine interactions. For example, what is the freedom of network owners, cloud providers, system architects, developers, and possible groups of end users? Insights that enhance transparency about levels of freedom can beneficially feed the debate about how humans relate to systems.

### 8.6.3 Value-Sensitive Design

Value-sensitive design is a method of technological design in which ethical values are protected by including them in the design process and building them into technology. Designing human–machine interactions rest on ethical principles that protect values such as privacy, justice, welfare, personal development, and autonomy. If technological progress is to be linked to ethical progress, reflecting on harm reduction and pursuing desirable improvements must be an integral part of the design.

The idea of value-sensitive design acknowledges that technology is not value-neutral and is always embedded in a social context. Such design transcends instrumental values, such as user efficiency, safety, reliability, and user-friendliness, being equally responsive to fundamental human values, such as justice, welfare, and autonomy. Value-sensitive design starts from the proposition that human values are essential in and by themselves, regardless of the individual, specific group, or company they are associated with. However, universal human values are, they are perceived and acted upon differently by people at different developmental levels and living in different cultures.

A pragmatic issue related to ethical design, as well as the unfolding of adult-developmental potential through apps, is that of net neutrality, which has to do with degrees of freedom of broadband owners to prioritize internet traffic based on user identities. Users themselves must be able to decide what to do with the intellectual and relational capabilities offered by the Internet. Overall, distinguishing levels of freedom in the design of systems is important since it leads to more thoughtfulness and in-depth debate, including research, on how to deal with informed citizens' questions.

In a humane organization (as we understand it), the value-sensitive design would be a central focus especially in the business model We-Space where highly different expertise and stakeholders—including ethical professionals, lawyers, engineers, cryptographers, ICT employees, and end users—work closely together. Their goal is to produce a design in which as many people as possible have a direct and indirect interest: education, industry, public life, privacy, and work environments. In such an approach to design, consideration is given to which values are prominent in a specific design, who has a foremost interest in it, and how the number of stakeholders benefitting from the design can be further increased.

## 8.7 Contours of a Humane Organization

### 8.7.1 Open Questions

Digital technologies are increasingly used to facilitate employee connectivity, structure project operations, make decisions, and develop relationships with customers and suppliers. The range of applications supporting the evolution toward self-direction is also growing. Digital support applications are now available in each of the quadrants in our overview of practices (see Chap. 1). The best-known at present are Slack, Facebook, and Microsoft's SharePoint, which focus on facilitating internal communication and collaboration. Others, such as Holaspirit, offer a set of templates that promise to make it easier to make agreements on role-fulfillment, project management, and meeting approaches.

Paradoxically, the architecture of these tools assumes that employees are self-authoring and, at the same time, that a set of principles, protocols, agreements, and pertinent infrastructure is required to steer coordination and cooperation in the right direction, as would be more appropriate for employees functioning at an other-dependent level of development. Often, these tools are simply digital versions of analog templates regarding which it is unknown how employees functioning from different development levels interpret them in real time. Nor is there a sufficient understanding of the efficiency and effectiveness logic embedded in templates. In addition, it is not unusual that a hierarchical logic creeps back into how systems are used in an instrumental and other-dependent culture.

These issues do not gain any clarity when difficulties in using digital technologies are attributed to insufficiently developed behavioral "skills" with no attention paid to the developmental resources that underlie the exercise of skills. Kane (2019) gives a pertinent example of such thinking when he speaks of an absence of "digital maturity," defined by him as "aligning an organization's people, culture, structure, and tasks to compete effectively by taking advantage of opportunities enabled by technological infrastructure, both inside and outside the organization."

According to Kane, building "digital maturity" (a handy label) is a strictly behavioral process of skill development, to enable a company to continuously adapt to changing environments by constantly realigning its employees, culture, tasks, and structure. He never stops to inquire what all of these abstractions mean for work in real time, given that employees work from an internal dialogue with themselves. The different components of his organizational model are, as it were, mechanical cogs that require continuous fine-tuning, so that ambiguity is reduced as much as possible to achieve maximum effectiveness and efficiency in interactions. In Kahn's argumentation, engineered determinism prevails, heaping abstractions upon abstractions. For him, digital collaboration applications determine resources and objectives, paths and destinations, as well as the structures on which collaboration is built (whatever that may be).

In short, engineered determinism dominates both the design of so-called intelligence systems and the remedies being created for making such systems more effective in collaborative work. Once again, the blind are leading the blind.

### 8.7.2 Six Principles of Intelligent System Design

What might be alternatives to *engineered determinism* in designing artificially intelligent systems that enhance human flourishing? Our answers to this question are based on arguments put forward throughout this book. We summarize these ideas by formulating six principles, all of them focus on the issue of creating opportunities for high-quality team dialogue and, by extension, vertical development in organizations. We formulate these principles as imperative cultural attitudes that either support or bring to life value-sensitive designs:

1. Adopt a stance of vulnerability and imperfection as a standard of self-development.
2. In tools, model, templates, and habits, pay attention to gaps.
3. Share your internal dialogue in communication with others.
4. Compose teams in such a way that they embody an "upward" dynamics.
5. Replace control functions by critical facilitation.
6. Make the role of "sense-making officer" an integral part of every manager's mandate.

The six principles above sketch a rough contour of what we call a "humane organization." Such an organization is characterized by a culture in which the development of reflective practice is centrally supported by every manager's function as a "sense-making officer." Reflective practice entails that every contributor is encouraged and enabled, to reflect on the gap between "how humans think" relative to "how the real world works." Working from that point of view, building collaborative intelligence becomes feasible when grounded in collective learning.

#### 8.7.2.1 Adopt a Stance of Vulnerability and Imperfection as a Standard of Self-Development

Logical-analytical thinking is, by nature, geared to a kind of illusory perfection and denies both the thinker's and the real world's fragility and complexity. It is, therefore, an insufficient guide to achieving true perfection. Combined with a view of language as only describing, rather than also creating, reality, it is a recipe for misconstruing how the real world works and turning it into a VUCA world. Thinking purely logically and monologically, the illusion is created that "everybody understands" what I am saying, which, from a dialogical perspective, is not cogent since everyone listening to me follows his or her developmentally sourced interpretation.

Paying attention to insufficiencies in tools one works with requires more than logical thinking, too, since it presupposes a holistic perception of how one's tools work, and thus is nearly impossible to achieve based on logical thinking alone. One needs to become aware that viewing the real world from a vantage point of control, rather than a multidimensional viewpoint such as laid out in DTF, is a sure bet to miss how reality works (Bhaskar et al. 2016). One would think that the developmental diversity of teams would provide a natural incitement for adopting a broad variety of world views, but the uniformity of our educational system, focused on "competences," makes that an illusion.

For this reason, one can imagine that safeguarding a "critical facilitation" point of view might be served by amplifying each manager's role identity by putting him or her in charge of broader ways of sense-making. He or she could be referred to as a "sense-making officer." His or her task would be to find stimulating opportunities for employees to become aware of their present way of interpreting not only the environment they work in but also the structure of the tools they work with. This book could become a guide for developing organizational programs aiming to bring that about (which would be the best use of the book we could imagine).

#### 8.7.2.2 In Tools, Model, Templates, and Habits, Pay Attention to Gaps

Since templates imported from the outside—whether models, theories, platforms—strongly influence what and how people think, it is vital to becoming aware of the limitations associated with the logical-analytical structure of all presently produced templates. To understand such limitations, the following guiding questions (derived from the four moments of dialectic in DTF) should be entertained:

1. Which contexts, dimensions, or variables, implicitly or explicitly, are essential parts of a template?
2. What are the different notions of "change" employed in using a template, and what are the associated time horizons within which organizationally meaningful changes are seen to arise by way of using a model?
3. What are the relationships between the dimensions and concepts assumed or neglected by a template?
4. How can areas of tension and conflict associated with using a template become grounds of reflection for strengthening collaboration?

In our estimation, answering questions like the above cannot be accomplished through best practices, or any preprogrammed or control-based debate formats. Rather, as expressed by the six principles above, corporate cultures must be shaped such as to encourage employees to take responsibility for their work, as well as for building bridges between each other without a fixation on "controlling" rather than "understanding" things. This imperative entails developing trust in each others' capabilities, as well as knowing something about colleagues' motivation in delivering work.

#### 8.7.2.3 Share Your Internal Dialogue in External Communications

Sharing one's internal dialogue—what one is thinking in this very moment—in exchange with others is of outstanding importance in trying to achieve such a work attitude. Following this principle entails making it an organizational norm to share opinions about ideas (rather than people) and to have face-to-face discussions with colleagues (rather than replacing them by email or texting). Unless one can learn not to consider criticism as a personal attack, not much of such a culture is in place.

#### 8.7.2.4 Compose Teams in Such a Way that They Embody an "Upward" Dynamics

Organizing teams in such a way that they embody what we have referred to as an "upward" developmental tendency is a matter of how teams are put together in the first place. Of overriding importance is not to leave team composition to deliberations of mere "competences," given that these by themselves create fiefdoms of ego-centrism when they are not considered against experts' adult-developmental level. As a rule, the mix of developmental levels of team members should be such that it is above the center of gravity required for enabling the team to meet its mandate. One way to achieve this is to mandate developmental assessment through semistructured interviews of team members, for the sake of getting a "big picture" of developmental levels present in a team.

More informally and behaviorally, putting in place "upward" directed teams entails that team members clarify for themselves what are the tasks which for them create an opportunity of achieving added-value optimally. In addition, employees should have an awareness of the specific We-Space they feel they belong in, and what it entails for them to assume a specific role in that space. "Organizing teams upwards" also implies that team members are free to choose roles requiring wide-scoped perspective-taking, so that the team is exposed to an optimal number of divergent perspectives transcending mere expertises.

#### 8.7.2.5 Replace Control Functions by Critical Facilitation

This principle concerns reporting relationships in which, traditionally, the emphasis is one-sidedly put on controlling. By contrast, in what we call a *humane organization*, supervisory roles are defined as critical facilitator, not control, functions. This reconception of vertical roles primarily serves to promote self-organization which does not happen by the command from above but is self-generated according to the level of adult maturity.

A *critical facilitator* is a person who works based on his or her internal dialogue sourced by intense listening to self and others. Internally, her mandate is to be steadily aware of her own movements-in-thought in response to that of team members. Externally, her task is to increase the complexity of a team's thinking by critically questioning team members, transcending their present perspectives, and keeping differences and tensions on the table productively for as long as possible—all to guide a group to arrive at more and more nuanced choices based on nuanced world views. A facilitator like that is a "critical" thinker to the extent that he or she is capable of detachment from ego-centric attitudes, a schooled "interviewer" of team members who works as an "observer" of others' movements-in-thought, rather than maintaining a control perspective or fixating on team members "behavior." He or she considers himself or herself an integral part of the organizational system, pays attention to how participants develop role identity, facilitates development toward maturity, and prevents downwardly divided team dynamics. To be able to do so, he or she must be a person with a high level of self-awareness about his or her frame of reference.

#### 8.7.2.6 Make the Role of "Sense-Making Officer" an Integral Part of Every Manager's Mandate

With this last principle, we want to draw attention to a role that does not currently exist in organizations but is urgently needed. It is a role that one can interweave with any senior management function. This role concerns monitoring the quality of the dialogues discussed in this book that together constitute "organizational work": the dialogue on taking ownership of one's role, ensuring coherence in action, creating common ground for collaboration, developing growth tasks for employees (while coaching double listening), and calibrating the quality of dialogue in a wide variety of meetings.

This role must ensure that in each dialogue space, the quality of discussions gradually improves, leading to more integrative decision-making and growth, both for individual employees, teams, and the organization as a whole. The various levers we have described in the different chapters of this book can be the first source of inspiration for bringing this about.

### 8.7.3 Positive and Negative Freedoms in Different We-Spaces

The two notions of freedom introduced in this chapter—positive and negative freedom—find their empirical justification in findings of adult-developmental research that show that every adult strives to leave his or her dependency on others behind, thus becoming self-authoring. According to empirical findings, this transition to self-authoring is achieved by no more than 25% of the population, depending on its national culture (Cook-Greuter 1999). This transition is made in human consciousness when an individual "realizes" that his or her authentic voice is different from, and may be in contrast to, the internal voices of others, thereby detaching from other-dependence. To abide by this experience—which dramatically changes an individual's world view forever, leaving no option to go back to other-dependence—takes courage since it entails that the individual might be shunned by others, or even killed.

A self-authorer is thus a person who has developed an authentic "theory of self" grounded in a unique value system that requires making decisions based on one's own (rather than others') values, and doing so even at the risk of losing others' support or being abandoned by them. While a self-authorer is rarely aware of the limitations of his or her own value system (that become clear only in transitioning to a self-aware position), his or her system of values makes for acting as a decision-maker able to take responsibility for his or her mistakes and deficiencies, and as being aware of a team's total mandate and integral function in an organization, as is the hallmark of an upwardly directed team.

Striving to act according to one's own value system is full of difficulties. Not only are there intrinsic limitations of doing so, there are also real-world pressures and constraints that make the journey to self-authoring psychologically as well as developmentally tricky and can even lead to abandoning the journey for reasons of convenience and comfort. It is these pressures and constraints that we subsume under the paradoxical notion of "negative freedom."

For instance, in previous chapters, we showed Robert to follow conflicted commitments, some of them deriving from his incipient self-authored value system while others swayed him to act in an other-dependent way, mainly for the sake of strengthening his social reputation (thus complying with what he assumed to be others' expectations of him). Robert lost his ability to distinguish between his espoused theory and this theory-in-use (Argyris and Schon 1978). At any moment of his life, it is therefore unclear, to himself as well as others, whether he will make decisions in tune with other-dependence (3/4) or self-authoring (4/3→4). His negative freedom is rooted in his person, not just in the environment he is acting in. There are no purely behavioral interventions (e.g., learnings) able to restore his positive freedom. If Robert's social environment exacerbates this situation, he may find it hard or impossible to develop a fully self-authored value system (4) and may have to move to a different job and environment to do so. Negative freedom thus is both intrinsic to a person as well as deriving from the organizational environment a person chooses to be in.

When, to simplify matters, we restrict the meaning of negative freedom to constraints imposed by the environment (seen as something *interpreted* by individual employees rather than something absolute), the form taken by the constraints in question is different in different We-Spaces. However, every We-Space, even the business model one, is associated with a set of constraints that may hinder a team member from achieving a self-authoring stance.

We-Spaces are mental spaces tied to the level of consciousness which underlies behavior. Their differences are "epistemological," i.e., are characterized by levels of self-awareness. Accordingly, a member of the continuous improvement space is more likely, on account of his adult-developmental level but also the kind of work he or she does, to use templates and digital systems more unreflectively than a team member in the value stream or transformation of business model space. Team members' negative freedom is thus built into the environment in which he or she works. His or her journey to self-authoring is full of obstacles that members of a more highly developed team would not encounter, both for internal and external reasons.

By contrast, a member of a team focusing on business model transformation has most likely reached not only the self-authoring level but also a commensurate level of cognitive maturity (fluidity of thinking). As a result, his emotional and cognitive "equipment" much less easily lends itself to supporting unreflective uses of digital systems, as is the rule in the continuous improvement space. In light of this contrast, we can speak of a tendency toward greater positive than negative freedom as we approach business transformation teams.

Evidently, positive and negative freedoms in the sense here defined stand in a complex relationship with each other on each level of self-development as well as employee deployment. As a consequence, the meaning of the six principles formulated in Sect. 8.7.2 as guiding principles for developing a "humane organization" is starkly different in each of the We-Space we distinguish. The interpretation of these principles is likely to shift considerably as positive freedom overtakes negative freedom in a particular We-Space over the course of adult development.

To summarize, continuous improvement We-Spaces (in which most individuals work) privilege negative, while business model transformation We-Spaces privilege positive, freedom. The shifting proportion of positive and negative freedom goes along with steady empowerment of thoughtful dialogue, compared to routinized movements-in-thought in lower We-Spaces. In tandem, the ability to hold and interpret multiple perspectives, to be aware of the "big picture" of the workflow one is embedded in, and the quality of dialogue characterizing a team—all of these aspects of work delivery are dramatically different in different We-Spaces, even disregarding different psychological profiles and role identities. In the business model space, positive freedoms tend to gain the upper hand because the team's mandate requires its members to question their own routinized vision of the future, let go of attachments and ideas not resonant with self-authoring, and in addition become aware of their present value system's limitations as they journey to a self-aware stance of meaning-making.

**Key Insights and Practice Reflections**

During our journey toward better understanding human–machine interactions in Chap. 8, we have visited a fair number of organizational practices to show the impact exerted on them by levels of adult development and their downwardly or upwardly oriented mix in teams. Compared to conventional organizational theories, our journey has been significantly different in its tenor given that we have firmly embraced empirical findings of adults' development over the life span, both of a social-emotional and cognitive nature. On account of our stance, we have been able to show that organizational research methodologies that restrict themselves to a behavioristic perspective also tend to adhere to logical-analytical schemes and templates that leave wide areas of corporate culture and transactions in darkness. We have characterized this restrictive approach to the nature of work and work delivery as rooted in remnants of Taylorism. This holding on to Tayloristic persuasions is in our view a stark hindrance both to achieving self-organization and integration of human with algorithmic intelligence.

In our view, the basic flaw in the restrictiveness of behavioristic approaches to organizational functioning is not primarily testimony to a lack of critical thinking, but rather of sensitivity for the fact that human work is embedded in human life, and an acknowledgment that human life developmentally determines the ways humans deliver work (not the other way around). For this reason, we have made short shrift of "competency models," precisely because they are Tayloristic in that they reduce broad human capabilities to "expertises" that tend to engender ego-centric fiefdoms more than create deep dialogue spaces.

The reduction of developmentally sourced human capabilities to what fits with machine- and logic-derived notions of efficiency and effectiveness is particularly unwarranted in our time because of the urgent organizational need, of integrating algorithmic intelligence into human work delivery. Aware of this need, we have undertaken it to "rehabilitate" ways of thinking of a different kind than logic-analytical reductions of human thinking permitted to emerge. Concretely, we have shown, both theoretically and practically, that human thinking is a capability under development over individuals' entire life span that increasingly transcends and transforms mere logic-analytical ways of thinking whose peak is reached early on in life when human consciousness has barely begun to mature. Calling this ability to think holistically, systemically, and transformationally *dialectical*, we have linked higher-level thinking to the ability for deep dialogue that grows with the level of both emotional and cognitive maturity. In fact, in following Laske's DTF, we have merged the meaning and practice of "dialectical" and "dialogical" thinking.

The merger of two aspects of higher-level thinking is of crucial importance for us when it comes to answering the question of what thinking is "all about." We have maintained throughout this book that human thinking by definition and unceasingly references the real world (which it constructs), and thus cannot be reduced to a play with thoughts and words inside people's heads. Instead, "thinking" pursues the truth and, at any point, requires distinguishing "how the real world works" and "how humans tend to think," thus making it a root of *critical realism* (Bhaskar et al. 2016).

The gap between how reality works and how humans think is becoming increasingly important since logic-based templates swamp organizations under the guise of "(fantastic) business software." Put in place by engineers who found it unthinkable to doubt their own logical thinking, it seems designed to let people forget that they are actually unceasingly thinking in ways beyond formal logic, being engaged in an internal dialogue that grounds their communication with others. What is neglected by software engineers is that since humans can never speak about the real world without simultaneously speaking about themselves, "dialogue" with self or other and "thinking about the real world" are essentially the same. This tenet calls for building "dialogically savvy" apps, none of which have yet been sighted.

What are the practical consequences of our conception of thinking as being simultaneously "dialectical" and "dialogical"? We would nominate as a primary consequence that kinds of work delivery that emaciate internal (and thus also external) dialogue between employees (and people generally) are pernicious for quality of teamwork and, in the long run, to organizational functioning as a whole. We would name as a second consequence that conceiving of organizational contributors as "instruments" as is the essence of Taylorism was never more mistaken and counter-productive than in the twenty-first century when humans at work are increasingly expected to "think for themselves" and "bear the burden of self-development themselves," not least to hold on to their positive freedom vis-à-vis algorithmically intelligent systems.

In light of our rehabilitation of human thinking as transformational and dialogical, rather than purely logical—which is, by nature, critical of behavioristic approaches to work delivery—we would in conclusion like to formulate some decisive insights reached by us as:

1. "Work" is based on the unfolding of developmental capabilities in the direction of different levels of adult maturity and is thus an ingredient of "composing a life," subject to the latter's development over the life span.
2. "Work delivery" is based on interpretive systems constructed by individuals that are in complete harmony with an individual's present level of adult development (or "world view"), both from a social-emotional and cognitive vantage point.
3. A "humane" organization is, consequently, a gathering of individuals of different capabilities and maturity levels that are composed of teams intrinsically (not only externally) linked to other teams, forming a network by which organizations define themselves culturally.
4. Due to the merger of discrepant levels of adult development in teams, two tendencies come into being that we have called "downwardly" and "upwardly" divided, respectively. The term "divided" refers to the relationship of team majority to minority, calibrated in terms of developmental level.
5. The structure of the developmentally sourced We-Spaces we distinguish has a mighty influence on what is habitual, possible, and unthinkable in a team. The three We-Spaces we have distinguished are characterized by dramatically different relationships between "interpersonal" and "task" process, with the outcome that only in the highest We-Space, of business model transformation, is the task process—what the team needs to get done, its mandate—safe from being subordinated to its interpersonal process. In short, "team maturity" manifests in the relationship of interpersonal to task process in teams.
6. The impact of adult-developmental levels on work delivery effectiveness and efficiency pervades all organizational practices including the board of directors.
7. Upwardly divided teams, in which a more highly developed team majority prevails over a less-developed minority, have an optimal chance to work in broad and deep dialogue spaces and therefore excel in producing propitious solutions rather than social-emotional haggling, in each of the three We-Spaces we have distinguished.
8. The time of "human resources" as a Tayloristic appendix to technology is over, since digital technologies require not only users of increasing

sophistication in their thinking but also their bonding as colleagues pursuing shared goals.

9. The blatant inefficiencies of instrumentalist notions of human–machine interaction are due to continuing Tayloristic misconceptions of what is human work, largely on account of separating "work" from "life," where life is the source of work, not the other way around.
10. The "epistemology of organizational work" found in this book is the result of 20 years of research in adult development and the application of its findings to understanding organizational functioning holistically and systemically. This discipline clarifies that, and in what way, "work" is a knowledge-based enterprise whose outcomes derive from developmentally differentiated interpretations of goals, tools, physical workspaces, and social role identities. These outcomes have a "truth value" in that they ultimately derive from organization members' understanding of the gap between "how the real world works" in contrast to "how humans think."

**Practice Reflections**

1. In your experience, what is the impact of developmentally sourced differences in interpreting work environments and role mandates on the work of teams?
2. In envisioning your own career trajectory over the life span, how closely do experiences made in doing different kinds of work match the book's description of differences of levels of adult maturity?
3. When thinking about what an organization could do for your self-development, how do you position mere competences against broader emotional and cognitive capabilities you want to strengthen in composing your life?
4. When thinking of yourself as aided in your work by algorithmic intelligence, what kinds of freedom do you envision becoming available to you that you find exciting in terms of not only work accomplishments but also personal mental growth?
5. How will you go about determining whether a particular work environment offers you the mental space to grow as a person, rather than merely delivering specific kinds of work whose accomplishment remains external to you?

# References

Amit R, Zott C (2001) Value creation in e-business. Strat Manag J 22:493–520
Anderson FH (1978) Francis Bacon: His Career and His Thought. Greenwood
Argyris C (1993) Knowledge for action: guide to overcoming barriers to organizational change. Jossey-Bass, San Francisco, CA
Argyris C, Schon DA (1978) Organizational learning: a theory of action perspective. Jossey-Bass, San Francisco, CA
Arora A (2019) Requisite agility unsymposium. https://requisiteagility.org/raunsymp/. Accessed Dec 2019
Basseches M (1978) Beyond closed-system problem solving: a study of meta-systemic aspects of mature thought. #79/8210. Dissertation, Harvard University. UMIO, Ann Arbor, MI
Basseches M (1984) Dialectic thinking and adult development. Ablex, Norwood, NJ
Beer S (1985) Diagnosing the system for organizations. Wiley, New York, NY
Bhaskar R (1993) Dialectic: The Pulse of Freedom. Routledge, London
Bhaskar R et al (2016) Metatheory for the twenty-first century. Routledge, London
Birk K (2019) The Nature of Work. Working paper
Blokdyk G (2018) Ishikawa diagram: a complete guide. 5STARCooks
Boyd G, Laske O (2018) Chapter 8. Human developmental processes as key to creating impactful leadership. In: Chatwani N (ed) Distributed leadership: the dynamics of balancing leadership and followership. Palgrave MacMillan, New York, NY
Brousseau E, Pénard T (2007) The economics of digital business models: a framework for analyzing the economics of platforms. Rev Netw Econ 6(2):81–114
Campbell A (2019) Kanban: the ultimate complete guide about agile project management with Kanban. Independently published
Clark A (2004) Natural-born cyborgs: minds, technologies, and the future of human intelligence. Oxford University Press, New York, NY
Cohen J (2012) Configuring the networked self: law, code, and the play of everyday practice. Yale University Press, New Haven, CT
Commons M (1984) Beyond formal operations. Praeger Publishers, New York, NY
Cook-Greuter S (1999) Post-autonomous ego development: a study of its nature and measurement. Dissertation, Harvard Graduate School of Education, Cambridge, MA. Bell & Howell, Ann Arbor, MI
Covey S (1989) The 7 habits of highly effective people. Simon & Schuster, London
Dalio R (2017) Principles: life and work. Simon & Schuster, New York, NY
Davenport TH (2018) The AI advantage. How to put the artificial intelligence revolution to work. MIT Press, Cambridge, MA
Davenport TH, Kibey J (2016) Only humans need apply. Harper Collins Publishers, New York, NY
Dawson-Tunik TL, Commons ML, Wilson M, Fisher KW (2005) The shape of development. Eur J Dev Psychol 2(2):163–196



J. De Visch, O. Laske, *Practices of Dynamic Collaboration*, Management for Professionals, https://doi.org/10.1007/978-3-030-42549-4

De Prins P, Leetens G, Verweire K (2018) Six batteries of change: energize your company. Lannoo Campus, Leuven

De Visch J (2010) The vertical dimension. Blueprint to align business and talent development. Connect & Transform Press, Mechelen

De Visch J (2014) Leadership: mind(s) creating value(s). Connect & Transform Press, Mechelen

De Visch J (2018) Dynamic collaboration playbook. In: 33 Ideas to strengthen self-organization and collaborative intelligence in teams. Connect & Transform Press, Mechelen

De Visch J (2019a) Re-thinking game. A powerful tool for challenging and opening minds. Connect & Transform Press, Mechelen

De Visch J (2019b) What can you do to foster your inner dialogue? A landscape of identity questions. Internal paper

De Visch J (2019c) How to teach managers to think: a testimony. https://interdevelopmentals.org/?p=6870

De Visch J, Laske O (2018) Dynamic collaboration. Strengthening self-organization and collaborative intelligence in teams. Connect & Transform/IDM Press, Mechelen

Dewar C, Doucette R (2018) Culture: 4 keys to why it matters. https://www.mckinsey.com/business-functions/organization/our-insights/the-organization-blog/culture-4-keys-to-why-it-matters

Drucker P (1967) The effective executive. Routledge, New York, NY

Felin T, Powel TT (2016) Designing organizations for dynamic capabilities. Paper submitted for California Management Review. Special Issue on Dynamic Capabilities. http://eureka.sbs.ox.ac.uk/5728/1/CMR%20paper.pdf

Finlayson G (2005) Habermas: a very short introduction. Oxford University Press, Oxford

Fischer KW (1980) A theory of cognitive development: the control and construction of hierarchies of skills. Psychol Rev 87:477–531

Frischmann BM, Selinger E (2016) Utopia?: a technologically determined world of frictionless transactions, optimized production, and maximal happiness. UCLA Law Rev 64:372–391

Frischmann BM, Selinger E (2018) Re-inventing humanity. Cambridge University Press, Cambridge, MA

Gabriels K (2016) Onlife. Hoe de digitale wereld je leven bepaalt. Lannoo, Tielt

Hawkins RE (1970) Need Press interaction as related to managerial styles among executives. Dissertation, Illinois Institute of Technology, Chicago, IL

Heidegger M (1977) The question concerning technology and other essays. Garland Publishing, New York, NY

Hirschhorn M (1988) Workplace within: psychodynamics of organizational life. MIT Press, Cambridge, MA

Hoda R, Murugesan LK (2016) Multi-level agile project management challenges: a self-organizing team perspective. J Syst Softw 117:245–257

Holbeche L (2015) The agile organization: how to build an innovative, sustainable and resilient business. Kogan Page, London

Hopkinson K (2019) Landscape of the mind - applying complexity in organisations. EMK complexity Group. http://emk-complexity.org/projects/landscape-of-the-mind.html

Horkheimer M (1947) Eclipse of reason. Martino Fine Books, Eastford, CT

Jaques E (1989) Requisite organizations. In: A total system for effective managerial organization and managerial leadership for the 21st century. Cason Hall & Co, Baltimore, MD

Jaques E, Cason K (1994) Human capability: a study of individual potential and its application. Cason Hall Publishers, Falls Church, VA

Kahneman D (2011) Thinking fast and slow. Allen Lane, London

Kane GC (2019) The technology fallacy. The MIT Press, Cambridge, MA

Kant E (1781, 2009) Critique of Pure Reason. Penguin Modern Classics, London

Karasek R (1979) Job demands, job decision latitude, and mental strain: implications for job redesign. Adm Sci Q 24(2):285–306. https://doi.org/10.2307/2392498

Keely L, Pikkel R, Quinn B, Waters H (2013) Ten types of innovation. The discipline of building breakthroughs. Wiley, Hoboken, NJ

Kegan R (1982) The evolving self. Problem and process in human development. Harvard University Press, Cambridge, MA
Kegan R, Lahey LL (2009) Immunity to change: how to overcome it and unlock the potential in yourself and your organization. Harvard Business Press, Cambridge, MA
Keith JE (2018) Where the action is: the meetings that make or break your organization. Second Rise, Portland, OR
King PM, Kitchener KS (1994) Developing reflective judgment. Jossey Bass, San Francisco, CA
Kowalkowski C, Kindström D (2014) Service innovation in product-centric firms: a multidimensional business model perspective. J Bus Ind Market 29(2):96–111
Lanier J (2018) Ten arguments for deleting your social media accounts right now. Bodley Head, London
Laske O (1999) Laske's 'transformative effects of coaching on executives' professional agendas'. https://interdevelopmentals.org/?p=6870
Laske O (2005) Measuring hidden dimensions: the art and science of fully engaging adults ('MHD volume 1'), 1st edn. IDM Press, Gloucester, MA. http://www.interdevelopmentals.org/?page_id=1974
Laske O (2008) Measuring hidden dimensions of human systems: foundations of requisite organization ('MHD volume 2'), 2nd edn. IDM Press, Glouccester, MA. http://www.interdevelopmentals.org/?page_id=1974
Laske O (2011) Measuring hidden dimensions: the art and science of fully engaging adults ('MHD volume 1'), 2nd edn. IDM Press, Gloucester, MA. http://www.interdevelopmentals.org/?page_id=1974
Laske O (2015a) Dialectical thinking for integral leaders. Integral Publishers, Tucson, AZ
Laske O (2015b) Laske's dialectical thought form framework (DTF) as a tool for creating integral collaborations: applying Bhaskar's four moments of dialectic to reshaping cognitive development as a social practice. Integr Lead Rev 11(3):72
Laske O (2017a) Measuring hidden dimensions: the art and science of fully engaging adults ('MHD volume 1'), 3rd edn. IDM Press, Gloucester, MA. http://www.interdevelopmentals.org/?page_id=1974
Laske O (2017b) Improving management by design: novel tools for expanding and deepening the business model design space. https://interdevelopmentals.org/?p=5026
Laske O (2017c) In: Snow A (ed) DTFM: dialectical thought form manual, 1st edn. http://www.interdevelopmentals.org/?page_id=1974
Laske O (2018a) The vurdelja-laske dialectical thought form workbook. https://interdevelopmentals.org/?p=6621
Laske O (2018b) A greatly delayed departure: notions of competence are finally fading since they are seen as pernicious in a distributed-leadership environment. https://interdevelopmentals.org/?p=6542
Laske O (2018c) Early warnings that competence models would not sustain survival or innovation. https://interdevelopmentals.org/?p=6528
Laske O (2018d) How teams works: a straightforward developmental hypothesis. https://interdevelopmentals.org/?page_id=4266
Laske O (2018e) Suggestions for a pedagogy of dialectical thinking. https://interdevelopmentals.org/?p=6494
Laske O (2018f) A new paradigm of team work: engaging the power of dialogue. https://interdevelopmentals.org/?p=6422
Laske O (2018g) On the practice of cognitive interviewing, cognitive coaching, and text analysis. https://interdevelopmentals.org/?p=5680
Laske O (2018h) Collaborative intelligence in teams: the view from CDF. https://interdevelopmentals.org/?p=5660 (Collection of papers)
Laske O (2018i) Developmental coaching: a curtailed discipline squashed by behaviorism. https://interdevelopmentals.org/?p=5186
Laske O (2018j) Can coaches nurture and increase team maturity? https://interdevelopmentals.org/?p=5176

Laske O (2018k) What coaches should know about their clients. https://interdevelopmentals.org/?p=5166
Laske O (2019a) Cognitive coaching as a tool for building enabling environments in distributed-leadership organizations: an introduction to the dialectical thought form framework (DTF). https://interdevelopmentals.org/?p=7026
Laske O (2019b) Grundlagen potenzial-orientierter Unternehmen: Einleitung in Dialektisches Denken in Organisationen. https://interdevelopmentals.org/?p=7033
Laske O (2019c) A social-emotional team typology for self-organizing organizations. https://interdevelopmentals.org/?p=7011
Laske O (2019d) An artificially intelligent CDF coach: considerations regarding app-based executive coaching. https://interdevelopmentals.org/?p=6930
Laske O (2019e) Exploring movements-in-thought: the experiential and historical roots of qualitative data acquisition in the constructive developmental framework. https://interdevelopmentals.org/?p=6919
Laske O (2019f) On the difficulty of letting thinking 'appear'. https://interdevelopmentals.org/?p=6837
Laske O (2019g) Balancing dialogue and text analysis in teaching dialectical thinking. https://interdevelopmentals.org/?p=6829
Laske O (2019h) Making a cognitive case study following the IDM cohort method. https://interdevelopmentals.org/?p=6819
Laske O (2019i) Is there a bridge between social-emotional and cognitive capability? https://interdevelopmentals.org/?p=6798
Laske O (2019j) Frankfurt school hauptseminar teachings from the perspective of laske's dialectical thought form framework (DTF). https://interdevelopmentals.org/?p=6763
Laske O (2019k) Barriers to using CDF. https://interdevelopmentals.org/?p=6744
Mayo E (1933) The human problems of an industrial civilization. Routledge, New York, NY
Mc Gregor D (1960) The human side of enterprise. McGraw-Hill Companies Inc, New York, NY
McMorland J (2005) Are you big enough for your job? Is your job big enough for you? Exploring levels of work in organizations. Univ Auckl Bus Rev 7(2):75–83
Middleton-Keller E (2011) Identifying the multi-dimensional problem-space & co-creating an enabling environment. In: Andrew T, Richardson KA (eds) Moving forward with complexity. Emergent Publications, Litchfield Park, AZ
Osterwalder A, Pigneur Y (2010) Business model generation: a handbook for visionaries, game changers, and challengers. John Wiley, Hoboken, NJ
Porter M (1980) Competitive strategy: techniques for analyzing industries and competitions. Free Press, New York, NY
Possert B, Possert J (2019) Mindopeners vs. brainfrost a playful endeavor. http://www.mindopeners.net/. Accessed Jun 2019
Rau T, Koch-Gonzalez J (2018) Many voices one song: shared power with sociocracy. Sociocracy for All, Amherst, US
Ricci A, Omicini A, Drenti E (2003) Activity theory as a framework for MAS coordination. Conference Paper in Lecture Notes in Computer Science. https://www.researchgate.net/publication/221029921_Activity_Theory_as_a_Framework_for_MAS_Coordination
Robertson BJ (2016) Holacracy: the revolutionary management system that abolishes hierarchy. Penguin Randon House, London
Roos LL, Starke FA (1981) Organizational roles. In: Nystrom PC, Starbuck WH (eds) Handbook of organizational design, vol 1. Oxford University Press, Oxford, pp 290–308
Samygin-Cherkaoui A (2005) McKinsey 7S Framework: boost business performance, prepare for change and implement effective strategies. https://www.50minutes.com
Schakel JK, van Fenema PC, Faraj S (2016) Shots fired! Switching between practices in police work. Org Sci 27:391–410
Schein EH, Schein P (2018) Humble leadership: the power of relationships, openness, and trust. Berrett-Koehler Publishers, San Francisco, CA
Schiller F (1794) On the esthetic education of man. Penguin Classics, London

Schwab K (2019) Why we need the 'Davos Manifesto' for a better kind of capitalism. https://www.weforum.org/agenda/2019/12/why-we-need-davos-manifesto-for-better-kind-of-capitalism/
Schwartz M (2015) On Bhaskarian and Laskean dialectic. Int Lead Rev 6(16):83
Sisodia R, Wolfe J, Sheth D (2007) Firms of endearment: how world-class companies profit from passion and purpose. Pearson Education, Upper Saddle River, NJ
Stewart J (2016) Review of Otto Laske's work. https://interdevelopmentals.org/?p=4204
Stray V (2014) An empirical investigation of the daily stand-up meeting in agile software development project. Dissertation, Department of Informatics, Faculty of Mathematics and Natural Sciences University of Oslo
Sull D, Sull C (2018) With goals: FAST beats SMART. https://sloanreview.mit.edu/article/with-goals-fast-beats-smart/
Taylor FW (1911) The principles of scientific management. Harper & Brothers, New York, NY; London. Published by Suzeteo Enterprises in 2014
Tomasello M (2014) A natural history of human thinking. Harvard University Press, London
Van Clieaf M (2016) Designing performance for long-term value. Aligning business strategy, management structure and incentive design. In: Leblanc R (ed) The handbook of board governance: a comprehensive guide for public. Private and not for profit board members. Wiley, New York, NY, pp 514–535

MIX
Papier aus verantwortungsvollen Quellen
Paper from responsible sources
FSC® C105338

If you have any concerns about our products,
you can contact us on
**ProductSafety@springernature.com**

In case Publisher is established outside the EU,
the EU authorized representative is:
**Springer Nature Customer Service Center GmbH**
**Europaplatz 3, 69115 Heidelberg, Germany**

Printed by Libri Plureos GmbH
in Hamburg, Germany